Africanness – Inculturation – Ethics

FORUM INTERDISZIPLINÄRE ETHIK

Herausgegeben von Gerfried W. Hunold

Band 26

Frankfurt am Main · Berlin · Bern · Bruxelles · New York · Oxford · Wien

Simon Kofi Appiah

Africanness Inculturation Ethics

In Search of the Subject
of an Inculturated Christian Ethic

PETER LANG
Frankfurt am Main · Berlin · Bern · Bruxelles · New York · Oxford · Wien

Die Deutsche Bibliothek - CIP-Einheitsaufnahme

Appiah, Simon Kofi:

Africanness – inculturation – ethics : in search of the subject of an inculturated Christian ethic / Simon Kofi Appiah. - Frankfurt am Main ; Berlin ; Bern ; Bruxelles ; New York ; Oxford ; Wien : Lang, 2000
  (Forum interdisziplinäre Ethik ; Bd. 26)
  Zugl.: Tübingen, Univ., Diss., 2000
  ISBN 3-631-37164-0

D 21
ISSN 0937-3861
ISBN 3-631-37164-0
US-ISBN 0-8204-4826-5

© Peter Lang GmbH
Europäischer Verlag der Wissenschaften
Frankfurt am Main 2000
All rights reserved.

All parts of this publication are protected by copyright. Any utilisation outside the strict limits of the copyright law, without the permission of the publisher, is forbidden and liable to prosecution. This applies in particular to reproductions, translations, microfilming, and storage and processing in electronic retrieval systems.

Printed in Germany 1 2 4 5 6 7

Contents

Acknowledgements VII

Introduction 1

Chapter One
1. Inculturation reconsidered 9
1.1. Inculturation: A basic Reality of Religion 9
1.2. Inculturation and the Christian Religion 11
1.3. Inculturation in the African context: A Missionary
 Concept or an African way of being Church 17
1.4. A critical Appraisal of Inculturation in Current Theology 26
1.5. A New Approach to the Elements of Inculturation 37
1.6. The Existentialist Model of Inculturation and Vatican II 41
1.7. Chapter Resume 47

Chapter Two
2. Working Backwards: In Search of a New Narrative 49
2.1. The Formation of the Conventional Narrative 51
2.2. African Ethos and the Conventional Narrative 56
2.3. African Ethos and Tradition 64
2.4. African Ethos: Which African? In Search of other Paradigms 82

Chapter Three
3. African Theology and Inculturation Ethics 98
3.1. Africanness, Christian Theology and Inculturation Ethics 100
3.2. The Question of Method in Ethics 105
3.3. Ethics and other Terms relating to Inculturation 116
3.4. Ethics, Enculturation and Acculturation 121
3.5. The Role of African Traditions in Enculturation Ethics 129

Chapter Four

4. Where Theory and Praxis meet: Inculturation Ethics and Politics in Africa	132
4.1. Sketch of a Political Ethic	133
4.2. Indigenous African Systems of Leadership	137
4.3. The African Political Climate: An Overview	143
4.4. Reactions to the current Political Climate in Africa	146
4.5. Reviewing the Problem of Leadership in Africa Today in the Light of the Personalist Criterion	151
4.6. The concrete Contribution of Inculturation Ethics	162
5. Conclusion	167
Bibliography	171

Acknowledgements

Once the seed matures and bears fruit, it is enjoyed by many, but the joy of the harvest belongs to those who planted and nursed the seed. In the case of this study, the laborers have been many. Though space will allow me to mention only a few, I wish that all who have contributed to the completion of this study share in the joy of the harvest.

I am indebted to my moderator, Prof. Dr. G. W. Hunold, who showed interest in my area of study and patiently accompanied and encouraged me on this journey. I am most grateful to Sr. Barbara Linen (HCJ) who made time to come all the way from the US to read through the whole work. Her valuable suggestions have greatly improved the work. I thank Frau Sigrid Müller, other course-mates and friends who also read through the work and offered helpful suggestions. My gratitude goes also to the staff of the department of Theologische Ethik 1, especially Frau Hildegard Mattes.

I thank Bishop Gabriel Mante and others engaged in pastoral work in the Diocese of Jasikan for the support given me, and for the opportunity to be away for this period of time to undertake this study. I owe special gratitude to the Diocese of Rottenburg-Stuttgart for supporting me financially and giving me a home in the parish community of St. Maria, in Stuttgart. To the parish priest, Herbert Schmucker, the parish staff, Andreas and family, and the many good people of St. Maria, I offer my sincere thanks for their kindness and encouragement. I am also indebted to the Kolpingsfamilie and the catholic community of Markelsheim for their friendship and assistance.

To the three Ghanaian brother-priests also studying in Tübingen, Mike in Vienna and Cletus in Rome, I say special thanks for your brotherliness.

Finally, it remains for me to express my heartfelt gratitude to my family. My three mothers: Grace Ama Appiah, Resi Bokmeier and Ulla Overkamp deserve special thanks for their relentless love and care for me, and for their support during this period of studies. I thank in a special way, Fr. Jos Smits and Br. Peter Arnold for their fatherly care and support. To Bro Tommy, Dada Attaa and the many other brothers and sisters, I say thank you for your love and support.

Kofi Appiah

Stuttgart, July 2000

Introduction

The term Ethos describes the total construct of a people's way of life. It is the fruit of a complex structure of processes – experiencing, reflecting planning, experimenting, judging, deciding and acting.[1] The term regards especially the socially worked out pattern of behavior in relation to 'the good' or 'the bad' in a given society. This pattern must be taken seriously by individuals in organizing their life if they wish to be recognized as properly belonging to the group. Ethos contains traditions, customs and mores that are practiced as a matter of convention or out of a kind of intuitive realization of the acceptable way of acting in the various circumstances of life. The content of ethos is thus not codified into written laws.[2]

There is a certain tension between the social and individual, the objective and situation-subjective aspects of ethos, since ethos poses as a binding and enduring ought, often against the individual and subjective wishes. The binding nature of an ethos derives from the fact that it embodies the fundamental questions that confront human beings and the answers they have found to such questions at a given time and place. People have always had questions about themselves and their life, about their origins and destiny and about the world around them. The way such questions and their solutions are concretely conceived are determined by the context, geographical location, religious attitudes, scientific development and history of the people concerned.[3] We could say that an ethos is group specific and involves a people's practical reason about basic questions concerning human existence. Ethos has its own rationality.[4]

As a characteristically human phenomenon, ethos possesses a constitutive element which I wish to call questioning. This questioning may take various forms, but it always involves the basic question: "What is the good to be done?" It is a question that demands a systematic reflection on what people do. A systematic analysis of a people's way of life, by the application of a scientific methodology, in view of the good to be done or the evil to be avoided is what the term ethics describes.

Contemporary studies emphasize the need to avoid an abstract approach to ethics and insist that ethics is valid insofar as it takes the totality of what constitutes humanness seriously. Ethics must be based on questions arising from the concrete biographical, cultural, and historical experiences of people

---

[1] See N. Dzobo, "Introduction to Indigenous Ethics of the Ewe of West Africa", in: Oguaa Educator, Vol. 6, no. 1, October 1975.
[2] E. Höffele, Lexikon der Ethik (München: Verlag C. H. Beck, 1997), p. 204.
[3] See W. Kluxen, Ethik des Ethos (Freiburg/München: Verlag Karl Alber GmbH, 1974), pp. 12ff.
[4] Kluxen, Ethik des Ethos, pp. 23ff.

at a given time and place. Consequently ethics could be said to arise from ethos, it is an "ethics of ethos".[5] The claims of ethics would be more or less convincing in the extent to which such claims remain related to the concrete attempts at humanizing humanity. The aim of ethics is the 'maximization of the humanum'.[6]

At the core of the ethos of African communities is the same intention of the qualitative maximization of humanness.[7] The Ewes of Ghana for instance say '*ame nyuie ye wo ame*' (literally meaning: the good person is human), and '*ame vondi mewo ame o*' (the evil person is human only by appearance and not in essence).[8] Here African morality has much to share with other moral systems and with Christian morality in particular.

The social, economic, political and cultural situations in Africa raise serious moral questions because they tend so often to dehumanize the African on many levels. On the one hand, many African communities can boast of laudable moral systems. Besides, the people of these communities are admired for their spirit of endurance and hopeful attitude of joy in the face of intolerable suffering, humiliation and death. On the other hand, the seriousness of the deplorable conditions of life of the majority of Africans cannot be winked at. Africa has serious problems which seem to embrace nearly all aspects of life. Ethically it is possible to talk of many situations of evil in Africa. Situations of evil minimize rather than maximize the humanum, and the role of Christian ethics in such a situation cannot be overemphasized. For Christian ethics to be relevant in Africa, it must have something to say to the situations of evil in Africa and to Africans who experience these situations of evil. In this way we can speak of an African Christian morality.

There are observable points of convergence between African and Christian morality which could help Africans respond appropriately to their concrete problems. These points of convergence notwithstanding, both moral systems have had a rather complex pattern of relationships in the history of African Christianity in which African and Christian moral systems have tended to run in separate tracks. This problem is compounded when considered in the light of the rejection of African moral systems by missionary Christianity on account of ethnocentrism. The rejection of African moral systems led to ex-

---

[5] Kluxen, Ethik des Ethos.
[6] W. Korff, "Normen als Gestaltungsträger menschlichen Daseins", in: A. Hertz et al. (eds.), Handbuch der christlichen Ethik, vol. 1 (Freiburg: Herder, ²1993), p. 114.
[7] See N. Dzobo, "Introduction to Indigenous Ethics of the Ewe of West Africa", in: Oguaa Educator, vol. 6, no. 1, October 1975; L. Magesa, African Religion. The Moral Traditions of Abundant Life (Maryknoll: Orbis Books, 1997); K. Wiredu, Philosophy in an African Culture (Cambridge: Cambridge University Press, 1980), p. 6.
[8] J. Hevi, Indigenous Leadership Among the Ewes of South-Eastern Ghana as a Moral Responsibility, Doctorate Dissertation (Rome: Pontificia Universitas Lateranensis, 1980), p. 114.

periences of humiliation arising from a systematic isolation of Africans and their way of life from the community of cultures. This background has had tremendous influence on much of the work that has been done in the area of African ethics.

From the beginning of the 20th century we find works that begin to show some sympathy towards the African way of life, although these works largely remained within the evolutionist mind set. These were mainly works of anthropologists and missionaries or colonial administrators living and working in the colonies. One could mention here works such as A. B. Ellis, The Yoruba Speaking Peoples of the Slave Coast (1894), R. S. Rattray, Ashanti (1923), and Ashanti Law and Constitution (1927), J. Spieth, Ewe Stämme (1906), A Kagwa, Old Customs of the Baganda, in Man, vol. X no. 3, (1910), Leo Frobenius, Kulturgeschichte Afrikas (1933), and others.

After this period followed the works which John Mbiti calls "intermediate and current studies."[9] There is a relatively long list of works with different accents. Some of the popularly known works of this period which could be mentioned include: P. Temples, Bantu Philosophy (1945, French edn.), J. Jahn, Muntu (1958, German edn.), and J. V. Taylor, The Primal Vision (1963). Others are G. Parrinder, H. Deschamps, E. Dammann, E. E. Evans-Pritchard and G. Lienhardt.[10] Peculiar to the works of this period is their interest and concentration on African religion and culture. African ethos and morality is thus usually treated in tandem with African religion and culture. The same is true of indigenous African scholars who undertook African studies, revealed for instance in the title of Mbiti's book: *'African Religions and Philosophy'*. As pioneers in this field, many of the African scholars felt a strong need to defend the integrity of the African and the African way of life as such. In their apologetics they were disposed to the very Western categories of thought with which Africans and their way of life had previously been dismissed as backward. This often led to certain observations that sometimes tend to be incoherent, and reactionary or romantic. African scholars that have devoted time for African religion, culture and ethics include among others E. B. Idowu, G. M. Setiloane, J. O. Awolalu, K. A. Opoku, J. Mugambi, V. Y. Mudimbe and many more. Among these is J. B. Danquah's Akan doctrine of God (1944). Except that the work was limited to Ghana with particular attention to the Akan, it is one of the works that attempts to address the issue of ethics directly. It was originally meant to be part of a three-volumed work entitled *Gold Coast Ethics and Religion*.[11]

The works mentioned above did not concern themselves with African *Christian* morality particularly. This was to begin with the rise of African the-

---

[9] J. S. Mbiti, African Religions and Philosophy (Oxford: Heinemann, ²1989), pp. 10ff.
[10] Mbiti, African Religions and Philosophy, p. 12.
[11] See C. A. Ackah, Akan Ethics (Accra: Ghana Universities Press, 1988), p. 6.

ology in the second half of the 20th century. All the same, work in this area has remained relatively slow. As Bénezét Bujo notes, "one of the reproaches most often levelled at African Christian theology is that it has failed to develop a Christian ethic which corresponds to the aspirations of the African."[12] Bujo is one of the scholars who has concerned himself greatly with African Christian morality. His works include African Christian Morality at the Age of Inculturation (1989-90), Die ethische Dimension der Gemeinschaft: Studien zur theologischen Ethik (1993), "Can Morality be Christian in Africa?"; in: African Christian Studies (1988), "A Christocentric Ethic for Black Africa", in: Theology Digest (1985). Some other works relating to African Christian morality include: H. Haselbarth, Christian Ethics in the African Context (1976), J. W. Sempebwa, African Traditional Moral Norms and their Implication for Christianity (1983), C. Villa-Vicencio and J. de Gruchy (eds.), Doing Ethics in Context: South African Perspectives (1994), D. A. Rader, Christian Ethics in an African Context: A Focus on Urban Zambia (1991), J. N. K. Mugambi and A. Nasimiyu-Wasike (eds.), Moral and Ethical Issues in African Christianity: Exploratory Essays in Moral Theology (1992).

Except in the case of Bujo, many of the scholars who try to do African Christian ethics would seem to depart from an understanding of inculturation as the need to integrate Christian morality in African moral traditions. Since much of the talk on inculturation deals with authenticity, there is the tendency to suggest that inculturation ethics must be about sorting out the good traditions of Africa and making them the bases for fruitful Christian practice in Africa. By and large scholars apply the comparative method to show the value of African moral systems and to establish the equality of African and Western moral systems. Much attention is therefore devoted to African tradition, and to the development of a concept of an African Christian ethic based on what might be called ethno-theology. Thus many scholars would seem to be addressing the question of cultural identity in Christian practice, while taking that same identity for granted. One can note something paradoxical here.[13]
Even in doubting one's identity, one presumes knowledge of what that identity is or should be. If we pay attention to the concrete experience of people, it becomes difficult to believe that we shall solve this paradox in the African context by appealing to tradition alone. It is a paradox that has wide and complex moral implications.

In recent times morality has been shown to be greatly concerned with the question of identity.[14] In its Western philosophical understanding, how-

---

[12] B. Bujo, African Christian Morality at the Age of Inculturation (Kenya: St. Paul Publications, 1990), p. 11.
[13] K. Wiredu, "Problems in Africa's self-definition in the Contemporary World", in: G. F. McLean (ed.), Person and Community. Cultural Heritage and Contemporary Change Series, II. Africa, Vol. 1 (Washington: CIPSH/UNESCO, 1992), pp. 59-70.
[14] See T. Laubach, "Identität als Grundproblem ethischer Reflexion", in: T. Laubach, Ethik

ever, the term identity connotes the meaning of the nature of an individual and all that constitutes his or her self-definition as a person. In this context one may not limit the meaning of identity in the first place to cultural identity, the latter being what is mostly implied in this study. However the place of culture in the formation of a person's identity is a general phenomenon that cannot be under estimated. Gerfried W. Hunold depending on studies in sociology and psychology has in different publications made important contributions for understanding the intricate correlation between culture and nature in human persons. Hunold insists that the consideration of the human person as a "*Naturkulturwesen*" (nature-culture species) is a crucial point of departure for ethical inquiry.[15]

Identity relates closely to morality since there is no morality in vacuum. Moral responsibility presumes an identifiable subject who in turn has a practical self-understanding in relation to his or her choices and actions. For the way we conceive ourselves as human beings plays an important role in the way we define our morality. Thomas Laubach observes that identity could be considered as the point of departure and the goal of ethical reflection. He explains that the practical attempt to answer the question "who am I?", usually corresponds to the practical answer we find for the question "what must I do."[16] At the same time identity can be seen as the goal of moral reflection by departing from the tension between what we are and what we must be or wish to be. In this case we are confronted with the same question from the opposite end. The answer to the question "what must I do?" corresponds to the answer we give to the question "who must I be?"[17]

Insofar as Christian ethics seeks to understand how human beings strive to maximize their humanness in response to God's call, it is possible to say that Christian morality is concerned with the process of humanization and so constitutes in itself a paradigm of humanization. Christians believe that God's call to full humanness has been concretely made in the person of Jesus. He is God's gift to human beings. Because of its concern with how human beings realize their own humanness, the faith in the incarnation of Jesus is central to Christian ethics. It is on this acceptance of Jesus as God's gift and his incarnation as the ultimate paradigm of humanization *par excellence* that Christian ethics and inculturation converge.

---

und Identität. Festschrift für Gerfried W. Hunold zum 60. Geburtstag (Tübingen und Basel: Francke Verlag, 1998), pp.11-25, a good source for relevant literature on the topic of identity and ethics.
[15] See G. W. Hunold, Identitätstheorie: "Die sittliche Struktur des Individuellen im Sozialen", in: A. Herz, et al. (eds.), Handbuch der christlichen Ethik, vol. 1 (Freiburg: Herder, 1993), pp. 117-195.
[16] Laubach, 'Identität als Grundproblem', p.13.
[17] Laubach, 'Identiät als Grundproblem', pp. 13-14, referring also to G. Böhme, Anthropologie in pragmatischer Hinsicht, (Frankfurt a. M.: 1985), p. 30.

In view of the immeasurable importance of the identity question, therefore, the main thesis of this study suggests that besides studying the value of African moral systems and traditions, inculturation ethics has to address itself to two primary questions:

(1) How African must Africans be, if their morality is to be at once Christian and authentic? This question implies that the identity question and the question of subjectification[18] are essential to an African Christian ethic. It is argued that doing ethics of inculturation is not, in the first place, the justification of norms or of African moral systems. More important is the anthropological question: 'who is the actor?' In other words, who is the African who bears the inculturated Christian morality?

(2) How can we achieve a more integral consideration of the African which allows for the application of a personalist criterion for doing inculturation ethics?[19] It is proposed that an adequate consideration of the African is possible when inculturation ethics is based on an anthropology with the following postulates:
(a) Africans need many of their indigenous moral traditions for an authentic African Christian morality. However they need not be traditionalistic in order to be authentic Africans.
(b) The search for African identity needs a theory that broadens the horizons beyond the western mental categories. Such a theory should aim at assisting Africans in telling their own story, in remembering the multiple sources of their culture and the moral demands that such inherent cultural pluralism makes on their choices and actions.

Two main terms, which in addition to inculturation, recur in this study are 'Afrinanness' and ethics. Africanness is used here to connote the vast range of anthropological and theological themes which African theology considers. Thus the term describes the desire for authenticity and the struggles to redress the state of alienation that resulted from the historical experiences of cultural domination, slavery and colonialism in Africa. In this sense, Africanness directs our attention to the complex web of issues involved in the African struggle for the rehabilitation and integral liberation of Africans, as basic topics of African theology. Positively, the term stands in opposition to these

---

[18] The word is coined to emphasize the need to understand 'subjectivity' more in the sense of a process than the static and fixed connotations sometimes associated with the term subjectivity.
[19] The idea of the human person more adequately considered is given ample expression in Vatican II's Gaudium et Spes. Its development as criterion for doing moral theology, however, is the work of Janssens on whom we shall greatly depend for developing our thoughts on the importance of ethics in inculturation.

negative historical and anthropological experiences of Africans. In connection with the incarnation of Jesus, the term connotes both the hope and challenge on which African Christianity is to be founded. When considered ethically, Africanness takes on meanings like subjectivity, self-discovery or self-consciousness and [cultural] identity. In the context of an integral African theological hermeneutic, Africanness is also a challenge to reconsider the various 'images' and presumptions that underlie the African search for authenticity. The term asks us to be wary of anachronism and romanticism. Africanness, therefore, denotes also the concrete African of flesh and blood, as against an ideal African of the 'pure-traditions'.

Ethics is conceived in this study as 'a hermeneutic of behavior', i.e. an operation in which people and their moral actions are apprehended and interpreted as 'texts'. These are not written texts, but actions and behavior. That means the study tries to reconsider some of the categories of interpretation applied to the African way of life in the search for the authentic African. It is argued that the conventional approach resulted in a dualistic interpretation that made the communication between African ethos and Christian ethics unfruitful. In order to be convincing, inculturation ethics must reinterpret the existing notions and concrete ways of being African and Christian.

The study proceeds in the following manner. Chapter one addresses recent developments in the concept of inculturation with particular attention to the developments in mission theology. The discussion is aimed at delineating the parameters of this study by accentuating some nuances of the meaning of inculturation which are only implicit in many of the explanations given to inculturation.

Chapter two considers the nature of the conventional interpretation of Africanness and delineates some of the reasons for the inadequate consideration of the African in the conventional interpretations. The discourse on and about the African in the conventional interpretation is described as a 'narrative' based on categories that use a partial interpretation of history. Since much of the information existing about Africans is the fruit of the anthropology and missiology of the early nineteenth century, the chapter shows how these sources themselves are burdened with biased schemes of interpretation. By exposing such schemes of thought it becomes possible to show how the crisis of interpretation has made it difficult not only for the outsider, but also for Africans themselves to understand the African reality. The chapter closes by referring to the plural nature of the African cultural identity based on 'the triple heritage' paradigm worked out by Ali Mazrui, presenting this paradigm as a useful alternative to the one-way definition of African cultural identity based on the so-called *traditional African*.

Chapter three deals with the theological implications of doing Christian ethics in Africa. Basically the chapter discusses the question of the Christian religious foundations of an inculturation ethics in the African situation. Since doing Christian ethics depends tremendously on the productivity of method, the chapter also considers two sample methods and explains their usefulness for doing inculturation ethics. Both samples insist on an adequate consideration of the human person. Concepts relating to inculturation, which also help to explain the social and anthropological implications of humanness are briefly discussed. The relevance of these anthropological processes in the development of a religious ethic is illustrated with three concrete examples.

Chapter four applies the insights arising from the theory worked out in the first three chapters to a specific and pertinent moral problem -political leadership- in Africa. The example calls for analysis on many different levels and reveals the complex nature of the African reality in the area of ethics.

It is our hope that this study will nurture further the interest to engage in African Christian ethics, based on the agenda of integral liberation of the African, which is the aim of theology in Africa. The study invites African Christians and Africans in general to broaden their horizons for their self-definition and attempt on that basis to evaluate the wealth of knowledge that exists today on the importance of African moral traditions.[20] In short the study is meant to challenge Africans to look beyond the merely *'traditional'* in their search for authenticity. A morality that remains closed within its own ghetto is not yet Christian. An African Christian morality with perspectives for the future is possible only when Africans allow their group specific ethos to enter into a fruitful correlation with the radicalism of the good news of Jesus.

---

[20] See B. Bujo, Die ethische Dimension der Gemeinschaft: Das afrikanische Modell im Nord-Süd-Dialog (Freiburg: Universitätsverlag, 1993); Bujo, African Christian Morality at the Age of Inculturation (Nairobi: St. Paul Publication, 1990); Bujo, 'Can Morality be Christian in Africa?', in: African Christian Studies 4(1988) 5-39; T. Sundermeier, Nur gemeinsam können wir leben: Das Menschenbild schwarzafrikanisceher Religionen (Gütersloh: Gütersloher Verl.-Haus Mohn, 1988). Some recent works include, K. Gyekye, African Cultural Values (Accra: Sankofa Publ. Corporation, 1996), L. Magesa, African Religion: The Moral Traditions of Abundant Life (Maryknoll: Orbis Books, 1997).

Chapter One

1. Inculturation Reconsidered

Many scholars have significantly explained the concept of inculturation in African theology. The intention of this chapter is to depend on some of such significant studies to prepare grounds for the discussion on ethics as an aspect of inculturation. The chapter begins by showing briefly how the concept of inculturation could be said to be a general religious phenomenon, then considers how inculturation is particular to Christian theological thought and to Christian religious experience. The second part of the chapter specifies further the nuances of meaning that inculturation receives when considered as part of an integral African theological hermeneutic. Some presumptions about inculturation usually taken for granted are also pointed out.

1.1 Inculturation: A basic Reality of Religion

The term inculturation concerns a phenomenon that is fundamental to religious experience. In principle religion becomes concrete through a given cultural embodiment. The myths, signs and symbols, institutions, language, and intuitions of people about themselves, their life and fate, and their questions about their origins and future are elements that concretely embody a people's religious experience.[1]

Religion must become culturally embodied because our humanness is the basic medium for appropriating to ourselves all reality.[2] Considering the fullness of meaning we can attach to the word 'reality', it becomes possible to appreciate the fullness of freedom to which the human being is disposed.[3] Yet, by nature, humanness implies at the same time a limitation to a given history, culture, geographical place, and to a body of knowledge about the world and about us. Human beings are finite.[4] This natural-cultural limitation of *human-*

---

[1] See. F. J. Streng (ed.), Understanding the Religious Life (California: Dickenson Publishing Company, ²1976), pp. 1-9.

[2] A. Gehlen, Gesamtausgabe, Bd. 3, Teilband 1, Der Mensch: Seine Natur und seine Stellung in der Welt, K.–S. Rehberg ed. (Frankfurt a. M.: Vittorio Klostermann, 1993), pp. 29ff.

[3] See J. G. Herder, "Ideen zur Philosophie der Geschichte der Menschheit" (1784), who described the human being as the creature that enjoys the greatest freedom in the whole of creation. In his view, the human being was as it were, 'left free' at creation. See also A. Gehlen, Der Mensch, pp. 30-31; W. Pannenberg, Anthropology in Theological Perspective (Edinburgh: T. & T. Clark Ltd., 1985), pp. 29-32.

[4] See W. Kluxen, Ethik des Ethos (Freiburg/München: Verlag Karl Alber GmbH, 1974).

being leaves its mark on the actual form that religion takes among a given group of people.[5] Thus an African myth of creation is different in many respects from an Ancient Near Eastern one.[6] Nonetheless both types of myth could be shown to be addressing similar questions of worry to different groups of people.

An *'uninculturated'* religion is therefore contradictory or at best fictive, because it can neither be concretely known nor lived.[7] When the religion concerned is intercultural (i.e. transferred from one culture to another) the need for appropriation in the recipient culture becomes more explicit and urgent. For example, one widespread indigenous religious cult among the Ewes of West Africa is the Yehwe-cult which was originally practiced among the Yoruba of Nigeria. From there it was transferred to Eweland through South Dahomey (now Benin) and then to Togo. An important characteristic of this religion is its insistence on purity of tradition. A change of word may render a whole incantation void. Thus Yehwe like many other cults developed its own secret language, known only to initiated members. It is interesting however to observe that even this secret language took variant forms corresponding to the dialectal variations of the Ewe language in which it was introduced. For instance, 'chicken' in the original Yoruba was called *'adiɛ.'* In receiving this cultic language in Agu Tavie (Dahomey, now Benin), the same word became *'adiyɛ'*, and in Tyve (Lome, Togo) the variant form *'adiye'* was used.[8] The history of religions abounds with many other examples especially with regard to the so-called world religions,[9] as shown in the specific variations of the Hindu religion in India and in China or Confucianism in Japan and in Korea.

The process involved in bringing about the actualization of a religion by (and for) a group of people can be conveniently described as inculturation. In

---

[5] E. Schillebeeckx, Gasammelte Schriften Bd. 1, Offenbarung und Theologie (Mainz, Grünewald Verlag, 1965), p. 327; Streng, Understanding the Religious Life, p. 3.
[6] For a Yoruba (Nigeria) variant of the many myths of creation in Africa, see G. Parrinder, African Mythology (London, Hamlyn, 1967), pp. 19ff. For Near Eastern as well as European myths of creation, see P. Bentley (ed.), The Hutchinson Dictionary of World Myth (Oxford: Helicon Publishing Limited and Duncan Baird Publishers, 1995).
[7] See M. Seckler, "Der theologische Begriff der Religion", in: W. Kern, H. J. Pottmeyer, M. Seckler (ed.), Handbuch der Fundamentaltheologie, Bd. 1 (Freiburg: Herder, 1985), pp. 173-194 here, pp. 182-188. Discussing the anthropological sense in which Aquinas applied the term religion, Seckler explains: "Anthropologisch ... werden für die Religion aus der leibhaftigkeit des Menschen Folgerungen gezogen. Es geht in der Religion um das >>Eingedenksein<< der göttlichen Dinge im Sinnenhaften,...ihre bezeugende Bekundung... und leibhaftige Vergegenwärtigung" (Seckler, p. 183).
[8] D. Westermann, Afrikanische Tabusitten in ihrer Einwirkung auf die Sprachgestaltung (Berlin: 1940), p.14-17; here p. 15.
[9] Cf. M. Eliade and J. Kitagawa (eds.), The History of Religions (Chicago, University of Chicago Press, 1959); E. J. Sharpe, Comparative Religion. A History (London: Duckworth, 1975); Sharpe, Understanding Religion (London: Duckworth, 1983).

the ideal situation the culture-religion-symbiosis occurs as a matter of course, even if not without frictions. In the study of religions the phenomenon has often been factually described and analyzed without applying the term inculturation.[10] But we can say that in general the phenomenon which inculturation describes is as old as religion itself.

1.2 Inculturation and the Christian Religion

Practicing the Christian faith, like all other religions, is possible only by way of a human culture.[11] However, to limit the concept of inculturation to a fundamental and general principle of religion does not do justice to the current use of the term in Christian theology. In considering the anthropological and cultural manifestations of religion, it is important to keep in mind that Christian theology builds on specific meanings of religion. As Max Seckler explains,[12] for Christian theology, the term religion obtains its proper meaning only when understood as the experience of a saving relationship with God. He shows how this originally thomistic interpretation of religion as *"ordo ad Deum"* or *"ordo hominis ad Deum"*[13] confers a more integral and essential meaning to the anthropological and cultural aspects of religion.[14]

In Christian thinking, therefore, the human-cultural appropriation of religion cannot be anything other than a real and existential process in which the whole of creation is drawn into and sustained in a saving relationship with God.[15] It is thus important to explain that inculturation developed as a specifically Christian theological concept and has, therefore, a proper Christian understanding. The term *per se* is a neologism since it gained admission into Christian theological terminology in the recent past.[16] Even as a neologism in

---

[10] See Streng, Understanding the Religious Life, pp.:3-5. See also G. Lanczkowski (ed.), Geschichte der Religionen (Frankfurt am Main: Fischer Verlag, 1980); H. Kishimoto, "An Operational Definition of Religion", in: Numen 8 (1961), pp. 236-240; P. L. Berger and T. Luckmann, The Social Construction of Reality (New York: Anchor Books, 1966). The explanation for the absence of the term inculturation in the philosophy of religion is probably due to the fact that the term inculturation was originally not part of the terminology of the science of religions. As we shall see later, the term is said to have been derived from the social sciences, specifically anthropology, where it appears as *'enculturation.'* In this form the term studies the process by which a person learns to become 'a cultural actor' of the culture to which he/she belongs.
[11] A. Shorter, Toward a Theology of Inculturation, (Maryknoll: Orbis, 1986), p. 59.
[12] M. Seckler, 'Der theologische Begriff', pp. 180-182.
[13] Seckler, 'Der theologische Begriff', p. 179, citing Th. Aquinas, S.th. II-II 81, 1.
[14] Seckler, 'Der theologische Begriff', p. 181.
[15] Seckler, 'Der theologische Begriff', p. 181. For Seckler the emphasis lies not on the relational aspect of the *ordo ad Deum*, but on the saving nature of such a relationship.
[16] See G. Collet, "Inkulturation", in:P. Eicher (ed.), Neues Lexikon der theologischen Beg-

Christian thinking, the term still describes an old aspect of the life and growth of the Christian religion, which is probably as old as the Church herself.[17] Basically the concept describes the processes through which the good news of Christ takes root in a given culture.[18] It is about the way the Jesus event and the faith in the God of Jesus takes on the human face of the culture in which it is inserted.

1.2.1 The Incarnation as specific basis for Inculturation

The Christian theological specification, however, lies in the fact that this manifestation of a general principle of religion is not just due to the given anthropological conditions of our humanness. Christian theology emphasizes that inculturation is actually God's own way of making himself known and loved. By virtue of the incarnation of Jesus, inculturation could be said to be

---

riffe, Bd. 3 (München: Kössel-Verlag, 1991), p. 396.

[17] See A. Shorter, Toward a Theology of Inculturation, p. 3. Shorter refers to an anonymous and apologetic letter, 'The Epistle to Diognetus'. The letter must have been written around the mid-second-century and would seem to belong to the beginnings of the writings of the Church Fathers who were later called Apologists. The Epistle bases on Platonic dualism, which as Shorter rightly observes, is "a doubtful model for inculturation". But because the letter attends to the religious faith of Christians vis-à-vis the anthropological constants of their daily life (e.g. language, dress, food, laws and general manner of life), it is an early "witness to the distinction and interaction between faith and culture on which the notion of inculturation rests" (Shorter, Toward a Theology, p. 3). Shorter took his quotation of the Epistle from H. Bettenson (ed.), The Early Christian Fathers (Oxford, 1956), pp. 74-5. Another instance of inculturation at the time of the Church Fathers, which Sorter mentions is St. Justin and his idea of the 'Logos spermaticos' (Shorter, Toward a Theology, p.75ff; referring to Justin, 'De Fide ad Petrum', quoted in:Kung, 1967, p. 32). This was a period in which Greek philosophical concepts were being introduced into Christian thought as a means of conceptualizing the Christian world view and understanding of reality. One could even go beyond the period of the Fathers and find examples in the Old and New Testaments. A famous NT example is the Council of Jerusalem. See P. Schineller, A Handbook on Inculturation (New York: Paulist Press, 1990), pp. 29. The Council could be said to have addressed issues pertinent to the self-understanding of non-Jewish communities evangelized by Paul and their search for a Christian identity without necessarily becoming stereotype Jews (through circumcision or the observance of other Jewish prescriptions). Major sections of the OT also reveal a process of a people in search of a theonomous identity, based on the faith in Yahweh, in the midst of Semitic Mesopotamian cultures. See A. Heidel, The Babylonian Genesis (Chicago & London: University of Chicago Press, 1974. Heidel offers typical examples of how OT revelation was handed down as Scriptures in forms and traditions borrowed from the Semitic Mesopotamian cultures. The Jewish Bible then presented the traditions in monotheistic categories replacing the original polytheistic categories of the Mesopotamian cultures. Especially interesting in this regard are the rules of worship, institutions of prophecy and kingship.

[18] See Collet, Shorter, Schineller, Martey.

first and foremost the initiative of God. In the incarnation God becomes a person and lives his godly life in the human way.[19] By becoming this particular person, Jesus of Nazareth, and living in this particular culture of the Jews, the reality of God becomes part and parcel of human history in its various particularizations.[20] Human history (because it is the locus of divine revelation) becomes the history of salvation.[21] In the Christian understanding of the concept, then, inculturation rests fundamentally on the paradigm of the incarnation of Jesus[22] as the culmination of God's self-communication with humanity and as the goal of the Christian's endeavor to become more human.

1.2.2 Theology of Incarnation

A theology of incarnation departs from the basic principle that revelation itself is God's self-communication among men and women in a concrete historical setting. It elucidates revelation by taking seriously the factor of embodiment based on the mystery of the incarnation of Jesus. Of importance is the central datum of human existence as incarnate (embodied) being.[23] Objectively, we experience and know God through other persons, historical events, in our given cultures, through the groups to which we belong and other forms of objective embodiments of God's presence –word and sacraments, Ecclesial communities and forms of concrete expression given to religious feeling. Subjectively incarnation theology emphasizes the fact that the human being is

---

[19] Schillebeeckx, Offenbarung und Theologie, p. 310. His own German expression of the idea is: "Gott ist persönlich Mensch und lebt sein göttliches Leben auf menschliche Weise."

[20] P. Turkson, "Inculturation: a Biblical Perspective", in:P. Turkson, F. Wijsen (eds.), Inculturation: Abide by the Otherness of Africa and the Africans (Kampen: 1994), p. 6. Referring to Beauchamp, Turkson reminds us that besides the general meaning of incarnation, inculturation "adds the precision that God *became this particular man: Jesus of Nazareth*, unlike all men; and the Word became *this particular flesh and assumed a particular culture*, unlike all other cultures (Turkson's italics). See P. Beauchamp, "The Role of the Old Testament in the Process of Building up of local Churches", in:Inculturation (III), Bible and Inculturation (Rome: 1983), pp. 3-4. See also Vatican II, Gaudium et Spes, no. 18, in:A. Flannery (general ed.), Vatican Council II: The Conciliar and Post Conciliar Documents (Leominster: Fowler Wright Bks. Ltd.).

[21] This way of understanding human history is one of the major points which inculturation theology shares with liberation theology. As we shall see later, the point has far reaching implications, especially in relation to questions of liberation and salvation. See G. Gutierrez, A Theology of Liberation (Maryknoll: Orbis Books, 1973), p. 483.

[22] See Vatican II, *Dei Verbum*, 2; General Catechetical Directory, (London: Catholic Truth Society, 1971), paragraph 10.

[23] N. Sharkey, "Incarnational Theology", in:New Catholic Encyclopedia, Vol. 7 (Yew York: McGraw-Hill Book Company), pp. 415ff. See also Schillebeeckx, Offenbarung und Theologie, p. 310ff.

both a conscious-self (i.e. not only biological) and a corporeal-self. Corporeality means human persons do not just have, but are body. Besides, they also form part of the objective embodiments of revelation. We are in the world and need the things of the world not just for survival, but also to know and communicate with and about God. To a great extent our knowing and speaking about ourselves, about God, and about our relationship with him and with each other usually take place in our situation as human beings. The incarnation of Jesus therefore validates the fact that God reveals himself to us and we come to know him from the position of our humanness.[24]

1.2.3 "The Word in germ"

Christians assert that God is to be found in every culture because they express faith in Jesus as the Word through whom all things were made (Jn 1,1ff). By virtue of human creatureliness the Word exists in germ[25] in and among all groups of people, no matter how latent or diffuse the people's apprehension of this germ may be. The incarnation of Christ is thus the concrete expression and fullness of God's self-communication to all human beings from the beginning of time. The general phenomenon, which is defined in religious studies as religion is thus given a specific *terminus* in the Christian God.[26] For Christian theology, religion in all cultures is an innate, even if nebulous and remote, response to the one God who communicates himself as the principle of life and

---

[24] Schillebeeckx, Offenbarung und Theologie, p. 232ff. Given the brevity of the discussion undertaken here, we have to remind ourselves once more (see earlier reference to Seckler and his explanation of the anthropological and cultural relevance of religion in section 1.2. of this study) that in stressing the anthropological and cultural aspects of religion, the intention is not to reduce inculturation to culturalism, where religion is ascribed purely to human virtue or merit. As Schillebeeckx explains, the point about the anthropological and cultural implications of religion is that God's gratuitous self-communication always takes shape within "the created and time-circumscribed" conditions of human beings. This explanation applies also as a basic principle underlying the idea of inculturation. See Schillebeeckx, Christ the Sacrament of our Encounter with God (London: Sheed and Ward, 1963).

[25] Shorter (Toward a Theology, pp. 75ff) reminds us that the expression "seeds of the Word" was used in connection with the concept of inculturation in Vatican II, Ad Gentes 11, 22. However, the expression itself goes back to St. Justin and his idea of Logos spermaticos. Justin taught that the ‚seed-bearing Word' exists in the heart of every culture. He like other Apologists of his time, was making use of ideas stemming from non-Christian (pagan) Greek philosophy. See Justin, Apologia I, 44, tr. Bettenson 1956, p. 83; and Apologia II, 13, tr. Bettenson 1956, pp. 87-8. Both quotations are found in Shorter (1988:76-77), from whom the reference is borrowed.

[26] Seckler, ('Der theologische Begriff', pp.186-187), states that for Christian theology, religion is without compromise theocentric.

salvation.[27] We could say that God is to be found wherever human persons are found, so that one does not make God known to any group of people *ex nihilo*. Every attempt to make God known is always preceded by God's own initiative.[28]

1.2.4 The Fruit of God's Word

The Church understands herself as a grace filled community in which the Word, which elsewhere exists only in germ, now grows to fruition – the people of God.[29] Consequently Christian theology emphasizes the special relation that exists between the incarnate Christ and the Church.[30] She is seen as the concrete fruit of God's self communication in Christ.

Biblically and traditionally, the Church is described as the body of Christ, and Christians are members of this body. These members however are human beings of flesh and blood. They are governed by their given biological, psychological, physical and anthropological constitution. Hence they think, feel, form groups, have cultures, etc. Saying that these people form the body of Christ, therefore, is an attempt to grasp the reality of the Church by way of the principle of mediation in which God begins with human beings where they are, i.e. with our humanness and all that it implies to be human.

Without going into much detail, it is possible to say that the Christian specification of that phenomenon which is described as inculturation goes beyond the socio-anthropological concerns of how culture and faith interact. Inculturation concerns the process through which human history becomes the context for the revelation of the love of God. In short inculturation is about salvation history.[31]

---

[27] Schillebeeckx (Christ the Sacrament, p. 8, footnote 2) explains in this connection that a religion based on a purely human design, "natural religion" is not possible. Religion, phenomenologically considered, always presupposes a relation between the Divine (God) and the human person. Therefore all religion is founded on "an *instinctus divinus* arising from the deepest foundations of human religious psychology as influenced by the attraction of divine grace". See also Lumen Gentium, 16.

[28] St. Augustin is mostly quoted in this regard. He explains that the service of God (religion) which we know in the Church is as old as the world, and graduates the coming into being of the Christian Church in three major phases. (i) the "Church" of the heathen, (ii) the pre-Christian "Church" of the chosen race of Israel, and (iii) the Church of the first born, which is the mature Church (see St. Augustine in:Pigne, Patrologia Latina [PL], 44, cols. 161, 315 and 974; PL, 43, cols. 609-10; cited in:Schillebeeckx, Offenbarung und Theologie, p. 7). As Schillebeeckx puts it, "In a nebulous but nonetheless discernible fashion the sacramental Church is already present in the life of the whole of mankind."

[29] See Lumen Gentium, 9ff.

[30] Lumen Gentium, 3-9ff.

[31] Compare Schillebeeckx, Christ the Sacrament, p. 5.

1.2.5 The Church is by nature missionary.

As the concrete fruition of a 'generative Logos' in the world, the Church cannot end in herself. Her mere presence in the world is mission. She points beyond herself to the pre-existing love of God, found among all peoples.[32] She bears the hope of the fullness of life resulting from God's presence in human history. She reminds us of the salvation that arises from the encounter of God with people and leads people to enter into this union more consciously and concretely. Together with Schillebeeckx it is possible to say, "[the] >>Church<< as the visible presence of grace, is a world-reality."[33] She is an inculturated Church called to inculturate.

Inculturation belongs as much to the nature of the Church, in the extent to which she is missionary in nature. Although the treatment of the topic here has been brief, it is clear enough that the Church's missionary vocation has implications for inculturation and vise versa. An investigation of such implications has been done in many of the works on the subject of inculturation, some aspects being taken up at relevant points in this study. At the same time it is difficult as hinted in the paragraphs above (and as we shall see more concretely later in the discussion) to limit inculturation to evangelization, because inculturation concerns the whole Christian experience which is more than evangelization. The foregoing paragraphs have therefore focused more on pointing out where a theology of inculturation sinks its roots in the Christian faith.

1.2.6 Inculturation (Incarnation) is non-militant

The unnerving aspect of the biblical narrative of the birth of Jesus is the subtlety and simplicity characterizing the event. The nativity stories of the NT would seem to show that the incarnation of Jesus did not occur in such a dramatic manner, as we would often want to believe. The incarnation was not a militant activity wrought through power and might. Apart from the biblical elements such as the angels, the star, and prophecies employed to emphasize that Jesus' birth was a theophanic revelation, Jesus is shown to have been born into the most ordinary of conditions. Thus we obtain the picture of a *permeat-*

---

[32] The statement on the missionary nature of the Church in *Ad Gentes* makes it clear that the Church's mission "flows from 'the fountain-like love' of God the Father." It is God's plan to call men and women together and in so doing offer them a share in his life. Thus the Church is called to proclaim this hope by inviting people to share consciously in the fullness of life which God offers.

[33] Schillebeeckx, Christ the Sacrament, p. 10.

ing process through which humanity is drawn into godliness.[34]

Similarly, inculturation based on the paradigm of incarnation can only be founded on the same principle of non-militancy – less drama, more reality. The real state of human beings is what incarnates and is incarnated. The philosophy of a people, for example, becomes a medium for thinking about God.[35] Some form or manner of dress assumes special meaning. Habits and attitudes or the sum total of a people's way of life that comes to be associated with the faith will gain sacred and new meanings.[36]

These traditions, habits and attitudes are measured and challenged by the new self-interpretation arising from the perspective of the people's relationship with God. These traditions and attitudes become at the same time the means of custody and further transmission of this relationship. So, for example, is St. Justin's idea of 'Logos spermaticos' the fruit of Greek philosophy become the medium of Christian theology. Latin became the language of Roman Christianity, and the style of dressing in the King's court in medieval Europe became the symbol of clerical authority in the medieval Church. In view of this permeating relationship between culture and religion, it is possible to say that given the normal situation, every culture is capable of 'incarnating' the Christian faith according to its own internal dynamism and freedom. It is therefore proper to infer some form of hindrance if inculturation does not occur in a given culture at a particular time.

1.3 Inculturation in the African Context: A Missionary Concept or an African way of being Church?

In the paragraphs that follow, the discussion turns away from inculturation as a basic Christian religious experience in general and concentrates on the theme of inculturation with specific reference to the African experience. In studying inculturation with specific reference to Africa, we shall base ourselves on the

---

[34] The genre of the 'infancy narratives' (Matthew 1, 18-2, 23; Luke 1, 5-2, 52) would seem to suggest that the writers probably drew on independent traditions that are "more typical of a Greco-Roman biography." The heroic elements of such Greco-Roman tradition must have been used by Matthew and Luke because of their preoccupation with the "divine exaltation of Jesus", especially emphasized in the resurrection narratives. The heroic elements to be found in the 'infancy narratives' therefore fit into a scheme with which the evangelists sought to establish the "universal validity of Jesus' teaching." See P. Perkins, "The Synoptic Gospels and Acts of the Apostles: Telling the Christian Story", in:J. Barton (ed.), The Cambridge Companion to Biblical Interpretation (Cambridge: Cambridge University Press, 1998), pp. 242-243.

[35] Vatican II, Gaudium et Spes, 44.

[36] Vatican II, Gaudium et Spes, 58.

thesis that inculturation as a normal result of the religion-culture correlation was prevented in Africa due to the negative cultural history of African peoples. From this point of view, the history of the term as such, its application as a missionary concept on the one hand, and as part of an integral African theological hermeneutic that seeks the liberation of the African on the other hand, are briefly considered.

1.3.1 A brief History of the term Inculturation

The use of the term 'inculturation' as a theological concept is relatively new. The term developed mainly due to the genuine concerns of Churches in 'mission countries', especially Africa. Concrete beginnings of this movement date to the 1950s, when the long existing desire for an African expression of the Christian faith began to be taken seriously. Attempts were made to relate Christian praxis as much as possible to local situations, based on the cultures of the people being evangelized.[37] The main focus was to translate Western Theology into African cultural concepts. Other terms that came to be used in both Catholic and Protestant circles included indigenization, localization, Africanization, contextualization and adaptation. On the Catholic side, it was adaptation that gained official recognition at Vatican II.[38]

The role of the Protestant Church in the development of the theology of inculturation has been no less significant. Especially after 1963 when the All Africa Conference of Churches (AACC) came into being, the Protestant Church, and individual Protestant theologians have contributed immensely in shaping the concept of inculturation.[39] Among Protestant thinkers around this

---

[37] *Des Prêtres noir s'interrogent*, 1956. This work was done by a group of African Priests studying in Europe at the time, who joined together to discuss and write regularly about what the Christian faith could be about in the light of the African situation. The 'spirit' of their thrust was in many ways similar to the work of Placide Tempels, who sought to translate Christian thought into Bantu Philosophy. See P. Tempels, Bantu-Philosophie: Ontologie und Ethik (Heidelberg: Wolfgang Rothe Verlag, 1956). We are also reminded of the European precedence of such attempts in the previous century (Schreiter, Constructing Local Theologies, pp.7ff). These attempts were mainly in the form of "de-Hellenization" of Western Christianity, based on the translation model. For a study on inculturation in different regions, see J. Gremillion, Proceedings of the Catholic Theological Society of America 38 (1981), pp. 113-124.

[38] Ad Gentes, 22; Lumen Gentium 13; Gaudium et Spes, 44. The word adaptation was also used by Paul VI in his allocution at the canonization of the Martyrs of Uganda (AAS 1964:908), and again in his apostolic exhortation, Evangelii Nuntiandi, 1975.

[39] For a detailed study on the Protestant contribution towards the development of inculturation theology, see Haleblian, 'The Problem of Contextualization' in:Missiology, 11 (1983), pp. 95-111. Schreiter (Constructing Local Theologies, p. 2, footnote 3) refers to the same author. See also Martey (African Theology, p. 63-69) who gives a short but precise over-

time, however, it would seem that more emphasis was laid on the terms Africanization and indigenization.

By the mid-1970s new theological awareness led African theologians to question the implications of basing African theology on the adaptation model. It had become clear that this model was itself a Western missionary invention, which did not allow theology in Africa to go beyond certain external trappings (for example liturgical dress and hymns).[40] At the 1974 Synod of Bishops in Rome the bishops of Africa and Madagascar therefore rejected the term adaptation, returning to the original paradigm of incarnation for developing Christian thought and praxis in Africa. The bishops "considered as being completely out of date the so-called theology of adaptation. Instead they adopt the theology of incarnation."[41] The response of Rome dismissed this *votum* of the bishops, notwithstanding its consistency with scripture, and the fact that Vatican II's document *Gaudium et Spes* would seem to have the incarnation as its point of departure in speaking about the need for relating the faith to the various "socio-cultural regions".[42]

Since Adaptation was rejected by African bishops and theologians, incarnation by Rome and indigenization was not received with enthusiasm in Protestant circles any more, there arose the need for a new term that could

---

view of the development of the concept in both Protestant and Catholic circles.

[40] Like the translation model, adaptation has a basic weakness because in trying to express local ideas using Western categories, it presumes a method in which an articulated philosophical system forms the basis for a systematic theology. Schreiter (1985:10ff) makes it clear that such a theology has its roots in 13th century theology of the West, which important as it may be is limited in scope. It is a theology addressed principally to the academy. Yet "Church and academy are not coextensive institutions". The Adaptation model is bound to force cultural data into foreign categories.

[41] AFER, vol. 17, No. 1, 1975, p. 58, quoted in:Shorter, Toward a Theology, p. 80. See also Shorter, African Christian Theology, p. 150, referred to in:Martey, African Theology, p. 66. Martey also informs us about the same misgivings concerning the theology of adaptation on the Protestant side, as made clear by the AACC. See AACC, The Struggle Continues, (Nairobi: 1975), p. 52, in:Martey, African Theology, p. 66, footnote 15.

[42] Shorter, (African Christian Theology, p. 14) cites portions of the response to the bishops in L'Osservatore Romano, no. 45, 7 November 1974, p. 9. Among others, the Pope's response considered the idea of a theology of incarnation "dangerous" and enjoined the African bishops to find "a better expression of faith to correspond to the racial, social and cultural milieux." More than two decades later, as Shorter further observes, Cardinal Ratzinger, Secretary of the Congregation for the Doctrine of the Faith, also dismissed African theology, considering it "more a project than a reality" (p. 244). These references are also mentioned by Martey, African Theology, p. 66. His critical eye does not miss the contradictions that surface when one tries to reconcile these negative official reactions with the papal statement that there was need to find an expression of faith corresponding to the cultural milieu. Besides, Martey believes that these reactions undermine "Vatican II theology and the Pope's own promise of the 1969 Kampala address."

adequately express the shift in theological awareness, self-understanding and Christian religious experience of Africans.[43] This need found its satisfaction in the term inculturation, which gained currency by the end of the 1970s.

In the Catholic Church the introduction of the term inculturation is credited largely to the members of the Society of Jesus. Beginning with Joseph Masson of the Gregorian University, who probably first used the term in 1962, inculturation was used and discussed at length at the 32nd Congregation of the Society in Rome (December 1974 – April 1975). In 1978 the term became popular following the publication of the letter of the Jesuit Superior General, Pedro Arrupe, in which inculturation was defined and explained.[44] Since then there have been several conferences and seminars on inculturation,[45] and the term has since been added to current theological lexicons.[46] Arrupe described inculturation as: "[t]he incarnation of Christian life and of the Christian message in a particular cultural context, in such a way that this experience not only finds expression through elements proper to the culture in question but becomes a principle that animates, directs and unifies the culture, transforming it and remaking it so as to bring about a >>new creation<<."[47] Inculturation thus implies the appropriation of Christian life to a given culture. This appropriation of the Christian life gives the culture concerned a specific orientation, and effects in the long run a renewal and transformation of the culture. Arrupe's definition, therefore, tries to capture generally and essentially what inculturation is about.

To appreciate the concrete import of inculturation in African theology, however, we must search for the reasons which prevented inculturation from taking place at the inception of evangelization, and why inculturation is now considered as an urgent need and task of the African Church. The thesis be-

---

[43] Martey, African Theology, p. 67.

[44] See Arrupe, "Letter to the Whole Society on Inculturation", in: Studies in the International Apostolate of Jesuits, 7 (June 1978).

[45] Examples of such conferences and seminars, on national and international frontiers, include the Boston Conference on inculturation, indigenization, and contextualisation (see Schineller, constructing Local Theologies, Chap. 1, footnote 4), the series of seminars at the Gregorian University in Rome between 1977 –78; 1981 in Jerusalem and Yogyakarta in 1983 (see Shorter, Toward a Theology, p. 8). For detailed information on the historical development of the term inculturation, see Shorter, Toward a Theology, pp. 10ff and Schineller, Handbook, pp. 5ff.

[46] See Collet, 'Inkulturation', p. 396. Besides, there is currently quite a long list of literature on the theology of inculturation. *Missio* for instance offers a bibliographical entry of about 498 books and articles dealing directly with or related to the theme of inculturation in Africa. This collection covers only the period between 1980 – 1994 (see ThiC Supplements 9 (1994), pp. 27-63.

[47] Arrupe, 'Letter', p. 172, cited by Schineller, Handbook, p. 6 and in:Shorter, Toward a Theology, p. 11.

hind this desire to relate inculturation to the particular situation of Africa was given earlier (see paragraph 1.3 of this study): namely, inculturation as a normal result of the religion-culture correlation was prevented in Africa as a result of the negative cultural history of African peoples. Some concrete aspects of this thesis are taken up in the paragraphs that follow.

1.3.2 Why Inculturation in Africa?

Why after all is there a need for inculturation if, as we saw earlier, it is a phenomenon that accompanies every religious experience anyway? Why inculturation in Africa of all places, with its rich religious traditions and feeling? Why could African cultures not incarnate the Christian faith from the very moment the Christian message first reached the African soil? These are fundamental questions that we can ill afford to overlook. They compel us to look for the phenomena that must have militated against a religious process that should have occurred as a matter of course. Such phenomena, we would suggest, are to be found in the cultural and religious history of the people concerned.

To understand inculturation therefore one should cautiously select from the history of Christian evangelization on the one hand, and from the cultural and political history of African peoples on the other hand, those factors, which must have hindered the process of inculturation in the first place. The presentation that follows presents briefly the background to missionary activity in Africa and suggests that this background is the context that helps us to test our understanding of inculturation in the particular context of Africa.

1.3.3 Christianity and Christian Conquest

As the Church grew in her own consciousness, she used the Jewish, Greek and Roman cultural elements, which had influenced her formation from the beginning to give expression to her self-understanding and to shape her identity. From humble beginnings of communities of believers grouped probably according to different traditions of the Jesus event,[48] the Church grew into a community with a great tendency towards homogeneity. For such homogeneity however the Church had to pay a price. The Church of the apostolic era, marked by prophetic dynamism in the midst of persecution had by the 4th and

---

[48] Bible scholars make us understand that the Gospels represent different but related traditions of communities. In addition to these are the Pauline communities, which he founded through his ministry to the gentiles.

5th centuries become "the Church of Christian times," marked by the Empire and Christian conquest.[49] A long and complicated history of what is referred to as Christendom had begun. The development of Christian identity became intricately tied up with imperial Roman culture, civilization and identity.[50] The context of local communities ceased to be the domain for reflecting on the faith; immediate concerns of the communities were now only of secondary importance and answers were sought for questions that were not real or directly related to the experience of particular communities.[51]

Beginning with the Emperor Constantine, the practice of Christian religion became more a matter of tradition than of faith.[52] By the time of the Emperor Theodosius around 400CE there ensued a thorough and persistent attack on the indigenous Roman religion and every form of heresy in the wake of an official enforcement of Christianity.[53] The result was to confuse faith with a 'political principle' and "to identify God with the maintenance of a specific human institution."[54] The Emperor now represented Christ and a person became Christian on the basis of imperial legislation.[55] The last two decades of Theodosius' rule saw the completion of Christian militancy and victory. Theologies developed in favor of the Empire (as representing the reign of god on earth) and there was an "integration of the Roman past based on the perceived religious victory of Christianity over the old religion."[56]

From now on, the Church would operate (especially regarding her missionary mandate) on stringent dichotomous categories for understanding peoples and cultures – Christians versus heathens, "inner barbarians and classical

---

[49] G. M. Bediako, Primal Religion and Biblical Religion: Addressing a Problem of Relationship (Sheffield: Academic Press, 1997), p. 20.

[50] Bediako, Primal Religion, pp. 20ff.

[51] It has been mentioned above that this tendency towards homogeneity was already present in NT times as shown in the events leading to the Council of Jerusalem (Acts 15).

[52] Bediako (Primal Religion, p. 20) cites A. D. Nock, Conversion: The Old and the New in Religion from Alexander to Augustine of Hippo (Oxford: Oxford University Press, 1933), pp. 1-10. We are made to understand that "religion of tradition [implies] an intrinsic aspect of social organization. A prophetic religion is one originating from a prophetic movement that provides an ethical critique of existing religious tradition."

[53] Bediako (Primal Religion, p. 20) referring to C. N. Cochrane, Christianity and Classical Culture, (London: Oxford University Press, 1957), p. 3; N. Q. King, The Emperor Theodosius and the Establishment of Christianity (London: SCM Press, 1961).

[54] Bediako (p. 21) referring to M. H. Shepherd. Jr., "Before and After Constantine", in:J. C. Brauer (ed.), the Impact of the Church upon its Culture (Chicago: Chicago University Press, 1968), pp. 17-38; Cochrane 1957:336.

[55] Bediako, Primal Religion, p. 21.

[56] Bediako, Primal Religion, p. 21. The comment of A. R. Markus, (Christianity in the Roman World [London: Thomas & Hudson, 1974]), makes it clearer: ">>Christian<< had come to define the inner quality of the Roman world, >>Roman<< had come to define the outer edges of Christendom." Cited in:Bediako, Primal Religion, p. 21, footnote 8.

civilization"[57], orient and occident, etc. It is interesting to note however that these dichotomous categories for understanding reality did not, in the first place, have anything directly to do with Africans. The home of such categories and their limits of application remained for a long time within the Roman world.[58] As history would have it, however, the gulf established between peoples by virtue of such categories healed in favor of 'Europe',[59] but at the expense and to the detriment of other peoples and cultures among whom are Africans.[60]

Beginning with the idea of 'Europa' under Charlemagne around 800CE, the identification of Christianity with imperial Rome shifted to identification of Christianity with Europe. Christendom gradually became Eurocentrism and European consciousness became the basis of Christian identity.[61] In the process it was only the Empire that diffused into a new structure of political and geographical organization—Europe. The identification of this new social entity with Christianity and the dualistic categories for interpreting reality however survived the demise of the Roman Empire and gained greater importance in the European paradigm. Thus Europe became all that the Roman Empire was and the world beyond the boundaries of Europe took the place of what the 'inner barbarians' used to be within the Roman world.[62] For our purposes in

---

[57] P. Brown, The World of Late Antiquity from Marcus Aurelius to Muhammad (London: Thames & Hudson, 1971), p. 112; cited in:Bediako, Primal religion, p. 22.

[58] We are informed that for a long time Roman Christianity remained within its own walls, not wanting to have any contact with peoples beyond the borders of the Roman Empire. Such people were considered too uncivilized to be fit for a religion that had come to be associated with urban life and civilian ethics. Thus within the Western world of the fourth and fifth centuries, Christianity had already "assumed its general stock of prejudices. Questions such as 'What place would God have in a savage world?' and 'How could Christian witness survive among barbarians?' were common" (Bediako, Primal Religion, p. 22 citing Brown, The World, p. 112). The same sources make clear, therefore, that the expansion of Christianity in the Roman world itself around this time materialized only after the gap between the ">>inner barbarians<< and classical civilization" had been bridged. See also E. A. Thompson, 'Christianity and the Northern Barbarians', in: A. Momigliano (ed.), The Conflict between Paganism and Christianity in the fourth Century (Oxford: Clarendon Press, 1963), pp. 56-78, cited in:Bediako, Primal Religion, p. 22.

[59] Both the name and the creation of geographical boundaries of what came to be known as Europe has its own history. See Denys Hay, Europe: The emergence of an Idea (Edinburgh: Edinburgh University Press, 1957).

[60] See A. Mazrui, The Africans, A Triple Heritage, (London: BBC Publications, 1986).

[61] Bediako, Primal Religion, p. 28.

[62] The reasons for this development and the process itself are beyond the limits of this study. For a good overview of some of such reasons, see Bediako, Primal Religion, pp. 22-45, especially 35-45. See also D. Hay, Europe: The Emergence of an Idea; Maurice Keen, The Pelican History of Medieval Europe (Harmondsworth: Pelican, 1969); W. M. Watt, The Influence of Islam on Medieval Europe (Edinburgh: Edinburgh University Press, 1972); A. Mazrui, The Moving Cultural Frontier of World Order: From Monotheism to

this study it is sufficient to conclude that by the time Christian missionaries arrived in Africa the dichotomous consideration of peoples tended to apply to 'civilized Europeans' and 'primitive Africans', 'Christian Europe' and 'heathen (pagan) Africa' etc. Europe was now the new Kingdom of God on earth,[63] and the Christianizing motive accorded European conquerors the freedom to operate *sicut miles Christi*.[64] We are thus at the threshold of the history of Christian evangelization in Africa, relevant parts of which are discussed later in the study.

If we make the historical setting of evangelization in Africa the context for analyzing the concept of inculturation,[65] it becomes justifiable to make certain inferences. The first inference is that much of missionary activity in Africa depended on, or at least cooperated closely with European militancy on the continent.[66] Secondly, we can further infer that the speed with which Afri-

---

North-South Relations, World Order Models Project, Working Paper No. 18 (New York: Institute for World Order, Inc., 1982). Most of these sources are mentioned in Bediako, Primal Religion. Bediako concludes that the emergence of Christian Europe was only the continuation of Christendom in a wider context of the world (p. 39).

[63] In the seventeenth century, an English Protestant minister, the Reverend Samuel Purchas observed: "Europe is taught the way to scale Heaven, not by Mathematicall principles, but by Divine veritie. Jesus Christ is their way, their truth, their life; who hath long since given a Bill of Divorce to ungrateful Asia where hee was borne, and Africa the place of his flight and refuge, and is become almost wholly and onely European. For wee find of this name in Asia, lesser in Africa and nothing at all in America, but later European gleanings." See S. Purchas, His Pilgrimes (Hakluyt Society Extra Series, 1905), Introduction, I, p. 215, quoted in:Hay 1957:110, and in:Bediako, Primal Religion, p. 39.

[64] In 1494 Pope Nicholas V authorized the King of Portugal to "invade, conquer and submit to perpetual slavery the people of Africa." See E. L. Bute and H. J. P. Harmer, The Black Handbook: The People, History and Politics of Africa and the African Diaspora (London and Washington: Cassell, 1997), p. 325. Before this authorization, there existed an earlier one, which had a more universalistic tone, as shown in the Papal Bulls, *Dum Diverses* in 1452, *Romanus Pontifex* in 1455 and *Inter Caetera* in 1456. See C. R. Boxer, The Portuguese Seaborn Empire 1415-1825 (London: Hutchinson, 1969), pp. 21-22, cited in:Bediako, Primal religion, p. 40, footnote 84. It is important to note that these papal documents are often given dates that do not always tally. J. M. Ela, for instance dates *Inter Caetera* to 1493, he also believes the authorization of Nicholas V to the King of Portugal was given in 1454. See J. M. Ela, African Cry, (Maryknoll: Orbis Books, 1986), p. 11. A good source of information about the Bull, *Inter Cetera* is R. Aubenas and R. Richard, La chiesa e il rinascimento (Torino, 1972), pp. 166-167. See also J. M. Bonino, Doing Theology in a Revolutionary Situation (Philadelphia: Frotress Press, 1975), pp. 2-9.

[65] Theology is meaningful only if it provides a faithful reflection of events that make up history, including the history of the life of the Church. A notion of inculturation that generates from a vision of a yet-to-be-lived experience will lack any reference to the practical experience of African peoples, whose aspirations inculturation is supposed to answer. Hence inculturation theology, like all theology must be a reflection modeled on the concrete stuff of lived experience. See Ela, African Cry, p. 28ff.

[66] Many books on the history of the Church in Africa give this impression, which is cer-

can peoples were christianized was not so much the result of the inner dynamism of the faith per se.[67] Certain external factors did play a major role. From this inference it becomes possible to conclude that from the onset of evangelization, African peoples and cultures were denied the freedom to interact with the Christian message in such a way that would yield an African incarnation of Christianity.[68] The emphasis of this study, however, is not just the fact that much in the history of evangelization in Africa had negative and detrimental effects. Most important is the fact that behind the form which evangelization took lies a *narrative*[69] based on a stringent dichotomous category for understanding reality and for considering human persons. In the area of morality and ethics, as in other areas life, this dualistic consideration of the human person has its toll on the Western Church, but its effect is very pronounced in the African context. We shall now direct our attention to some important nuances of meaning of inculturation on the basis of the background described above.

---

tainly based on facts of history. The impression is further confirmed in other books on African history and culture. At the same time we have to remember that the Christian Churches in Europe and the missionary congregations in Africa did confront the colonizers and sometimes challenged the injustice of the situation. Nevertheless, the Church could not extricate herself from her identification with Europe and the European zeal for conquest. If she criticized the injustice of aggression, she nonetheless depended on the conquered territories of the various European nations for Christianizing African peoples. See Ela, African Cry, pp. 9-38, see also J. V. Taylor, The Primal Vision (London: SCM Press, 1963), pp. 5-12.

[67] L. P. Ngongo, "Pourvoir politique occidental dans les structures de l'Eglise en Afrique," in:Civilisation noir et Eglise catholique: Colloque d'Abidjan, 12-17 Septembre 1977 (Paris: Présence Africaine, 1978), cited in:Ela, African Cry, p. 22, footnote 12.

[68] What F. Kamphaus says about the Church in this regard is directly applicable to Africa. "Oft hat [die Kirche ... ihre] Berufung zum Universalismus mißverstanden; sie hat die Lokalkirchen und ihre Kulturen überfremdet, andere Religionen verteufelt, sich in ihrer Mission viel zu sehr an den europäischen Imperialismus angekoppelt.... Sie hat ihre Berufung, dem anbrechenden Reich Gottes zu dienen, als Herrschaftsanspruch mißbraucht." F. Kamphaus, Eine Zukunft für alle (Freiburg: Herder, 1995), p. 22.

[69] We mentioned that we intend to approach morality and ethics, the main concern of this study, by considering ethical action as 'texts'. This idea stems from the tradition that attempts to study and teach ethics as *narrative*. Details about this approach and its contribution to the study of ethics are taken up in the next chapter. In addition the word narrative is used here to paint a picture in which the whole process of evangelization is seen as a pattern of dialogue in which the Western world has often told the 'life story' of Africans on the basis of a dualistic category for understanding reality. Based upon the same category, the West has often failed to understand the story even when Africans told it. What is worse, Africans themselves have been drawn into the same dichotomous category of thought, which they willy-nilly apply in telling their life story.

1.4 A critical Appraisal of Inculturation in Current Theology

In this section some of the nuances of meaning in the theory and praxis of inculturation are considered. On the basis of some underlying notions that are taken for granted, it is proposed that care should be taken not to assume all too quickly that inculturation attains its fullness of meaning when considered only as an essential theology of mission. Using the idea of Models as a method for doing theology,[70] the various approaches to inculturation are classified under two main models – the essentialist model and the existentialist model. The former considers inculturation from the point of view of a theology of mission, and the latter as a process of rehabilitation and liberation. These two sets of meanings need not be mutually exclusive, but they could be and are on occasion mutually opposing.[71]

1.4.1 The Essentialist Model

The essentialist model understands inculturation as having fundamentally to do with a theology of mission. It is a matter of evangelization. Its purpose is to respect cultures, "seek to know the essential components" of the cultures to be evangelized, respect their particular values and riches and so endeavor "to bring the power of the Gospel into the very heart of culture and cultures."[72] The Post-Synodal Apostolic Exhortation, *Ecclesia in Africa,* on the Special

---

[70] The idea of using models in theological methodology was introduced and popularized in contemporary times by Avery Dulles. See Dulles, Models of the Church (Dublin: Gill and McMillan, 1974); and Models of Revelation (Maryknoll: Orbis Books, 1983). Models are intellectual representations for evaluating the strengths and weaknesses of theological propositions. They help to structure the motives underlying specific patterns of thought with respect to the facts and experiences which compose the subject matter of theological reflection. Models are an effective means for judging the relevance of theological procedure. See also Lornegan, A Third Collection, (Paulist Press, 1985), pp. 116-119 passim. Schreiter (Constructing Local Theologies, pp. 6ff) mentions a variant form of this method, which he calls 'Mapping'. He warns, however, that this use of models as theological methodology has the danger of superficial taxonomy.

[71] Such opposition does not exist only between the official Church and local Churches in Africa, but also between theologians in the local Churches themselves. This, for example, is the issue that Martey addresses, by pointing out the opposition that seems to exist between South African Black Theology and the theology of inculturation in sub-Saharan Africa. The former emphasizes liberation and takes the social-political situation as its point of departure, while inculturation concentrates on the cultural aspects of liberation (see Martey, African Theology). The disagreement looks greater between the official Church and local Churches. Real signs of such differences, not only about the meaning of inculturation, but also about its praxis can be deduced from the comment of Cardinal Ratzinger, and the Pope's designation of a theology of incarnation as dangerous, earlier referred to.

[72] John Paul II, Apostolic Exhortation, Catechesi Tradendae, 1979.

Assembly for Africa of the Synod of Bishops teaches clearly in this regard. Chapter three of this document treats "Evangelization and Inculturation."[73] *Propositio* 59 speaks specifically of "the importance for *evangelization of inculturation*"[74] which is explained to mean "the process by which "catechesis >>takes flesh<< in the various cultures."[75]

Here inculturation has as its objective, first and foremost, the originality of faith expression, so that the mysteries of faith are lived and expressed in and by means of the culture concerned. The same document therefore explains that the goal to be achieved through inculturation is "the synthesis between culture and faith[76] ... without compromising what is of divine right and the great discipline of the Church."[77] Essentially inculturation as a means of evangelization is urgent "because in Africa there are millions who are not yet evangelized."[78] Inculturation in the essentialist model is therefore expected to provide the medium for full evangelization, so that *many* will come to receive the good news of Jesus for their salvation. An important aspect of salvation is the acceptance of baptism and the practice of a good Christian life.[79] Inculturation must busy itself with finding the proper or essential way of bringing about evangelization in all its aspects. For that matter there is need to study the receiving culture in all its complexity so as to infuse all facets of life of the peoples being evangelized with the gospel.[80]

---

[73] John Paul II, Post Synodal Apostolic Exhortation, *Ecclesia in Africa*, (Nairobi: Paulines Publications. 1995), pp. 41-56.

[74] Ecclesia in Africa, p. 44; my italics.

[75] Ecclesia in Africa, p. 44, referring to Catechesi Tradendae, p. 53.

[76] Ecclesia in Africa, p. 61, no. 78, referring to John Paul II, Address to the Italian National Congress of the Ecclesial Movement for Cultural Commitment (16 January 1982), 2: Insegnamenti V/ (1982), p. 131.

[77] Ecclesia in Africa, p. 61, referring to Vatican II, Constitution on the Sacred Liturgy, *Sacrosanctum Concilium*, 37-40.

[78] Ecclesia in Africa, no. 74. This formulation smacks of the classical theological preoccupation with the quantitative "salvation of the pagans" (G. Gutierrez, A Theology of Liberation, Maryknoll: Orbis Books, 1973, pp.150-152). As Gutierrez rightly observes, there are two basic issues behind such preoccupation with quantitative salvation: "The terms of the problem are, on the one hand, the universality of salvation, and on the other, the visible Church as the mediator of salvation" (Gutierrez, A Theology, p. 150). Although inculturation certainly aims at a *"qualitative and intensive* approach" (Gutierrez, p. 151, author's emphasis) to the Christian faith, we realize from the language of the Synod that the concept of inculturation, in its essentialist form has not been freed of the '*dichotomous narrative'* described earlier.

[79] Ecclesia in Africa, no. 78. It is clear that the document presumes that people know what 'a good Christian life' entails, and that once the culture of the people becomes the means of expressing their faith, it will be easier to obtain the fruit of a 'good Christian life.' It remains unclear how 'the good Christian life' is to be defined, but from the tone of the Document, it is possible to infer that this definition is reserved to the Official Church.

[80] Ecclesia in Africa, no. 62.

This model also expects the principle and function of inculturation to be essentially the same, the world over, "because the gospel is never an internal product of a particular country but always comes 'from outside', from on high."[81] The receiving culture must therefore open to the challenge and total transformation (conversion) required by the gospel. And the gospel in turn must take on the nature of culture in which it is preached in order to become relevant and authentic.[82] In the final analysis inculturation is accomplished, in and through the power of the Holy Spirit, for the benefit of the universal salvation of all.[83]

When one critically considers the material available on inculturation, one cannot avoid to take note of the tendency of seeing inculturation as a means of doing evangelization well. This tendency can be found even in literature that is rather critical of the essentialist model of inculturation. Two influential books on inculturation by Shorter and Schineller respectively could help to illustrate the point.[84] In the case of the former, there is no doubt that (considering how often Shorter is cited in much of the literature on the topic of inculturation) Shorter's book is of indisputable importance in the study of inculturation theology. For example, he shows his awareness of the fact that inculturation could be misunderstood as a one-way process, where faith is transferred from one culture to another, rather than as a process of mutual transformation. He therefore suggests the use of the term 'interculturation.'[85] How-

---

[81] Ecclesia in Africa, no. 74. This statement could be understood to mean that the Gospel has a divine and therefore supracultural character – which is not the same as saying the Gospel is extra-cultural. Hence the statement is in order as long as it stresses the element of conversion expected of cultures that come into contact with the Gospel. However, it is difficult to miss the 'high christological' tone of the statement. The formulation almost robs the statement of its value. As Shorter (Toward a Theology, p. 82) puts it, an inculturation modeled on a Christology from above "encourages in practice a one-way view of inculturation. ... [It is] essentially [a] model of the Eternal Logos, a pre-existent divine being, taking human flesh. ... One is immediately tempted by the analogy to think of inculturation in terms of a disembodied essence being injected into a concrete human culture. ... [Yet] there is no world of essences. The Christian message –Christ himself– is transmitted from culture to culture, from history to history."

[82] Ecclesia in Africa, nos. 55, 57, 62.

[83] Ecclesia in Africa, no. 78.

[84] A. Shorter, Toward A Theology of Inculturation (Maryknoll: Orbis Books, first published in 1988, fourth printing 1995); P. Schineller, A Handbook on Inculturation (New York: Paulist Press, 1990).

[85] Shorter, Toward a Theology, p. 3. Shorter believes many missiologists are dissatisfied with the term inculturation because of the danger of evoking this one-sided meaning of evangelization. The word 'interculturation' is borrowed from Bishop Joseph Blomjous, whom Shorter acknowledges to have coined the term in 1980. See Blomjous, "Development in Mission Thinking and Practice 1959-1980: Inculturation and Interculturation", in: AFER, Vol. 22, No. 6, pp. 393-398. Reference taken from Shorter, Toward a Theology, p. 273. It is interesting to realize that Blomjous coined this term against the background of a

ever, he does not take pains to illustrate how the very restriction of inculturation to the essentials of evangelization alone yields that danger.

Again, Shorter makes use of Lonergan's distinction between classicist and contemporary approaches to understanding culture.[86] He observes that the former is more normative and the latter more dynamic and plural. Shorter fails, however, to apply the same categories to the concept of inculturation as a whole. This would have revealed the two models operative in the discussion on inculturation. Namely, inculturation as a search for normative and universally applicable means of evangelization on the one hand, and on the other hand, as one part of a complete theological hermeneutic and awareness which remain incomplete without the motive of liberation. Hence even though Shorter is not at all silent about the liberation aspect, the motives of rehabilitation and liberation do not receive the emphasis that one would expect from the detailed knowledge Shorter displays concerning the concept of inculturation. It would seem that these motives are given only an implicit importance in the statement that inculturation is "nothing other than the profound evangelization of a people in their culture."[87]

In general the book of Schineller overlaps with many of the issues presented by Shorter. A valuable addition however is Schineller's chapter on Method. It is clear from this chapter that Schineller's concern, i.e. what he considers as the basic and most important purpose of inculturation, is that evangelization is done and done well. The three fundamental elements in "*the how of evangelization*" (title of Chapter 5 of Schineller's book) therefore are 'the Christian message', 'the situation' and 'the pastoral agent or minister.' Like Shorter, Schineller also has a section on Liberation Theology. Here, he discusses the importance of liberation in inculturation. All the same his general approach makes it impossible to escape the impression that liberation is strongly subordinate to the motive of evangelization. In order words, it is presupposed that a good evangelization entails liberation. His approach would seem to tie in well with the assertion that the term inculturation developed as a result of the self-reflection of the missionary on the successes and failures of his efforts in evangelization.[88] This view forgets the important place occupied by the people being evangelized. The point is therefore clear that if inculturation developed as result of the missionary's evaluation of his work, then the

---

distinction between what he called 'traditional mission' and 'the mission of the future'. See Shorter, Toward a Theology, p. 13.
[86] Shorter, Toward a Theology, p. 14.
[87] Shorter, Toward a Theology, p. 63.
[88] Such an assertion is deducible, for example, from the statement of Arrupe (Letter, p. 9). "We are now able to lament that at its inception, "Christianity did not realize that the African ground had long been carefully prepared by God for the reception of the Christian seed; and that that seed had in the course of the centuries inevitably put on the cultural garments of different civilizations, Jewish, Greek, Roman, etc." Cited in:Schineller, Handbook, p.12.

subject of inculturation par excellence is the missionary or pastoral worker, even if 'missionary' here implies being only a "facilitator", as Schineller would want us to understand.[89]

1.4.2 Limitations and Advantages of the Essentialist model

The fundamental weakness of this model is its tendency to reduce inculturation to a theology of mission. This weakness causes more worry when inculturation is given formulations that falsely presume a *neutral* African cultural history.[90] Many of the consequences for doing so have been mentioned in the discussion of the model above. We shall briefly reiterate some of the important points.

The model gives the impression that inculturation does not necessarily arise from any internal awakening to self, or from a shift in the categories with which the recipients of the gospel define themselves. Thus inculturation still carries with it the danger of imposition and/or paternalism.[91] The model is liable to operate on the basis of a *heteronomous pluralism*.[92]

Another danger is the tendency to overemphasize the 'quantitative and extensive' aspect of the missionary mandate to the neglect of the 'qualitative and intensive' aspects. In the African context, the model does not seem to accord

---

[89] Schineller, Handbook, pp. 68ff.

[90] The expression 'neutral cultural history' is used here to describe a culture that has (for the greater part) functioned and continues to do so on the basis of its own inner dynamism and freedom. The faith-culture dialogue on the African continent, however, cannot be said to have taken place on a neutral cultural foil. At the time of the contact African cultures were subjected to slavery, colonialism and cultural domination. The importance of cultural freedom if culture should effectively serve as a vehicle of faith is emphasized in Gaudium et Spes, no. 59. "Culture since it flows from man's rational and social nature, has continual need of rightful freedom of development and legitimate possibility of autonomy according to its own principles. Quite rightly it demands respect and enjoys a certain inviolability."

[91] See Martey, African Theology, pp. 7-9; Shorter, African Christian Theology, p. 150.

[92] By heteronomous pluralism is meant that system in which concession is made for difference (cultural or otherwise) based, however, on external factors (such as Church authority, social scientists or missionaries, etc.) and not on an internal hermeneutic of difference arising from the facts of life of a given group of people. This latter type of difference constitutes what we may refer to as autonomous pluralism. Heteronomous pluralism is formal, whereas autonomous pluralism is existential. Formal pluralism is used in the context of Africa, for instance, as compensation for the humiliation inflicted on Africans in the history of their contact with the West. For that reason heteronomous pluralism often stands the danger of romanticizing African cultures, and it is often paternalistic, even if unwittingly so. See Schreiter, Constructing Local Theologies, p. 39; See also T. Sundermeier, Den Fremden verstehen: Eine praktische Hermeneutik, (Goettingen: Vandenhoeck & Ruprecht, 1996).

the anthropological rehabilitation and liberation which Africans desire the importance and emphasis it deserves. These motives would seem to be subordinated to the motives of a supposed "profound evangelization". The narrative of Christian life is likely to continue to dependend on dichotomous categories for understanding the 'faith–culture' dialogue.

Finally, because of its interest in the systematic, the questions of concern in this model would center on what was done wrong in the process of evangelization, and not why something was done wrong. The model would seek to restrict the limits of authenticity rather than support authentic differences of peoples. Less attention would be given to the existential history of the people.

The strengths of the essentialist model of inculturation lie in the area of the systematic. The essentialist model insists on respect for church history and tradition. It seeks to relate the local experience to other local experiences in the larger union of communities of faith. The model also warns against culturalism and insists that gospel values should not be compromised. It is for that matter more normative, setting limits and warning of possible excesses.

Besides its importance for the systematic, the model reflects a positive growth of consciousness on the part of the official Church and missionary communities as regards their attitude towards non-western cultures. In the African context, for example, the movement from the *motu proprio* forgiving Africans the curse of Ham to the papal address (Uganda, 1969) commending the values of African cultures shows enormous progress.[93]

1.4.3 The Existentialist Model

The existentialist model sees inculturation as an aspect of a new theological hermeneutic, based on a fundamental shift in the theological awareness of the recipients of the gospel. Such an understanding of inculturation is being articulated more and more by various individual African theologians and by conferences of African theologians. The model demands that inculturation be considered a part of an integral African theological hermeneutic, which remains incomplete without the aspects of anthropological rehabilitation and liberation. I shall illustrate this by referring to E. Martey and J. M. Ela,[94] whose works, in the opinion of this study, are paradigmatic of what is here described as the existentialist model of inculturation. The reasons for this opinion will become clear in course of the discussion.

---

[93] See reference by Ela in his African Cry, (Maryknoll: Orbis Books, 1986), p. 30
[94] E. Martey, African Theology: Inculturation and Liberation (Maryknoll: Orbis Books, 1994); J. M. Ela, My Faith as an African (Maryknoll: Orbis Books, 1988), see especially Ela, African Cry (Maryknoll: Orbis Books, 1986).

Martey's contribution to the discussion on inculturation is his insistence that inculturation is not only 'culture-gospel (faith) dialectic', but also a process that seeks the integral liberation of the African using the instruments of faith *and* culture.[95] Inculturation begins with a new level of consciousness on the part of Africans seeking answers to their existential questions.

The concrete conditions of life in Africa, Martey argues, must form the *locus sine qua non* for any meaningful theological enterprise in Africa. To describe the 'African reality' Martey used the words of the Ecumenical Association of Third World Theologians (EATWOT):

"The social underdevelopment of Africa represents a fundamental aspect of the anthropological pauperization of the African person. If we define pauperization as the fact of becoming or making poor, namely being deprived of all that we have acquired, all that we are and all that we can do, we shall recognize that Africa is subjugated to structures which result in complete pauperization: political, economic, and social. When it is not a matter of being deprived of all that we own, but rather of all that we are – our human identity, our social roots, our history, our culture, our dignity, our rights, our hopes, and our plans – then pauperization becomes anthropological. It then affects religious and cultural life at its very roots."[96]

Against this background Martey laments the division of African theology into compartments of 'Africanisation'[sic] on one hand, and 'Liberation'[97] on the other hand. If the African reality that EATWOT describes is taken seriously, then the specific question which African theology must address is the question of *"anthropological poverty"*[98] Hence "the struggle against this anthropological pauperization of the African person is what gives Africa its theological agenda."[99] The themes of inculturation and liberation, Martey strongly suggests, are inseparably linked in any theology that would do justice to the African reality.[100]

---

[95] Martey, African Theology, pp. 7ff.

[96] The *African Report* presented at the Second General Assembly of EATWOT held in Oaxtepec, Mexico, 1986, in:K. C. Abraham, (ed.), Third World Theologies: Commonalities and Divergences (Maryknoll, N.Y.: Orbis Books, 1990), p. 47; quoted in:Martey, African Theology, p. 38.

[97] Africanization here refers to the theology of inculturation, found mainly in sub-Saharan Africa. Even here, the theology of inculturation is given a different accentuation in the francophone and anglophone zones. 'Liberation' refers to Black Theology, found mainly in South Africa.

[98] Martey, African Theology, p. 38.

[99] Martey, African Theology, p. 38.

[100] Martey, African Theology, pp. 38ff.

As an integral part of the African theological agenda, inculturation takes as its point of departure not only the self-reflection of the missionary Church, but especially and most importantly the revolutionary changes in the socio-political consciousness of many African peoples. The history of what is now called inculturation in Africa began according to this model, then, not in the 1950s but already towards "the end of the nineteenth century and, especially, the first decade of the twentieth, when a more organized black resistance to colonial oppression and racism [developed]."[101] Martey further makes clear that the movement responsible for this 'black consciousness' was not the missionary Church, but pan-Africanism and especially African nationalism in the period soon after World War II.[102] On the basis of this new consciousness the Pan African Conference of Third World Theologians expresses the purpose of African theology:

> "We believe that African theology must be understood in the context of African life and culture and the creative attempt of African people to shape a new future that is different from the colonial past and the neo-colonial present.... African theology must reject, therefore, the prefabricated ideas of North Atlantic theology by defining itself according to the struggles of the people in their resistance against the structures of domination. Our task as theologians is to create a theology that arises from and is accountable to African people."[103]

Unlike Martey who seeks a synthesis for the inculturation-liberation aspects of African theology, Ela argues strongly for liberation as the main task of African theology. In this regard he would seem sometimes to concentrate only on the motive of liberation in his treatment of the subject of inculturation. All the same he sheds much light on the existentialist model by way of the very down to earth examples he provides of the local situation from which his theology arises, and by insisting that inculturation cannot forget the aspect of liberation. He raises his voice against the many people, and especially missionaries in anglophone African countries who believe that liberation has no place in Africa. Ela's quotation of Amilcar Cabral succinctly pictures what is at stake. "In order to restore authenticity to Africans, great importance should be given to the cultural factors that inspired the initial resistance to foreign control."[104]

---

[101] Martey, African Theology, p. 7.
[102] Martey, African Theology, p. 7 and pp. 63ff. For a detailed presentation on the beginnings of the process which is today called inculturation, in the view of Martey, see pp. 7-26; and pp. 63-86.
[103] *Final Communiqué* of the Pan African Conference of Third World Theologians, in: K. Appiah-Kubi and Sergio Torres (ed.), African Theology En Route (Maryknoll: Orbis Books, 1979), p. 193; cited in: Martey, African Theology, p. 63.
[104] A. Cabral, Unite et lutte, (Paris: Maspero, 1967), in: Ela, My Faith as an African, p. xv.

To see culture only as an instrument of evangelization could backfire, if the culture involved is not also made an instance of liberation. This is especially clear if one remembers that evangelization affected African culture the way it did, because the missionary at that time in Africa, was to a great extent, (even if inadvertently) a 'co-administrator' of the forces that so negatively affected African peoples and their cultures.[105]

In contemporary times the Church must face the bitter truth that no matter how hard she tries to oppose the forces of oppression and culture domination, she finds herself always trailing behind such forces. Contemporary politics, industrialization and its unjust economic structures, scientific advancement propagating a godless humanism[106], etc. are forces that often baffle, perplex or subsume the missionary him/herself in the seemingly uncontrollable speed of modernization. The problem is compounded if we remember that the negative effects of these forces build on the capital of humiliation and oppression that Africans have experienced in history.

In the face of such realities Ela believes that inculturation can contribute to the integral liberation of Africans by employing those cultural factors that support an internal and conscious resistance to humiliation, poverty and oppression. Inculturation should not be seen as something 'coming from outside there'. It is rather a harnessing of African cultural potentials and combining them with the values of the Gospel to bring hope of fullness of life to African peoples.

Like Martey, Ela argues that such integral liberation necessarily requires a reconsideration of African cultural, political and religious history. Such a reconsideration of African history will entail a process in which Africans develop a new cultural psychology, "a rereading of our African memory."[107] Based on this new level of consciousness inculturation will necessarily question the existing dichotomous categories, which have become normative for understanding Africa and the African identity.[108]

---

[105] J. K. Agbeti, West African Church History, 2 vols.(Leiden: E. J. Brill, 1986). See also C. T. Groves, The Planting of Christianity in Africa, 4 vols. (London: 1948-58).

[106] See Shorter, Toward a Theology, pp. 51ff. Shorter observes that "Christianity may be on the way to becoming a sub-culture in the Western culture it helped to create" because of the Church's difficulty in finding means "to penetrate and permeate the modernization process" (here p. 52).

[107] J. -M. Ela, My Faith as an African, p. xvi.

[108] In expressing the same idea, Martey suggests that theologizing in Africa must begin with a 'hermeneutic of suspicion'. Martey cites Ricoeur who explains that 'a hermeneutic of suspicion' "begins by *doubting* whether there is such an object [so that] ... hermeneutics is not an explication of the object, but *a tearing off of masks, an interpretation that reduces disguise*" (P. Ricoeur, Freud and Philosophy: An Essay on Interpretation. Tr. Denis Savage [New Haven, Conn.: Yale University Press, 1977], p. 30, Martey's emphasis); cited in: Martey, African Theology, p. 56. The feminist theologian, Schüssler Fiorenza has also developed a methodology of interpretation aimed at achieving a paradigmatic change in bibli-

Inculturation according to the existentialist model, then, would no longer be merely a *modus operandi* for evangelization, but a *modus vivendi*, in which faith and culture are at the service of integral liberation and salvation. Inculturation in this context is about becoming African -*Afrikanerwerdung*, "not in spite of, but because of, being evangelized."[109]

1.4.4 Limitations and Advantages of the Existentialist Model

The strength of the existentialist model lies in the fact that it avoids the danger of conceiving an inculturation arising from nostalgia for a lost cultural childhood on the part of the so-called developed world, out of which the older Churches grew. It avoids the projection of "we-would-so-much-like-to-have" values on African cultures due to romanticism and anachronism. Another strength is that the model concentrates on "the questions, which the people themselves ask, and not those thought necessary for systematic."[110] In this way, the newness of inculturation, as Crollius puts it, is not "the question of the relation between the Christian message and the cultures of mankind, ... but the *status quaestionis*, the way the problem is envisaged, is new."[111] It is a newness arising from the correspondence of inculturation to the "state of those who ask the question", based on their "new historical situation."[112] It takes not only cultural history, but also the people themselves seriously.

There are weaknesses to the existentialist model. It is clear that it will place less importance on the systematic and normative evangelization. There could be the danger of reacting negatively to Church tradition and so throwing out the baby together with the bath water. There is also "the possibility of reflecting only after action has been taken, rather than making reflection a basis for action ... [and] the too close concentration on ill and the inability to see intermediate manifestations of grace can also be a problem."[113]

What Schreiter says here is important. It would seem however that the theology of inculturation (both in its existentialist and essentialist forms) suffers a deficit of praxis. Whereas the Latin American experience of liberation

---

cal interpretation. She lists the hermeneutic of suspicion (Hermeneutik des Verdachts) as one of the four main elements needed for such a paradigmatic change. See E. Schüssler Fiorenza, Bread Not Stone: The Challenge of Feminist Biblical Interpretation (Boston: Beacon Press, 1984).

[109] E.-J. Pénoukou, Églises d'Afrique Propositions pour l'Avenir (Paris:1984), cited in: Shorter, Toward a Theology, p. 78.

[110] Schreiter, Local Theologies, p. 13.

[111] A. R. Crollius, "Inculturation: Newness and Ongoing Process", in: J. M. Walligo et al., Inculturation: Its meaning and Urgency, (Nairobi: St. Paul, 1986), p. 31.

[112] Crollius, 'Inculturation', p. 31.

[113] Schreiter, Constructing Local Theologies, p. 15.

theology, for example, grew out of the day to day struggle against the forces of oppression, it would seem that in the case of inculturation, theory has overtaken praxis.[114]

1.4.5 Models of Inculturation and African Christian Ethics

The experiment (above) of explaining inculturation by the use of models is not intended to compartmentalize the meaning and/or function of inculturation to any specific mindsets. Nor is it an attempt to work out conclusively the clearest possibility for understanding the phenomenon. The caution, which Schreiter sounds, remains valid. "The lack of consistent terminology, the need for neologisms, and the problem of conflicting connotations suggest something of the state of this shift in theological reflection. It is still new; many of the problems involved have not yet been thought through; and there is still no consensus about some basic and important issues."[115] The explanations given here are meant to help in exposing only two of the many and complex sets of meanings that could determine the approaches a person chooses in applying the concept of inculturation to the concrete religious experience of people.

These sets of meanings are often taken for granted so that we become inattentive to the divergent points of departure for doing inculturation theology in Africa. The danger involved in this lack of attentiveness is the possibility of developing a theory-praxis of inculturation based on a fictive consensus of meaning.

Above all the explanation of inculturation above aims at servicing a particular line of thought. This study is basically concerned with moral inquiry, an investigation of questions about morality. It is therefore necessary to show how ethics forms an aspect of inculturation.[116] In order to do so, the experiment with models has helped us to make explicit two fundamental elements of inculturation –people and history- which usually receive only implicit attention in most of the literature on the subject. If in the essentialist model culture and faith form the elements of importance, in the existentialist model the people and their history (historical consciousness) are indispensable and must be

---

[114] See J. M Ela, African Cry, 1986. Ela criticizes Negritude and African Personality movements as ideologies of the elite which are propounded from an ivory tower. Ela would even dismiss these movements as having nothing to do with the real experiences of the ordinary African. One would have to make allowance here for exaggeration on the part of Ela, as a result of the anger and vehemence articulated in his theological reflection. At the same time one cannot dismiss the point he makes all together.

[115] Schreiter, Constructing Local theologies, p. 6.

[116] See especially chapter three of this study for the main discussion of this question of ethics as a theme of inculturation.

explicitly considered. It implies that if culture and faith provide the formal instance, the people concerned and their history constitute the moral import of inculturation.

There is no morality without a people. Morality and ethics then do not only raise questions worthy of consideration in inculturation; they go beyond that level. For, to the extent that ethical questions are factual, personal, cultural and historical, morality itself presents a paradigmatic process of inculturation, of becoming human (humanization, or for that matter, 'human incarnation') Thus ethics as an aspect of inculturation deals very much with the existentialist understanding and concerns especially, questions of identity and self-consciousness. In order to work out the importance of people and their history it is necessary to turn our attention briefly to the terms of inculturation

1.5 A New Approach to the Elements of Inculturation

The attempt has been made above to draw attention to the subtle and essentialist bias that often underlies the discussion on inculturation. Due to this bias the basic terms of inculturation are usually limited to culture and faith. As a result inculturation is conceived as 'culture-faith dialectic'. A renewed consideration however would seem to suggest that the idea of inculturation as the search for a proper cultural manifestation of the Christian faith is the minimum. Inculturation in the African experience must traverse this limit. In addition to faith and culture, the people of Africa as the bearers of their culture, and the history of African peoples as a constitutive part of their present must be explicitly addressed. This new approach to the terms of inculturation insists, then, that both pairs of elements constitute the fundamental subject matter of inculturation. These pairs of elements – faith and culture on one hand, and people and history on the other – will now be discussed in order to focus the discussion further.

1.5.1 Faith and Culture

Two terms of reference considered fundamental to the discourse inculturation is expected to initiate are the Christian religious term (or component) and the cultural component. The former is described among others as Faith or Christian message, or sometimes even as Christianity, or often as the Gospel, or the essence of the Gospel. Chapter five of Shorter's *Toward a Theology of Inculturation* (titled "The Christian term of Inculturation")[117] gives a good assess-

---

[117] Shorter, Toward a Theology, p. 59.

ment of some of the renderings of the Christian term of inculturation, showing their usefulness and limitations respectively. Shorter himself settles on the insight from Schillebeeckx that "Christianity is not the religion of a book but of a person"[118]. He therefore concludes, "there is a real sense in which it can be said that the message of Christianity is Christ himself, that he is the subject of his own message."[119]

Here Shorter makes an important contribution in explaining what the Christian term of inculturation involves. His plea that "it can be truthfully said that what is inculturated is Jesus himself"[120] is especially striking. And this plea gains relevance in our context when Shorter links it to Pope John Paul's address in Nairobi in 1980: "In you, Christ has himself become African."[121] In this way we are naturally reminded of the incarnation paradigm and given the basis for which inculturation is at all possible.

Nonetheless this Christ event has always needed mediation, so that seeing Christ and his incarnation as the subject matter of inculturation does not exclude the traditional instances of mediation in the history of Christianity. Thus the Christian term of inculturation necessarily implies also the means of mediation. It includes in that regard the Christian religious tradition, and institutional affiliation – the Church, which is the custodian of that tradition. The Christian term will also include the scriptures, catechesis, church teaching, ritual and ceremony.

Yet all these have no existence without a given culture. Like all other religions, Christianity lives within and is expressed through culture. Hence we could say inculturation involves a communication between 'faith-contained-in-culture' and a 'to-be-christianized-culture'. Culture, then, is to be found on both sides of the inculturation equation.[122] The study of culture, therefore, as an important and basic element of inculturation cannot be overemphasized. As was mentioned already such study could take place in a number of ways. Whichever approach is taken, however, the role culture is actually given in the process would depend on whether one understands the phenomenon of culture essentially or existentially.

There are many definitions of culture, as there are schools and approaches to the study of culture. On the phenomenological level, the understanding of culture has experienced a continuous evolution of thought in several directions. Thus "in reality, anthropology has lacked a single broadly accepted and theoretically productive definition of culture."[123] For the moment it

---

[118] E. Schillebeeckx, Christ, the Christian Experience in the Modern World (London:1980), p. 33, quoted in: Shorter, Toward a Theology, p. 59, 60.
[119] Shorter, Toward a Theology, p. 60
[120] Shorter, Toward a Theology, p. 61.
[121] Shorter, Toward a Theology; also Schineller, Handbook, pp. 42-44 passim.
[122] See Shorter, Toward a Theology, pp. 60ff.
[123] R. H. Winthrop, Dictionary of Concepts in Cultural Anthropology (New York: Green-

suffices to say that culture is understood in inculturation as the given component on the part of the group of people receiving, and of those transmitting the faith. Culture in this sense includes the factors with which human beings integrally secure their survival and transform themselves. It includes labor, various forms of social communication, custom, mores, and institutions of social life. It also embraces ideas, symbols and manifestations of the habits of a given community, which often determine the products of the community involved. It is necessarily historical and social.[124] It is also possible to say that culture is used in inculturation to designate the uniqueness and diversity of various human communities. In this case culture describes the many and different ways in which human beings organize their life, their divergent representations and interpretations of reality, and of history as a result of the different contexts and times in which different people live.

Tacitly, therefore, the term culture as used in the discussion on inculturation presupposes a 'hermeneutic of difference'. Depending on a person's emphases, the differences discovered would either be sporadic or organic. In the former instance, communities would be conceived to have differences without any commonality, i.e. non-communicable differences. In the latter instance the differences discovered would be seen as particularizations of a complex process of inter-cultural communications.

This latter idea of culture concedes to the historicity and uniqueness of different cultures. Nonetheless it also conceives of an already existing communication between cultures, seeing cultural difference as a difference that presumes an 'ecumenism of cultures'. It is thus a conception of culture, which in the discussion on inculturation, is neither paternalistic nor attempts to establish cultural difference only on the basis of formal or external categories.

1.5.2 People and History

> Our pasts have made us whatever we are
> and on that capital we have to live or
> else we must begin afresh.*
> [Lonergan]

With the statement above Lonergan establishes the essential connection between the human being and history. He declares, "man is a historical being" and argues that historicity is true not only of an individual but also of the group. For, "groups too live on their past and their past, so to speak, lives on in them."[125] Lonergan's concern is "existential history", which he defines as

---

wood Press, 1991), p. 50.
[124] Winthrop, Dictionary, p. 50ff. See also Gaudium et Spes, 53.
* Lonergan, Method in Theology, p. 181.

"the living tradition which formed us and thereby brought us to the point where we began forming ourselves."[126]

The idea Lonergan expresses here is not unknown among many communities in Africa. There is in Ghana, for instance, a popular proverb that says: "If you do not know where you come from, you might also not know where you are going to." Historical consciousness is relevant not only as a theological method. It is an unavoidable ingredient in all human reflection and praxis, without which there can be no qualitative leap in the process of humanization. If as we said earlier inculturation is about *becoming African*, certain questions become unavoidable. What type of past does the African (Christian) have? Is there a living tradition which has brought Africans or is bringing Africans to the point where "we begin forming ourselves"? Is inculturation in the African context a process of this self-formation of the African or just the search for better ways of evangelization and mission?

To show how relevant history is, as an element of inculturation, particularly in the African context, it might be helpful once again to refer to Martey. Together with the Ecumenical Association of Third World Theologians (EATWOT), Martey recognizes the fact that part of Africa's reality is constituted in the truth that Africans "have been expelled from the field of history by their oppressors." The same body stated that "Liberation, if true, must be a historical liberation."[127] Martey praises this methodological stance and suggests that "since the history of Africa is the result of western capitalist imperialism, whenever the question of African people's liberation is raised, there is always the need to begin with historical rehabilitation."[128] It becomes clear why the people concerned and their history constitute the moral instance of inculturation. The historical experience of Africans as the most humiliated of peoples,[129] the paradox of the inhabitable nature of their habitat, the fragmentation of African culture into a multiplicity of groups, languages and affiliations, the crisis of identity, the burden of under development and Africa's exclusion from world events[130] provide the "*Ortsbestimmung*" (definition of context) for inculturation in Africa.

Consequently, inculturation as dialogue between faith (Gospel) and culture must also be understood as the Gospel in dialogue with the people, with their knowing and feeling, i.e. with their states of consciousness. It is an attempt to reach to the psychology of the people. For, the Faith, which seeks to free people of all the forces that prevent them from being authentic, must also

---

[126] Lonergan, Method in Theology, p. 182.
[127] EATWOT, in: Martey, African Theology, p. 36.
[128] EATWOT, in: Martey, African Theology, p. 36.
[129] See A. Mazrui, The African Condition. A Political Diagnosis (London: Cambridge University Press, 1980), pp. 23-45.
[130] Mazrui, The African Condition.

touch their cultural psychology. Authenticity in this sense means no more than becoming what we are – human. Hence, if there is a proper sense in which we can say that the Christian term to be inculturated is the person of Jesus,[131] then there is equally a proper sense in which we can say that the culture term is the persons to be christianized.[132] Inculturation, then, is actually a communication between persons. It is a process in which Jesus comes to meet people where they are, in their historical situation. The liberation motive looses in this regard all suspicion of the subversive tendencies it is assumed to have, and assumes the biblical symbolic of healing, the metaphor that depicts integral human liberation[133] (See Lk 10, 19; 18, 42; Acts 27, 20, 34; Mk 5, 23; Mt 8, 25).

Thus the study of *culture texts*[134] in order to examine the values and vices of a culture, "by immersion in and familiarity with [the] situation"[135] is not yet a completed process of inculturation, unless it also includes an immersion in the levels of consciousness of the persons concerned. Cultural values could be praised and enhanced. Vices could be condemned and abandoned. But an anthropological casualty that affects the inner states of persons can only be healed. It is here that one can relate with their varied and complex processes of awareness, of knowing, of being intelligible, of judgement, and of making choices.[136]

1.6 The Existentialist Model of Inculturation and Vatican II

If this study gives preference to the existentialist model, it is because the model is open to a more integral consideration of the human person. The importance of considering the human person adequately is unequivocally expressed in the theology of Vatican II in the Pastoral Constitution, *Gaudium et Spes*. In what follows we shall base ourselves on the work of Janssens[137] and

---

[131] See previous reference to Shorter, Toward a Theology, p. 75.

[132] See. Shorter's citation of John Paul's statement to an African audience that "in the African, Jesus himself has become African", in:Shorter, Towards a Theology, p. 75.

[133] For a summary of the meaning of, and issues involved in, the liberation-salvation thematic in both OT & NT with special reference to Liberation Theology and African Theology, see: W. Amewowo, A Study of the Biblical Foundations of Liberation Theology, unpublished disser., (Rome: Faculty of Theology, Pontificia Universitas Gregoriana, 1976), especially pp. 60-67.

[134] See Schreiter, Constructing Local Theologies, Chapter three.

[135] Schineller, Handbook, p. 82.

[136] See Lonergan, Method in Theology, p. 231.

[137] See L. Janssens, 'Artificial Insemination: Ethical Considerations' in: Louvain Studies, vol. viii, no 1, (1980), pp. 3-29. Loius Janssens was professor of Moral Theology at the Catholic University of Louvain, where he lectured for some forty years, retiring in 1978. His article here referred to won international acclaim for its ingenuity in developing an

propose that Vatican II's notion of the "human person adequately considered" offers a sound foundation for understanding inculturation and for developing a theologically fruitful method for Christian moral inquiry.[138] It is generally accepted that Vatican II achieved a breakthrough in respect of the Church's self-understanding and in her appreciation of the reality in which people find themselves. In *Gaudium et Spes*, two main achievements could be underscored. On one hand the document treats anthropology in theological perspec-

---

ethical theory based on the "personalist foundation in the spirit of the Second Vatican Council". In this essay he builds on a previous work of his, "Personalist Morals" in: Louvain Studies, vol. iii (1970), pp. 5-15.

[138] In a discussion on this thesis, a colleague was quick to remark that using a document presented in greater part in Greco-Roman ways of thinking to express ideas about liberation in Africa is no more than "liberation into a Greco-Roman jail." This comment raises an important question: How far does a Church document such as *Gaudium et Spes* speak the language of the aspirations of the African Church? For many reasons *Gaudium et Spes* is a document that offers a basis for entering into dialogue with the Church, and which many people – Christians and non-Christians alike – will accept as such. Commentaries on GS show that the document could be said to have originated directly from the spirit of the council, by breaking away from many of the pre-formulated answers that used to be given to the questions it tackled (See K. Rahner & H. Vorgrimler, Kleines Konzilskompendium [Herder: 1966], p. 423). Secondly the formulation of the text shows that the council took notice of the great interest the world at large took in its proceedings and understood the expectations that the whole non-Catholic world had of the council. This trust inspired the bishops to work strenuously to meet the expectations of people the world over. The problems and hopes of people however could not be answered by appealing to the Church's dogmatic understanding of herself, and less still to any preoccupations with natural law and gospel principles, because these carry with them the *dichotomous narrative* of "we" and "they." The expectations of the world were exactly the opposite: How far is the Church capable of showing solidarity with the concrete person of today and how far is she aware of the real problems of the people of our times (Rahner & Vorgrimler 1966:424)? In GS the Church shows honesty and a realistic estimation of the situation without giving false assurances or ideals far removed from the reality. Above all the importance of the document stems from the fact that the "*world*" it speaks about is the *human person* (GS, 3) rather than a *system* (Rahner & Vorgrimler 1966:245). In relation to the African Church, it is important for African Christians and non-Christians to take this genuine offer for dialogue seriously and reciprocate the gesture, even if certain formulations still remain within the parameters of a given philosophical background. To the extent that the document does not impose any specific answers, but rather calls for dialogue, it would be reactionary to reject the document, just because it 'speaks a different language.' Besides GS is the document that most develops the theme of inculturation (albeit still based on the adaptation terminology and model). The care taken to emphasize respect for people and their cultures confirms the document's plea for an 'integral and adequate consideration of the human person.' That said however, the comment of my colleague remains useful when it is understood to mean that GS itself can not be exempted from the 'hermeneutic of suspicion' (Martey) that must accompany theological reflection in Africa. In rejecting the adaptation model in the 1979 Synod of Bishops, the bishops of Africa would seem to have been attentive to the 'hermeneutic of suspicion.' See also chapter one of this study.

tives with a newness. On the other hand the document succeeds in relating the Church to the world community and to different cultures without falling back on the dualistic categories in which such relation is traditionally defined.

1.6.1 'Human person adequately Considered'

For a long time Christian anthropology used a metaphysical argument to specify the uniqueness of human beings in the world. In distinction to animals and other creatures, human beings were considered to be fundamentally unique because they possessed an immortal soul. Based on platonic psychology the world of things was thought to be imperfect. The human body belonged to the cosmos and was therefore subordinate to the soul. The specialty about humanness lay in an other worldly designation and dignity in which the human person was elevated to the side of God and turned against the cosmos.[139]

Due to this metaphysical anthropology, the consideration of the human person also came to be strongly colored by the dichotomous frame of reference. A person was considered under the terms of body and soul. Thus the aim of many missionaries in Africa, for instance, was to "save souls." In the nineteenth century this metaphysical anthropology became questionable and attempts were made to find alternatives for understanding the specific difference of the human person in the world.[140] In doing so modern anthropology revived to some extent the stoic antiquity by establishing the uniqueness of human beings within the context of the cosmic order and not in an extraterrestrial world. The idea of understanding human persons from their relation to the world is traced to Democritus who first described the human being as "a world in miniature."[141]

Gaudium et Spes does not abandon the traditional definition of the human person by way of a person's special relationship with God. That human beings are created in the image of God, is a phrase that is repeated several times. At the same time the document clearly spells out principles for an integral Christian anthropology, which Janssens systematizes under eight important aspects: subjectivity, corporeality, being-in-the-world, sociality, institutionality, historicity, spirituality and the fundamental equality of all human

---

[139] W. Pannenberg, Anthropology in Theological Perspective (Edinburgh: T. & T. Clark Ltd., 1985), p. 27ff. Pannenberg makes an extensive use of the basic works in philosophical anthropology such as, A. Gehlen, Der Mensch (1940), H. Plessner, Die Stufen des Organischen und der Mensch (1928), J. v. Uexküll, Umwelt und Innenwlt der Tiere (1921), M. Scheler, Menschenbild und seine Grenzen (1972) among others.

[140] Pannenberg, Anthropology, p. 27.

[141] Pannenberg, Anthropology, p. 27.

beings.[142] Janssens elaborates on these elements in turns for the sake of clarification, but he makes clear that they belong together and must not be separated.

a. *Subjectivity* includes all that makes a person a conscious-self. Unlike objects or things of the world, the human person is a subject called to be conscious (GS, 15), he has a conscience (GS, 16) and enjoys freedom (GS, 17). In addition, the term subject is used in contemporary Western culture to imply a person's freedom of conscience and of religion, the right to participate and be responsible (GS, 31), the right to privacy and to human rights (GS, 26).[143]
The dignity of the human person as a subject finds full meaning in the light of Christian revelation. Each person is created in God's image (GS, 12, 17, 24, 29, 33, 37, etc.), redeemed by Christ from sin (GS, 13, 22, 37), called to become a child of God (GS, 22) and invited to share in the victory over death and in God's Kingdom (GS, 18, 21, 39, 45, 72, 93). The fundamental moral principle that arises from considering a person as a subject is that a person may not exploit others, nor be exploited by others as an object or as a means (GS, 27) for the purposes and pleasure of others.

b. *Corporeality* implies that the body is an integral part of our conscious-self. Janssens says we are "a conscious interiority, in corporeality." It is therefore morally incumbent to take care of and have respect for our body (GS, 14), for example, by ensuring good health (GS, 27). We also have to accept the limitations placed on us because we *are body*. For example, one may not overwork the laborer. Corporeality also implies that bodily needs and tendencies are not reducible to mere biological givens (GS, 51).[144]

c. *'Worldedness'*[145] is an integral element of the human person. The document explicitly states that "through his bodily condition man sums up in himself the elements of the material world" (GS, 14). By virtue of our corporeality "our being is a being-in-the-world."[146] Our survival and transformation depend to a great extent on our ability to transform the natural milieu (GS, 53-62) and put it at our service through our work, science and technology (GS, 5,

---

[142] Janssens, 'Artificial Insemination', p. 4.
[143] Janssens, 'Artificial Insemination', p. 5. Cites Vatican II's declaration on religious freedom, Dignitatis humanae, and H. Schelsky, "Zur soziologischen Theorie der Institution", in: Zur Theorie der Institution (Bertelsmann Universitätsverlag, 1975), pp. 9-26.
[144] Janssens, 'Artificial Insemination', pp. 5-6.
[145] This word has been coined in place of Janssens' phrase, "being in the world" as one of the basic elements not to be forgotten in the consideration of the human person. The word was coined to highlight the difference between Janssens' idea and the, often, pejorative connotations of the word 'worldliness'.
[146] Janssens, 'Artificial Insemination', p. 6.

9, 33-39).[147] We are however to be conscious of the ambiguities associated with our attempts to improve the world. The effects of human culture, science and technology can be at once instrumental and detrimental to the integral well-being of humanity. For example we are impressed with the positive contribution of technology – production and prosperity. At the same time we are worried about the purity of air, water and the safety of the environment in general. Besides there is the danger of becoming one-dimensional beings. Concentration on consumption of goods can make us forget "that our bodily-being-in-the-world embraces thinking and feeling as well as seeing, ... and therefore also involves the enjoyment and appreciation of things as well as aesthetic wonderment and contemplative reflection upon the deepest meaning of things and persons."[148] Thus our 'worldedness' also imposes a moral obligation on us by forcing us to keep an eye on the possible implications of our attempts to 'dominate and subdue the earth.'

d. *Sociality* means that human beings are essentially directed towards each other (GS, 25). "God did not create a solitary being. ... For by his innermost nature man is a social being, and unless he relates himself to others he can neither live nor develop his potential" (GS, 12).[149] So important is our openness to the other for our existence that Janssens states "to be man is to be fellow-man."[150] The biblical paradigm, 'male and female he created them' (Gen 1, 27) for instance, shows how the companionship of male and female establishes 'the primary form' of human sociality. Here also we are reminded of the double-sidedness of sociality. On the one hand society helps a person to fulfill his calling (even religious calling) in life. On the other hand the social environment sometimes turns a person away from the good, and urges towards evil (GS, 25).

e. *Institutionality*: By virtue of their sociality human beings live in social groups (GS, 23-32). In order to live in social groups we need structures and institutions (GS, 15, 25, 29), such as political structures (GS, 73-76) and international cooperation (GS, 77-90).[151] The moral implications of our sociality and our need to live in social groups are fundamental. An individualistic ethic is to be rejected (GS, 30), and it is obligatory to respect the just laws and other institutions (i.e. in so far as they are in the service of the common good) of society (GS, 26, 74).[152] Because these institutions are man-made, they are nec-

---

[147] Janssens, 'Artificial Insemination', p. 6.
[148] Janssens, 'Artificial Insemination', p. 6.
[149] Janssens, 'Artificial Insemination', p. 8.
[150] Janssens, 'Artificial Insemination', p. 8.
[151] Janssens, 'Artificial Insemination', p. 9.
[152] Janssens, 'Artificial Insemination', p. 9.

essarily limited, imperfect and changeable. They demand regular revision and accommodation "to changing circumstances, and [renewal] by dynamic development, according to the growing possibilities of human dignity" (GS, 26, 29, 30).[153]

f. *Historicity* emphasizes that "every human being is a history."[154] Our life unfolds in stages, our lives are bound to a given time and place, to given possibilities at a time. We are disposed to continual change and revision. Besides each personal history is defined in a given social context, so that we are constantly "involved in a cultural history."[155] We therefore have to work constantly "to order the laws and values of created things and of the human community itself"[156] (GS, 36, 2, 4, 5, 9, 54, 55). Since historicity affects all the essential aspects of a person, a personalist ethics must be dynamic. For Janssens, "the promotion of the humanum...becomes a moral obligation insofar as it becomes possible. Ethics is fundamentally a way of living and in its own growth must keep step with human life itself as it unfolds throughout history."[157]

g. *Spirituality* speaks of our creation in the image of God, whom we are called to know and love (GS, 12, 34).[158] Because of our fundamental openness to God, we live in faith, hope and love. Our spirituality directs our attitudes and activities towards the glory of God, so that our moral acts are at the same time acts of worship (GS 34, 36, 48, etc.). By virtue of our spirituality we bear a specific dignity (GS, 12, 17), which is brought to perfection in God (Gs, 21). Spirituality also accords our sociality and interdependence a deeper level of

---

[153] Janssens, 'Artificial Insemination', p. 9.

[154] Janssens, 'Artificial Insemination', p. 10. Janssens refers to developmental psychology (E. Erikson) which speaks of successive stages of life, which are respectively marked by special possibilities. It is the individual's duty to harness these possibilities at each stage of life in order to achieve integrity and wisdom.

[155] Janssens, 'Artificial Insemination', p. 10.

[156] Janssens, 'Artificial Insemination', p. 10.

[157] Janssens (pp. 10-11) cautions; however; that ethical dynamism does not imply that we endorse every novelty gratuitously, just because its newness. But at the same time we may not too quickly dismiss a value just because it is new. He cites H. Thielicke, Theologische Ethik II/1 (Tübingen: Mohr, 1959), pp. 240-241 to offer a couple of examples. When the use of the umbrella began in England, for instance, sermons were delivered to the effect that it was not right to prevent God's rain from falling "upon the just and the unjust." The use of the fork and spoon was also once condemned "because nature had given us hands to hold our food and a mouth to drink liquids." The organization of life insurance was against God, because man should entrust his safety and the care of his property only to God. In the wake of vaccination against smallpox Pope Leo XII declared, "Whoever allows himself to be vaccinated ceases to be a child of God. Smallpox is a judgment of God, the vaccination is a challenge toward heaven" (Janssens, citing from A. Jeannière, S.J., "Corps malièable", Cahiers Laennec, 29 [1968], p. 94).

[158] Janssens, 'Artificial Insemination', p. 9.

personal and communal fellowship, which in turn calls for a deep respect for the spiritual dignity of a person (Gs, 23). It is important to maintain a constant awareness of our spirituality, otherwise we stand the danger of either debasing ourselves "to the point of despair" or overestimating ourselves "as the absolute measure of all things" (GS 12).

h. Finally, there is the *basic equality* of all human persons (GS, 29). Created in the image of God, human beings are called to form one family, sharing a common beginning and a common destiny (GS, 24). We encounter each other on the same human levels of knowing, feeling, desiring, acting, caught up in the same values, etc.[159] For this reason it is possible to speak of universalizability of moral obligations. Yet *"in this framework* and *on this basis* of fundamental equality each person is simultaneously an originality, a unique subject."[160] Our temperaments, talents, capacities, drives and social milieu, etc. help to form a unique and original personality, and individual character.[161] That we are equal and original has implications for social life. As 'community-living together (co-existence)' we are challenged to promote each person's uniqueness to the full. As 'community-working (co-operation)' out a culture, we should take interest in common cultural values, and as 'community-sharing (co-participation)' the fruitfulness of our labor we must "be attuned to the needs of each and every person according to the demands of his originality."[162]

1.7 Chapter Resume

Doing ethics of inculturation presupposes an understanding of the concept of inculturation. This chapter has provided a sketch of the concept and meanings of inculturation as a general phenomenon of all religious experience, as a specifically Christian theological concept, and as a part of an integral theological hermeneutic particularly related to the experience of African Christians. In Christian theology, the term inculturation is still developing in meaning and praxis, but the phenomenon is as old as the Church. There are many sets of meanings underlying the concept. Two models, the existentialist and essentialist models, have been worked out to help focus the discussion on the main theses of the study. The essentialist model concentrates on the missionary aspect of inculturation, seeking normative approaches for 'good' and 'successful' evangelization. The existentialist model emphasizes the particular situation of

---

[159] Janssens, 'Artificial Insemination', p. 12.
[160] Janssens, 'Artificial Insemination', p. 12, author's italics.
[161] Janssens, 'Artificial Insemination, p. 12.
[162] Janssens, 'Artificial Insemination, p. 12.

Africans and takes the question of their anthropological rehabilitation and integral liberation seriously. Both models have strengths and limitations. They need not be mutually exclusive, but they could be mutually opposing.

The attempt to explain inculturation by way of the essentialist and existentialist models helped to point out the danger of becoming inattentive to the different sets of meanings. This inattentiveness in turn could lead to developing a theory-praxis of inculturation based on a fictive consensus. It is urgent to keep working toward better understanding, and proper application of inculturation in its various forms.

Since the question what is good to be done also implies who must a person be in order to be fully human, ethics and morality could be said to involve the same principle at work in inculturation. Both inculturation and ethics therefore demand an adequate consideration of the human person. Based on the work of Janssens, the chapter described some important elements for adequately considering the human person as worked out in Vatican II's *Gaudium et Spes*. These elements are used later as criteria for a new narrative on the African reality and the African identity, which form the basis for an inculturated ethic.

Chapter Two

2 Working Backwards: In search of a new Narrative

Around 200-120 BCE the historian Polybios argued that formerly history proceeded "sporadically". There were unconnected histories of different peoples and nations. Now however the events in Italy, Africa, Greece and Asia, he argued, have begun to interconnect, so that it is now possible to write a general history which considers the general connection of the separate events.[1] One must depart from this "organic" type of history, if one wished to understand the events in different nations.[2]

The presentation of world events however has not always followed the argument of Polybios. World events have often been communicated in a manner that would seem to have drifted from the interconnectedness of peoples and cultures, preferring a 'sporadic history' to an 'organic' one. We have mentioned, for instance, the division of peoples into Christian and pagan cultures.[3] The same division could be found in other areas. The social sciences developed the theory of the "Naturvölker" in distinction to "Kulturvölker" (the 'nature-cultures' and 'high-cultures').[4] In history and philosophy a similar distinction was made,[5] and not even international law could free itself from the

---

[1] Polybios, Historien, I, 3ff, cited in: W. Mühlmann, Homo Creator: Abhandlungen zur Soziologie, Anthropologie und Ethnologie (Wiesbaden: Oto Harrassowitz, 1962), p. 274. As Mühlmann cautions, one would have to make allowance for the fact that Polybios wrote out of his knowledge of the Roman World and the little information he had about peoples closest to the Roman boundaries. At the time he wrote, there were still many occurrences in other places and about other peoples which were unknown to him. At the same time his argument is in principle correct, and predates the discovery of a fact about human cultures of which we are becoming more and more conscious in contemporary times.

[2] Mühlmann, Homo Creator, p. 274.

[3] See earlier references in Bediako, Primal Religion, 1997. See also this study, pp. 13-17.

[4] Taking Mühlmann as an example, we realize that his awareness of Polybios' argument, did not prevent Mühlmann from being a man of his time and culture. Mühlmann's opinion about the difference between the so-called nature-folks and high cultures is rather characteristic of the trend of a "sporadic" presentation of events. According to Mühlmann, so distant apart are these two groups that the effect of the latter on the former in universal history could be compared to the effect of light on moths (See Mühlmann, Homo Creator, p. 276). He explains: "Ein "unendlich Kleines" im Vergleich zu einem "unendlich Goßen" sind eben die Naturvölker in ihrem Verhältnis zu den großen geschichtlichen Kulturen. Ihr Leben hat sich abseits der großen Zentren bewegter, heftig pulsierender Geschichte abgespielt, die wir Hochkulturen nennen" (Mühlmann, Homo Creator, p. 275). Paradoxically, Mühlmann develops his argument by using the citation of Polybios as his point of departure.

[5] Hegel, for instance, once wrote "what we properly understand by Africa, is the unhistorical, Undeveloped Spirit, still involved in the conditions of mere nature, and which had to be presented here only as on the threshold of the World's history" (G. W. Hegel, The Philosophy of History (New York: Prometheus Books, 1991), pp. 91-99, here p. 99). In the

tendency towards the fragmentation of history for the benefit of one group at the expense of another.[6]

Chapter two argues that this sporadic approach to history was used as a weapon to effect a systematic isolation of Africans from the community of cultures. The patterns of communication about and interpretation of Africans in anthropology and missiology demonstrate this systematic isolation. The chapter therefore concentrates on relevant aspects of anthropology[7] and missiology and attempts to expostulate the pre-constructed categories through which the African reality is interpreted. In doing so, some questions arise. How should we understand an African ethos? Were the imposed interpretations of African ethos perhaps a communication based on conventional patterns? When we speak of African ethos, which African do we mean, at which time and how should we measure Africaness? Besides the conventional notions, is it possible to find other paradigms for understanding the African?

---

same way H. Trevor-Roper wrote in 1963: "Perhaps in the future there will be some African history to teach. But at present there is none; there is only the history of Europeans in Africa. The rest is darkness... and darkness is not a subject of history", in West Africa, no. 2433, (London: 1964), p. 58; cited in Mazrui, The Africans, 1978, p. 87.

[6] J. S. Mill, for example, felt there could not be the same laws for the civilized and the uncivilized. He was of the opinion that "there is a great difference between the case in which the nations concerned are of the same, or something like the same, degree of civilization, and that in which one of the parties to the situation is of a high, and the other of a very low, grade of social improvement. To suppose that the same international customs, and the same rules of international morality, can obtain between one civilized nation and another and between civilized nations and barbarians, is a grave error, and one which no statesman can fall into, however it may be that those who, from a safe and unresponsible position, criticize statesmen... To characterize any conduct towards the barbarous people as a violation of the Law of Nations only shows that he who so speaks has never considered the subject." See Mill, "A few Words on Non-Intervention" in Dissertations and Discussions, Vol. 3 (London: 1967), pp. 153-158. Cited in Mazrui, The Moving Cultural Frontier of World Order (New York: Institute for World Order, Inc., 1982), p. 10.

[7] The choice of anthropology is because besides presenting a paradigm of the presentation made of Africans in all other areas in the cultural contact between Africa and Europe, anthropology was also the discipline that actually sought to provide information to all other disciplines on and about Africans and their way of life. Thus even the Christian missionary view of the African way of life is directly related to the image cast of African peoples on the basis of anthropological material. One could even speak of a reciprocity between missionary and anthropologist. Secondly we have mentioned that the term "inculturation" is related to the concept of "enculturation" in anthropology and sociology. Thirdly doing ethics in contemporary times demands a balanced anthropological foundation, an anthropology that recognizes its own time bound, and cultural contextual frames of reference, thus willing to respect and communicate with other specific anthropologies.

2.1 The Formation of the Conventional Narrative

As a systematic and empirical discipline of study Anthropology begun in the second half of the nineteenth century.[8] Nonetheless Anthropology was used in Africa as the most instrumental and comprehensive discipline from which other disciplines could gather "facts" about Africans and their cultures.[9] Yet Anthropology did not develop independently. It was a child of various historical, cultural and intellectual antecedents.[10] Underlying the methodology which anthropologists applied in Africa were many assumptions and pre-formed conceptual schemes about the development of the human species, society, religion, culture and civilization. It is possible to say that in its application in Africa Anthropology was a science in search of a laboratory for the confirmation of foregone conclusions. Africa, as it were, provided the laboratory and its peoples the experimental specimen. [11]

---

[8] See J. Beattie, Other Cultures: Aims, Methods and Achievements in Social Anthropology (London: Cohen & West, 1964), p. 5ff. Elsewhere Beattie refers to Anthropology as "the quite young science" (ibid, p. ix). For the history of anthropological theory see: M. Harris, The Rise of Anthropological Theory (Columbia University: Harper Collins Publishers, 1968); M. T. Hodgen, Early Anthropology in the Sixteenth and Seventeenth Centuries (Philadelphia: University of Pennsylvania Press, 1964).
[9] O. Onoge, "Revolutionäre Forderungen an die afrikanische Soziologie", in: R. Jestel (ed.), Das Afrika der Afrikaner: Gesellschaft und Kultur Afrikas (Frankfurt am Main: Suhrkamp Verlag, 1988), pp. 79-94, here p. 79.
[10] See Bediako, Primal Religion, p. 48ff. Before the material of missionaries and travelers became available in Europe, there had been earlier speculations about human development, culture, society, and religion. These speculations were based on conjecture arising from deductions made from the culture of the thinkers in Europe. Much of the conjecture was an attempt to replace the religious and metaphysical ideas about the meaning of the world and human life with explanations based on reason alone (Beattie, Other Cultures, p. 5). Thinkers like Adam Smith, D. Hume and Furguson in Britain or the Encyclopedists in France had written about 'primitive' institutions (Beattie, Other Cultures). To a great extent the rise of anthropology in the nineteenth century was a revolutionary touch to already existing theories about "human progress" traceable to the Enlightenment and beyond (Harris, The Rise of Anthropological Theory, p. 123ff). The argument that empirical anthropology begun in Africa as a reaction to the misrepresentations of the tales of missionaries and travelers often blends the Victorian beginnings and eurocentric categories of anthropology (Bediako, Primal Religion, p. 48ff). Anthropology actually needed a laboratory for the empirical study of human cultures. Just as metaphysics was rejected in defining the place of the human person in the universe, so did the Victorian era set God aside in explaining natural phenomena. Human affairs were explained not by reference to God or some unseen forces but by reference to purely natural processes explainable by reason. It was believed that by discovering the laws of nature and how they operate one could grasp the whole meaning of the universe. This fundamental assumption found application in all areas, but especially in geology (Lylle), in biology (Darwin, Wallace, Huxley) and in anthropology (E. B. Tylor, L. H. Morgan, H. Spencer, H. Maine).
[11] Nineteenth century anthropology built on the assumptions of "cultural evolution" to illustrate the meaningfulness of society and culture (Beattie, Other Cultures, p. 6). European

Besides the desire to [re]construct a universal history of human beings by tracing human development backwards from civilized Europe to the 'primitive' cultures, anthropology had an additional agenda in Africa. This agenda was to obtain and deliver information that would facilitate European imperial domination of African peoples.[12] It was within this context that the conventional conception of Africans, not only in anthropology but also in other disciplines like religion and morals, politics, sociology and the rest developed.

The result was the emergence of a conventional and circumscribed narrative with which the African reality was constructed. This narrative was detrimental to African peoples because it was based on an ethnocentrism in which European culture, aesthetic and ethic were used to judge and condemn

---

cultures were considered too advanced and complex for obtaining any insights into the beginnings of human beings and their institutions. The beginnings of human history were to be found among ‚primitive' peoples. E. B. Tylor argued that "In studying the phenomena of knowledge and art, religion and mythology, law and custom, and the rest of the complex whole which we call Civilization, it is not enough to have in view the more advanced races and to know their history... The explanation of the state of things in which we live has often to be sought in the condition of rude and early tribes; without a knowledge of this to guide us we may miss the meaning even of familiar thoughts and practices" (E. B. Tylor, Researches into the Early History of Mankind and the Development of Civilization, 1878, cited in: Bediako, Primal Religion, p. 47, footnote 5, from the abridged version of the third revised edition with an introduction by P. Bohannan; (Chicago: Chicago University Press, 1964, p. 1).

[12] The fact that anthropology arrived in Africa together with the colonial flag, is for many critics of nineteenth century anthropology no coincidence (Onoge, 'Revolutionäre Forderung', p. 79). Kathleen Goughs points out that "Vor dem Zweiten Weltkrieg wurde die praktische Forschungsarbeit immer in Gesellschaften durchgeführt, die zum Herrschaftsgebiet der Regierungen jener Länder gehörten, aus denen die Anthropologen stammten; hin und wieder auch in Herrschaftsgebieten einer befreundeten westlichen Macht. In der Alten Welt waren die Kolonialmächte klar als solche zu erkennen und hauptsächlich europäisch. Die Welt der meisten amerikanischen Anthropologen unterschied sich natürlich von der der Europäer, denn die primitiven Völker, die hauptsächlich von den Amerikanern erforscht wurden, waren besiegte Indianergruppen, die man in Reservate gesteckt hatte" (K. Gouths, "World Revolution and the science of man" in T. Roszak (ed.), The dissenting academy, New York: 1967, p. 128); cited in Onoge, 'Revolutionäre Forderung', p. 79. We are informed that Goughs' article originally appeared in Monthly Review under title: *Anthropology, child of imperialism* (see Onoge, footnote 4).

R. S. Rattray, himself in the service of the British colonial administration in the Gold Coast, undertook extensive studies of Ghanaian peoples, especially the Ashanti. In compiling his research findings, Rattray devoted the preface of his famous work entitled *Ashanti* to emphasizing the importance of Anthropology for the colonial powers. He wrote: "I have always maintained that necessary and valuable as anthropological training is to the [colonial] administrator or merchant it should be an indispensable adjunct to the training of the missionary... The matter affects not merely our own local or even national interests, but those of every great colonizing power... An anthropological department should ... be looked upon as in the nature of an 'Intelligence Department' to the administration" (Rattray, Ashanti, Oxford: Clarendon Press, 1923, pp. 1, 10, 5, 8 passim).

the African way of life.[13] Characteristic expressions common to the conventional narrative are terms like primitive, wild, native, animistic, barbaric, uncivilized and the like. The meanings of these terms vary slightly from one epoch to the other in the history of anthropology in Africa. Such variation in meaning is however cancelled out since all explanations of the terms depended on the myth of the inferiority of race and deficit of rationality on the part of Africans.

2.1.1 The presentation of Africans in History as Narrative

It might seem quite far fetched to describe the way Africans have been presented in the course of history in the various sciences as *"narrative"*. The point becomes clear however when we remember the importance of *narrative* in relation to questions of identity, religion and morality[14], history and culture. In current studies on ethics and in post modern philosophy *narrative* is presented as a vital point of convergence where value and truth, conception and being, theory and action, perception and interpretation integrate.[15] *Narrative* in this sense is to be understood more as narration, as a verb rather than as a sub-

---

[13] See Dundes, Every Man His Way, p. 23; A. Montagu (ed.), The Concept of the Primitive (New York: Free Press, 1968), both in Magesa African Religion, pp. 12ff.

[14] The study of ethics in contemporary times shows a philosophical turn to narrative. The presentation we make here is based on the essays of R. C. Allen, "When Narrative Fails" in Journal of Religious Ethics, vol.21, no. 1 (1993), pp. 27-67, and W. A. Barbieri, Jr., "Ethics and the Narrated Life", in The Journal of Religion, vol. 78, no. 3 (July 1998), pp. 361-386. Narrative ethics is based on the fundamental thesis "that morality is, at root, constituted by stories—that our judgements about right and wrong and good and evil, and our resulting actions, are dependent on the stories we tell and are shaped by (Barbieri, 'Ethics', p. 362). Both Allen and Barbieri inform us that the method arose as a reaction to conventional ways of doing ethics, which often pay little attention to the contextuality, historicity and subjectivity of morality. Conventional methods of doing ethics, these authors argue, lack contextuality because they are based on metaphysical principles that are distanced from daily experiences of people (Allen, 'When Narrative', p. 32; Barbieri, 'Ethics', p. 365, footnote 5). A narrativist ethics seeks to "broaden the horizons of contemporary ethics beyond its characteristic concern with moral principles, obligations and criteria for decision making" (Barbieri, 'Ethics', p. 361). Some of the main proponents of a narrativist ethics include, I. Murdoch, M. Nussbaum, S. Hauerwas and A. MacIntyre (Barbieri, 'Ethics', p. 361). Allen names H. Frei and G. Lindbeck in addition to Hauerwas and MacIntyre (Allen, 'When Narrative', p.27). In the German speaking world D. Mieth is one of the scholars that has concerned himself with narrative ethics. See D. Mieth, Dichtung, Glaube und Moral: Studien zur Begründung einer narrativen Ethik, mit einer Interpretation zum Tristanroman Gottfrieds von Strassburg (Mainz: Grünewald, ²1983); Mieth, Narrative Ethik, in Freiburger Zeitschrift für Philosophie und Theologie, 22, (1975), pp. 297-326.

[15] Allen, 'When Narrative Fails', pp. 32-33, Barbieri, Ethics and the Narrated Life, P. 32ff.

stantive.[16] The action of narrating includes not only a sequence of words, or written text. It also contains interactive silence, emotions, feelings, desires, unexpressed thoughts that establish connections to the past and to the present, movements of the body and of the mind. In short *narrative* is a world of being.[17] Narrative is so important because it creates the narrator. As Allen observes, "[the fact] that narrative is central, both for individuals and social wholes, to the project of recollection and hence to the foundation of identity is an insight that has been recognized and articulated repeatedly."[18]

An important aspect of narration is the ability to remember. Remembering is not only the ability to date and recount past events. It involves a processes of making oneself present to history and history to oneself. One establishes connections, awakens to new insights and reconstructs one's reality. Remembering is in a sense being and becoming present to oneself and to one's reality. The personal element involved in narration for individuals as well as for groups cannot be overemphasized.

It was unthinkable for OT Israel, for instance, to speak of itself as a people without a fundamental reference to its sacred history. Much of Israel's self identification is therefore set in rituals characterized by a fundamental confession of faith. Strikingly this confession of faith is usually set in narrative that reconstructs the past in the present. The narration prescribed for the presentation of first fruits is illustrative: "My father was a wondering Aramean. He went down into Egypt to find refuge there.... The Egyptians ill-treated us... but we called on Yahweh the God of our fathers. Yahweh heard our voice.... He brought us here and gave us this land, a land where milk and honey flow" (Dt 26,5b-10 passim).[19]

Like OT Israel the importance of narrative in African cultures is commonplace. For a long time whole communities lived on the memories of a

---

[16] Barbieri, 'Ethics', p. 367, footnote 6.

[17] See Allen, 'Where Narrative Fails', p. 28, referring to Oliver Sacks, The Man Who Mistook His Wife for a Hat, and Other Clinical Tales, (New York: Harper & Row, Perennial Library, 1987), pp. 110-11. Allen puts it thus: "a life narrative is more than a structured sequence of words; it is told in part "unconsciously," and it collects within itself both the nonverbal and the verbal—image, emotion, act, and word."

[18] Allen, 'Where Narrative Fails', p. 29.

[19] B. Anderson reminds us that the fundamental story that shapes Israel as a people lies in "her history as originating in a marvelous liberation from distress and oppression. A dispirited band of slaves, bound together only by their common plight, would never have become a people—a covenant community with a sense of historical vocation—had God not acted on their behalf when they were helpless and hopeless" (B. W. Anderson, The Living World of the Old Testament, England: Longman, 1984, 6th impression, p.46). If we try to reason away this narrative the essential content gets lost and what remains loses significance (see Anderson, The Living World, p. 12). We shall also see later that Isreal's life story is so fundamental that morality itself transcends the obedience of rules to become an act of worship.

fundamental narrative. "Spoken" narrative, especially as regards the religious, moral and cultural aspects of life, was almost imperative among many African communities. An important area in which we could find ready examples is leadership. The leader (chief) was expected to be totally shaped by the story upon which the communal identity was founded. The leader was to be the epitome of the community epic.[20]

2.1.2 The Conventional Narrative and Africans

In referring to the European conception of the African as narrative we are confronted with a narrative about the African.[21] The narrative is conventional because it reveals a repetitive pattern of communication whose effects are handed on from one generation to another. Notable among these effects on Africans is a certain loss of memory -amnesia. The conventional narrative succeeded to some extent in erasing the "inner narrative" that the African embodies.[22]

It is possible to parallel the African experience to that of one of Sacks' characters, William Thompson. Sacks presents Thompson as a patient of amnesia. Thompson's condition is so serious that he has lost all sense of the continuous flow of time. Since he is unable to remember, he lives only in the present which lasts only a few seconds. As a result of his condition, Thompson lacked any sense of personal identity.[23] There is a sense in which we can metaphorically relate Thompson's experience to that of many Africans as a result of the conventional narrative. We shall try to establish this relation using the words of Allen:

In the categories of the conventional narrative, Africans 'nimbly' con-

---

[20] J. Hevi, Indigenous Leadership among the Ewes of South-Eastern Ghana as a Moral Responsibility, Doctorate Thesis (Rome: 1980). I am aware that the author has reworked and published portions of this Thesis, although I have not yet laid hands on a copy of the publication. In some African communities the community-story was considered so personal that the actual narration sometimes yielded eruptions of ecstasy. Leadership is considered a moral value and is based on conviction rather than on law. In fact, parallel to OT Israel, many of the community stories are sacred histories among many African peoples. They are stories that are not just told but celebrated. In contrast to these indigenous narratives are the accounts given by Europeans about Africans and which Africans have received as a legacy. These Western discourses about the African, and of the African about himself as a result of Western cultural domination, is what we refer to here as dichotomous or conventional narrative. It is a narrative that cannot be celebrated for reasons here discussed.
[21] See L. Magesa, African Religion: The Moral Traditions of Abundant Life (Maryknoll: Orbis Books, 1997), p. 5.
[22] Allen, 'Where Narrative Fails', p. 27.
[23] Sacks, The Man who Mistook his Wife, pp. 108ff.

nect to the past. What they say of themselves is often 'a parody of narrative in which [they themselves] are hardly present.' The dichotomous narrative institutionalized 'spoken [and especially written] narrations effacing the African's perception, feeling, thought, and action.' "[There] is a resulting emptiness in which [the African] succumbs to [a] desperate concoction of story after story, none of which mean or matter more than any other, because all are equally detached from a world of lived experience."[24]

In view of the emptiness of the dichotomous narrative for African self-realization certain questions become pertinent. If ethics has to do with people who act consciously, how else should we understand *anthropological pauperization*,[25] if not in this sense of an "abyss of amnesia"[26] in which Africans hardly *remember* themselves? And if not in a sense in which Africans seek to broaden the horizons of their narrative, breaking through the limits set by the conventional narrative, what else could an ethic of inculturation be about?[27] In the section that follows we shall consider how the conventional narrative and its effects apply in the communication on African morality.

2.2 African Ethos and the Conventional Narrative

For a long time conventional consideration (in anthropology and missiology) held that morality in Africa functions essentially through religion and superstition, or tradition and social coercion based on the strong communal spirit of African peoples, where little room is made for individual freedom. By apply-

---

[24] See Allen, 'When Narrative Fails', pp. 27-29. I have tried to represent the African experience using the ideas and language of Allen as he presented them in his analysis of William Thompson, a character in Sacks' book earlier referred to. The lesson Allen calls us (as Africans especially) to learn in this analysis is that it is not enough just to "produce verbal [or written] constructs" (Allen, When 'Narrative', p. 28). To the extent that the story we tell fails to be a "continuous inner narrative" that enables us to "maintain our identity" (Sacks, The Man who Mistook his Wife, p. 112, in Allen, 'When Narrative', p. 28), what we say of ourselves has little relevance, because it lacks a foundational remembrance.

[25] EATWOT cited in Martey, African Theology, p. 38. The rhetorical question raised here is meant to echo Martey's discussion of the African reality. In the words of EATWOT he aptly observes that *"anthropological pauperization"* implies a deprivation of identity, social roots, history, culture, dignity, rights, hopes and plans (see full quotation in this study, chapter 1, p.24). Martey further explains, therefore, that inculturation (within the African context) addresses an aspect of a specific African question – that of *anthropological poverty*. And "the struggle against this fundamental poverty of the African person is what gives Africa its theological agenda" (Martey, African Theology, p. 38).

[26] Sacks, The Man who Mistook, p. 109, cited in Allen, 'When Narrative Fails', p. 27.

[27] Similar ideas have been expressed by many authors who handle the topic of African morality in its own right or in relation to Christianity and European cultures. See B. Bujo, L. Magesa, A. Shorter , J. Mbiti.

ing the conceptual patterns that inform the conventional narrative, morality in Africa was often subjected to an evolutionary taxonomy by which African communities were rated on a moral developmental scale in which morality is either totally absent, infantile, formally attributed, or romantically appreciated. This scale corresponds to the various stages of anthropological field research on the one hand and the various stages of the missionary enterprise in Africa on the other hand. However, the scale is not to be understood as constituting a lineal or historically synchronic pattern or theory. It is more like a recurrent force with ripples of varying extent. For the purposes of this study it is important to discuss how the conventional narrative portrays African morality. We shall do so from two main perspectives -religion and tradition.

2.2.1 Religion and African Ethos

The interconnectedness of morality and religion in Africa has been noted to be remarkably strong. The value of this close connection between religion and morality is being emphasized more and more in contemporary times.[28] Yet until recently, this connection often led to confusing opinions about the African as the subject of morality.

In anthropology it was theorized that the African was 'a thing' at the disposal of the society, exhibiting a merely mechanical solidarity in obedience to the society in which he lives (Durkheim), or an intellectually incapacitated being compensating his stupidity with religion and mythology (Tylor), or a pagan imbedded in crippling superstition and tradition (G. J. Christeller).[29]

That religion so negatively determined morality in Africa was not a view held only by non-African, but also by African scholars. Although some of them certainly intend a more positive and sympathetic interpretation of this view, their methodology and manner of theorizing about ethics in Africa illustrates the point we have been making about the effect of the conventional narrative on Africans. Let us take the example of Kudadjie[30] who writes: "Religion significantly influences what Africans consider good or bad....Religions determine much of the moral code of an African people, especially those val-

---

[28] See Magesa, African Religion; Bujo, African Christian Morality; Mbiti, African Religions and Philosophy, just to mention a few examples.

[29] In some cases (as was the case with the evolutionists) African morality was interpreted on the bases of race. It was believed that certain aspects of the life of the "native" were carried in blood, and were restricted to that level of evolutionary development. More about this later.

[30] For other views (sometimes vehemently opposed to those of Kudadjie), see for example, Kwesi Wiredu, "Morality and Religion in Akan Thought", in O. Oruka and D. Masolo (eds.), Philosophy and Cultures (Nairobi: Bookwise Publishers, 1983) pp. 6-13.

ues which may be called negative...the don'ts, the taboos"[31]. To illustrate his point Kudadjie quotes Harris and Sawyer (1968:93) who wrote the following about the Mende:

> "All Mende social customs are associated with some supernatural influence, God, or the ancestors, or some cultic spirit. All simple good manners also come under this category. Since contact with the cultic spirits and the ancestors is maintained through ritual acts, the various codes of behaviour sustained through the prescription of ritual prohibitions cover every aspect of life".[32]

So far one might say there is nothing wrong with this trend of thought. What is disturbing however is the characteristic conclusion which Kudadjie draws from the above conception of religion and ethics in Africa. He maintains:

> "Religion creates on the one hand fear, and on the other hand hope, on account of which vice is avoided and virtue practised. Because gods and ancestors bless and reward those who keep decorum."[33]

Kudadjie continues that together with tradition (to be considered below) and its legal sanctions, founded once again on the fear of the ancestors and spirits, conscience in the African ethical context is little more than the means of realizing guilt. It is the faculty of fear rather than of inner deliberation which helps a person to do the good and avoid evil.[34] Kudadjie further contends that since

---

[31] J. N. Kudadjie, 'Aspects of African Ethics', in J. S. Pobee (ed.), Religion, Morality and Population Dynamics, (Legon: University of Ghana, 1977), pp. 17-29. The place referred to here is p.20. We must mention in fairness to the author that he was treating the question of some important aspects of African morality within a given context -relation to population dynamics- in which he had limited room to espouse and defend some of the observations made and opinions expressed. Yet the very summary nature of the essay is precisely what marks it out as a good example of how much the conventional narrative has affected Africans in our way of telling our story, and how inadvertently unrelated to our personal experience the conception we make of ourselves could be. Kudajie's essay as a whole, and especially the ten points of summary could be said to epitomize a general tendency in certain quarters when it comes to the topic of African morality.

[32] Kudadjie, Aspects of African Ethics, p. 20.

[33] Kudadjie, Aspects of African Ethics, p. 20.

[34] Elsewhere ('Does Religion Determine Morality in African Societies? -A Viewpoint', in: Ghana Bulletin of Theology, vol. 4, No. 5, Dec. 1973, pp. 30-49), Kudadjie discusses the relationship between ethics and religion in Africa. He disagrees with the idea that religion is the source of ethics in Africa, and argues that such an opinion is neither logically correct nor commensurate with the actual experience of many African peoples. It is difficult to un-

moral Philosophy concerns not just consciousness of the good but the application of such consciousness in praxis, "African religions must be criticised [sic] for teaching the goodness of the gods and ancestors and the need for men to be good, while failing to teach that these gods also provide a person with the capability to do good."[35]

---

derstand why Kudajie in the present case would seem to be arguing almost directly against this conviction.

[35] Kudajie, Aspects of African Ethics, p. 21. There are quite a number of works on the idea of God and the gods in African religions. See Idowu, Olodumare, God in Yoruba (London, 1963); G. Parrinder, West African Religion, (London, 1968); E. Smith, African Ideas of God, 1966; J. Mbiti, Concepts of God in Africa, (Heinemann, 1970); W. R. Bascom & M. J. Herskovitz, Ifa Divination, 1969. I have however not yet come across any work that specifically treats Christian ontology vis-a-vis African religious ontology. Should we, however, decide to apply a classical Christian ontology (which is what Kudajie would seem inadvertently to be doing) to the question of the role of the gods in endowing people with the capability to do the good, then there is need for a more critical analysis. First, the lesser gods, and in particular the ancestors are hardly seen as playing any direct role in creation. One or the other god may be sent by the great God to carry out an errand in the process of creation (See Ibo and Yoruba myths of Creation; see also Parrinder, African Mythology, 1967, pp. 9ff; Rattray, Ashanti Proverbs, 1916, pp. 20-21). If that be so, it is difficult to see why one should expect the gods or ancestors to "provide a person the capability to do the good" as Kudajie argues.

Second, that the creator God directly endows human beings with moral capabilities is an idea clearly present in the beliefs of many African peoples. The Ewes of Ghana, for instance, believe that the individual is even invited to participate in the process through which God endows a person with the ability to lead a good life. This belief is expressed in the myth of the "ceremony of leave-taking" in *Bome* -the place of human origins- where a person was invited to co-determine his life-plan -*gbetsi*- for his or her sojourn on earth. T. Adzakpe (Penance and Expiatory Sacrifice among the Ghanaian-Ewe and their Relevance to the Christian Religion, Rome: Tipografia Olimpica, 1982, pp. 48ff) explains this belief, and informs us that a person is given an accompanying and protective spirit, *Aklama*, who helps in the fulfillment of a person's life program. J. Spieth (Ewe Stämme, 1906: 510ff) elaborates on the same belief using the term "*dzɔgbe*". Unfortunately, Spieth translates "*dzɔgbe*" in this context rather wrongly to mean 'Geburtstag' (birthday). The closest meaning might be the Greek '*tyche*' as it was understood in the Ethos of the ancient Greeks (Compare, L. Schmidt, Die Ethik der alten Griechen Bd. 1, Stuttgart: Frommann, 1882, reprinted 1964, p. 54; also M. P. Nilsson, Geschichte der Griechischen Religion, Bd. 2, München: C. H. Beck, 1955, reprinted 1967, pp. 200ff). Similar ideas could be found among the Ashantis of Ghana. The Ashanti maxim "*obi kwan nsi obi kwan mu*" (nobody's path [to God] crosses another's) is also understood to imply a person's direct connection to the creator God. The Ashanti also believe that the creator gave a bit of his spirit to each individual whom he sent into the world. This spirit was bound up with that individual's destiny and guided what he or she was to do or become. (Compare, K. A. Busia, "The Ashanti", in D. Ford, African Worlds, London: Oxford University Press, 1954, p. 192, 209).

Third, it would seem that Kudajie's criticism overlooks a more primary question, namely, to what extent does the culture of a people enable them live morally? The religious self-interpretation of a people usually follows as a second step to their cultural and histori-

Finally Kudadjie (here referring to Idowu 1962:168 who argues similarly) would want us to believe that as a result of this lack of innate capability to do the good, the African sacrifices ritually to compensate for breaching the moral injunction.

2.2.2 Is African Morality Moral Infantilism?

No wonder that such manner of argumentation above exposes the essence of African morality to distortion and doubt. Thus O'Donohue, for example, refers to similar patterns of 'narrative' by other African scholars like Mbiti and Kagame and concludes:

> "[their] testimonies cannot be simply dismissed, and it is probable that external rather than internal morality characterised the societies of traditional Africa, and this heritage remains visible today".[36]

The author is referring to Mbiti's remark that "something is evil because it is punished: it is not punished because it is evil." Kagame, on his part, says that the Banyarwanda word 'nibibi' (it is bad) "means no more than 'it is forbidden by law', and therefore likely to involve disagreeable consequences."[37] Both (Mbiti's and Kagame's) positions submit to an interpretation, which O'Donohue does not miss, namely, that in African communities, there is little "sense of personal responsibility for one's actions," and if that be so, then such morality "can be characterised [sic] as immature, even rudimentary morality."[38]

Of course, O'Donohue is aware of the fact that neither a totally external morality nor a purely internal morality could be found in any particular community. One will, under normal circumstances, find a mixture of heteronomy and autonomy in the moral history of societies as well as of individuals. All the same he concedes a hierarchical scale (in his own words, a kind of league table") of moral development, so that "the more internal the morality, the

---

cal experiences. The attribution of elements of their life to some supreme or divine power is more a matter of theological innovation which then sets the tone for their self interpretation and identity. This is why culture, religion and philosophy of life usually converge in a people's ethos. At this level, morality is more relational than rational.

[36] John O'Donohue, New Wine and Old Bottles: A Study of the Concepts of Traditional Africa and of Their Continuing Influence Today, (Upsala: Reprocentralen HSC, Upsala University, 1994), p. 118. It would be explained presently why we find O'Donohue's work paradigmatic of the application of the conventional narrative to African morality.

[37] Cited in O'Donohue, New Wine and Old Bottles, pp. 48, 117.

[38] O'Donohue, New Wine and Old Bottles, p. 118.

higher the position"[39] of that society. Hence based on the Africans' own story –"testimony" from African scholars- and on the author's own assessment of the moral situation in African communities today, based on classical functionalist analysis of Taboo, O'Donohue draws the following conclusions about morality in Africa:

> "An external morality, a morality, that is, based on fear of punishment, whether secular or transcendental, can only lead in the long run to Durkheim's anomie, and the absence of a tradition of internal morality is producing anomie in modern Africa. There is no reason to doubt that the moral potential of all human beings is the same, and that in Africa too there is a movement from external to internal morality, both in individuals and in societies generally. But the traditional moral system is a further obstacle to the building of modern nation-states in Africa, as well as to the integration of Africa as a whole into the world community".[40]

We may agree with O'Donohue if he implies that rather than following the conventional trend of analyzing Africa's moral problems extra- or interculturally, Africans should rather begin to do so more from the intra-cultural perspective. So it is for example mandatory for African communities to question the continuous oppression, exploitation, corruption and injustice they have suffered at the hands of indigenous political and religious elite since independence, despite any international collaboration these political or religious leaders may have enjoyed. But to allude, as O'Donohue does, to this "widespread exploitation and injustice in Modern Africa as confirmation [of the fact that] the morality of Africa is predominantly, perhaps overwhelmingly, external"[41], is a type of hermeneutic resembling what we have described above as conventional narrative. It is also a hermeneutic consisting of casuistry based

---

[39] O'Donohue, New Wine and Old Bottles, p. 117.
[40] O'Donohue, New Wine and Old Bottles, p. 120.
[41] O'Donohue, New Wine and Old Bottles, p. 118. It is important to remark that the authors criticized by O'Donohue belong mainly to the ethnographic school in the debate on African Philosophy and world view, and many of them (Mbiti, say) wrote as pioneers working in a given climate. The basic difficulty with this school of thought has been the question of method, and some other African scholars have shown their strong disagreement with the fact that the ethnographic school tends to compromise certain fundamental issues. It would have been interesting to see O'Donohue's position with regard to the positivist school of African philosophy. For a good exposition and review of both schools of thought, see Masolo, African Philosophy, (Edinburgh: Edinburgh University Press, 1994), pp. 194-246. See also chapter one of this study.

on the application of supposed universal norms.[42]

One realizes that O'Donohue is at pains to balance the anthropological truth that we can no longer set culture (*nomoi,* in the Greek sense of variegated laws and customs which vary from one region to the other) against human nature (*physis,* as the element that is universally valid for all humans -what was later called *psychic unity*)[43], with his strong conviction that the specific difference of Africans as regards morality, contrary to their Western contemporaries, is to be found in the Africans' essentially traditional nature, i.e. Africans' original inability to act out of personal deliberation and internal conviction. Hence O'Donohue's proposition that on the one hand, "there is no reason to doubt that the moral potential of all human beings is the same" on the other hand, however, the African moral system is so traditional that it lacks coherence with "the world community."[44] In the paragraph that follows he consolidates this conflict of thought:

---

[42] On Casuistry in traditional moral theology, see Manuals such as H. Nouldin, Questiones Morales: De Principiis Theologiae, 1899. It is important to note, however, that Casuistry is being re-worked in contemporary studies in Christian ethics. See the works of Keenan and Toulmin, for instance.

[43] R. H. Winthrop, Dictionary of Concepts in Cultural Anthropology, (New York: Greenwood Press, 1991), pp. 200-201. M. Harris, (The rise of Anthropological Theory [New York: Harper Corlins Publishers, 1968], p. 137) explains that the doctrine of Psychic Unity (common among Monogenists, e.g. Adolf Bastian) concerns the belief that the human mind is everywhere essentially similar. In the period of reaction against some of the racial theories established by evolutionism, the doctrine of psychic unity (which Harris contends goes as far back as the 'tabula rasa' theory of John Locke) was used to argue against people like Henry Morgan who firmly "believed that race and culture were interdependent [because] there are some customs of such a strikingly personal character that they may in a pre-eminent degree, be regarded as customs of the blood.... There are...three distinct customs or usages of this character, apparently transmitted with the blood.... These are, first, the custom of saluting by kin; second, the usage of wearing the breech-cloth; and third, the usage of sleeping at night in a state of nudity, each person being wrapped in a separate covering" (Morgan 1870: 274, cited in M: Harris, The Rise, p. 138). It is clear, looking at the sources he used, that O'Donohue was not unaware of this fallacious principle of race. All the same he seemed to have rejected such misconceptions (conventional narrative) of the evolutionists only theoretically and not consciously, since he would seem to have arrived at the same conclusions, even if with different arguments.

[44] It probably becomes clear now why O'Donohue has been selected to illustrate the way the conventional narrative applies in the area of African morality. The idea of a "world community" to which Africans do not yet belong is symptomatic of a dichotomous view of reality and of a "sporadic" historicity. I do not read O'Donohue as intending to cause any displeasure to the African. Yet despite his intention to contribute meaningfully to the discussion on the cultural dilemma of Africans, one wonders whether the nature of this contribution would not draw the African back into that "'narrational frenzy" -the endless and desperate concoction of story after story... [all of which] are equally detached from a world of lived experience' (see Allen, 'When Narrative, p. 28; cited earlier in this study).

> "*One is again obliged* (my emphasis) to append to these remarks the observation that the modern West too seems to be falling into a condition of moral *anomie*, (author's italics) and that more and more there is a convergence between the attitudes of people in traditional African societies and those of people in the West. But it seems correct to say that, whatever may be the actual moral situation, Western civilization was originally built on a widespread, internalized sense of "the good" and of "duty for duty's sake", and that, in spite of growing contemporary evidence of breakdown, large areas of Western society still operate on the understanding that people will do what is right whether anyone is watching or not."[45]

O'Donohue is proposing a general anthropology, which in turn implies a foundational anthropology because of the unity of the human race, but fails to reconcile both with a specific African cultural and historical anthropology[46]. We are therefore confronted with the position that whereas *anomie* could be a moral malady in all human societies, when it occurs in Africa it is an index of *traditionalism*, and the actual moral situation counts as confirmation thereof. But when *anomie* occurs in the West, as the author would seem to imply, it may be taken for anything except as proof of traditionalism, since western civilization was "originally built on a widespread, internalized sense of »the good« and of »duty for duty's sake«"[47]

2.2.3 In search of the African as the Subject of Moral Action

The discussion in the foregoing paragraphs make it difficult to identify the African as a mature agent of moral action. The question of agency, however, is of particular importance in an inculturation ethic. To begin with, it might be appropriate to reconstruct the image of the African as moral agent evolving from the conventional narrative. At least in the form illustrated above, one gets the impression that the morally engaged African:
-is a fear stricken person,
-enjoys probably just the minimum of any sense of personal direction,
-depends, as a result of this deficiency of reason, constantly on custom and tradition, crystallized in the dos and don'ts of taboo,

---

[45] O'Donohue, New Wine and Old Bottles, p. 120.
[46] See J. Komonchack, "Moral Pluralism and the Unity of the Church", in: Concilium 150 (10/1981), pp. 90/91, The importance of Komonchak's essay is taken up later in the discussion.
[47] O'Donohue, New Wine and Old Bottles, p. 120.

-is consequently at the beck and call of religious authority and
-essentially traditional by nature.[48]

This portrait of the African helps to point out, as Barbieri puts it, "that the locus of meaning and value lies not so much in words themselves, nor in what they signify, as in the dynamic between words and the people who employ them [we may add: and the people for whom the words are employed] in ordering and reflecting on the world in which they act."[49]

2.3 African Ethos and Tradition

Over the years scholars have found cause to contest much of the anthropological and missiological presentations of Africans and their way of life. Terms like animism, fetishism, ancestor worship, superstition, necromancy, and paganism, among others were accordingly rejected by Africanists because they petrify the African and mislead the non-African. Such terms are often referred to in African studies as misnomers.[50] In the light of such efforts it would seem

---

[48] See. E. E. Evans-Pritchard, The Theories of Primitive Religion, (Oxford: Clarendon Press, 1965), pp. 8ff. In extreme cases it was argued by some cultural psychologists, Mannoni for instance, that it is not every group of people that can be colonized. Africans were colonized because they are phylogenetically disposed to servitude. In this connection even the independence movements at the time of Africa's struggle for independence were seen as a mere psychological reaction on the part of Africans for fear that they might be deserted by their colonial masters. In a sense they were reactions to incite the colonial masters to perpetuate their rule. The idea evokes the picture of a child protesting against being deserted by its parents. See, O. Mannoni, Prospero and Caliban: The Psychology of Colonization, New York: 1964, p. 85; cited in Onoge, 'Revolutionäre Forderung', pp. 88-89.

Besides, Onoge informs us about two famous researches in African Studies conducted separately be Richie and Carothers. They were sponsored by the Rhodes-Livingstone-Institut and by UNESCO respectively. Both came out with the same finding which Onoge summarizes as follows: "in der Persönlichkeit des erwachsenen Afrikaners sind infantile Züge beherrschend. Die Schuld für diese 'hirnamputierte' Persönlichkeit wird nicht der Rasse zugeschrieben, sondern praktisch allen afrikanischen Gesellschaftseinrichtungen –der Familie, der Kindererziehung, dem Altersklassensystem, den Initiationsriten und der Religion." The purpose of this research, Onoge continues, could not have been other than the desire to portray Africans as everlasting children who always need external control (Onoge, 'Revolutionäre Forderung', p. 89. The Researches referred to are: James Richie, The African as Suckling and as Adult (Rhodes-Livingstone Publication), and James Carothers, The African Mind in Health and Sickness (New York: 1964).

[49] Barbieri, Ethics and the Narrated Life, p. 366.

[50] J. Mbiti, African Religions and Philosophy (Ibadan: Heinemann Educational Books, ²1990), p.7; chap 2 passim. See also J. N. D. Anderson, (ed.), The World's Religions (London: ³1960), p.9f. also referred to by Mbiti. See also Kofi Asare Opoku, West African Traditional Religion, (Hong Kong: FEP International Ltd. 1978).

improper to insinuate that Africanists[51] have been unconscious of the conventional narrative on African ethos and morality. At the same time, however, there is enough reason to believe that Africanists' attempts to combat misnomers have themselves been taken up in the spiral of conventionalism.

Behind the rejection of such terminology lies the identity question. In rejecting misleading presentations of Africans and their way of life, it devolves on Africanists to establish and appropriately conceptualize the authentic identity of the African. In the wake of African nationalism at the beginning of the 20th century, African spokesmen and women fell on race and 'traditional' culture as elements for establishing African identity. These attempts crystallized into the two movements of Negritude and African Personality in the French and English speaking Sub-Saharan Africa respectively.[52] Another characteristic of the works of this period is that while leading indigenous African writers tended to be reactionary, romantic and ideological, expatriate Africanists exhibited attitudes of superiority and paternalism as a result of cultural bigotry or of inflated sympathy, lacking critical analysis.[53]

Whatever the case may be, however, it would seem that after other negative descriptions of the African were believed to have been combated, there arose a new narrative, whose point of departure was *tradition*. The various directions of sailing into the proverbial 'African Sea of identity' were now to be worked out from the harbor of tradition. Hence descriptions like 'traditional African', 'African Traditional Religion', 'African Traditional Morality' and the like.

Interestingly, however, the use of tradition to compose an ode to the African way itself turned out to be only another fit of that "narrational frenzy", of story upon story, which hardly contains "an inner narrative" with which Africans could maintain their identity.[54] Somehow the traditional conditions under which major sections of African communities live seemed to have provided support both for the pros and cons in the debate on tradition as index of Africanness. By and large the African is the 'traditional person' and (to continue with O'Donohue as paradigmatic case study) indigenous African morality is

---

[51] The term Africanists is used here in an inclusive manner, (not withstanding the debate about who qualifies as an African philosopher, or for that matter as an Africanist in general) and implies those who do African studies with the view of contributing meaningfully to the discussion on the African cultural dilemma and providing adequate knowledge about and for Africa in other areas of studies. These people could be of African or non-African origins.
[52] See Chapter One of this study. For information and critical analysis on the nature and history of Pan-Africanism, see K. Appiah, In My Father's House.
[53] See Mbiti's short appraisal of studies on the subject in his African Religions and Philosophy, pp. 10-14.
[54] See. Allen, 'When Narrative Fails', pp. 27-29.

essentially 'traditional.'[55] To a certain extent, therefore, many scholars have emphasized the traditional aspect of the ethical identity of African peoples to the point of ontologizing tradition and making it the basis of ethical epistemology.

The question we have to investigate is how to justify logically the argument that a people's morality is essentially traditional because the people live under traditional conditions of life. Secondly, should we say that because African societies are still traditional, they are (in O'Donohue's scheme) on a lower moral indifference curve? Does that provide a sufficient reason to believe that all there is to African morality is tradition?[56] And should we, against all odds, decide to answer this question in the affirmative, does it not become obligatory to define the difference between a traditional African and a traditional non-African? This question is imperative since all human communities go through stages of moral development..[57] Besides, the stages of moral development are not as lineal as O'Donohue would want us to believe. Traditional patterns of thought, morality and world views can be found in large numbers of people in contemporary so-called advanced societies.[58]

The reduction of African morality to tradition is probably due to the fact that the 'new narrative' with which the African (or the interested non-African) tries to present reality is still based on the categories of the conventional narrative. The result is that tradition is often confused with traditionalism. There is enough reason, then, to argue that the terms *traditional* and *tradition* could not be said to be a more acceptable rendering in place of *primitive*. Assimeng suggests this when he says: ">>Traditional<< is apparently a much more acceptable adjectival description of the simple, unquestioning and taken-for-granted social structures and cultural systems, than 'primitive'; the latter is a term which scientific and value-free explications notwithstanding, still evokes the built-in connection of cultural grading."[59]

---

[55] O'Donohue, New Wine and Old Bottles, pp. 117f.

[56] Whoever argues this way should also show whether the identification of a traditional society is a judgement based on values or on technology. The multiplicity of related issues thereby are obvious, although beyond the scope of our study.

[57] One of the most influential studies available on the stages of moral development is found in the work of L. Kohlberg and A. Collby, Das Moralische Urteil: Der kognitionszentrierte entwicklungspsychologische Ansatz, in G. Sterner (ed.), Kindlers Psychologie des 20. Jahrhunderts, Bd. 1, (Weinheim und Basel: Beltz Verlag, 1984), pp. 348-364. See, however, the criticisms of this work by C. Gilligan and B. Bujo.

[58] If the social system of the society is so as not to tolerate such groups of people, they ultimately go underground and seek through all available means possible to live out their dream of life. The recurrent pattern of suicide religious(?) groups is more true to Western communities than African communities have known in recent times.

[59] M. Assimeng, Religion and Social Change in West Africa, (Accra: Ghana Universities Press, 1989), pp.48-49. Assimeng (p. 32) himself cautions that the terms 'African', 'traditional', and 'religion' should be seen as "operative variables [and] as such subject to a vari-

One would have to approach Assimeng's position with caution especially in the area of African ethos and religions. As will presently be shown, there is sufficient reason to believe that the terms traditional and tradition still remain open to the same set of problems as with other misnomers that were used to define what was thought to be authentically African.

To say, for instance, that it is proper to speak of African ethics 'if that implies considering ethics from the point of view of the *traditional African,*'[60] as Kudajie does, must be considered rather disputable, if not objectionable, in contemporary discussions on the subject. Such proposition is based on a myth which Masolo calls "*the ethno-philosophical cult of difference*"[61] and contains a subtlety that leads to some of the alarming conclusions of Kudajie.[62] It is appropriate therefore to consider some characteristics of traditionalism and how they apply to African communities, then attempt to differentiate tradition from traditionalism (as far as that is possible) and propose the thesis that although African traditions remain valid for an authentic African-Christian ethic, *traditionalism* is not and should not be the essence of African morality. In clearer terms the *African* as agent of an inculturated Christian ethic must not by logical necessity be synonymous with the *traditionalist* in order to be authentic.

---

ety of interpretations".
[60] See Kudajie, 'Aspects of African Ethics', p. 17.
[61] Masolo, African Philosophy, p. 204 (my emphasis).
[62] The ethnographic approach to ethics in Africa tends, according to Masolo (African Philosophy, p. 203), "to perpetuate, by translating into an ontological constitution (beyond temporality and change), what was in fact a product of a historical conjunct.... The other extreme of this position would be to resort to the institutionalisation [sic] of science in its dialectical form in the Marxist sense in order to counter the ontologisation [sic] of tradition and ethnology." Masolo discusses these positions in connection with the debate on African philosophy. His explanation of ethnophilosophy on the one hand and philosophy as a rigorous science (as proposed by Hountondji) on the other hand, make for interesting reading. A relatively milder nuance to the view of Hountondji is the position of Wiredu's scientific physicalism, based on Dewyan pragmatism. See Chapter 8 of Masolo's African Philosophy. See also Kwame Appiah, In My Father's House: Africa in the Philosophy of Culture (New York: Oxford University Press, 1992), pp. 85-106; H. O. Oruka, "African Philosophy: A brief personal history and current debate", in Contemporary Philosophy. A new Survey, vol. 5 (Dordrecht/Boston/Lancaster: Martinus Nijhoff Publishers, 1987), pp. 45-77. This last work contains other important essays and discussions on the current debate on the various schools of African philosophy.
* This sub-title is borrowed from Assimeng (Religion and Social Change, p. 48) who, however, uses the term 'dimensions' and not characteristics. The latter is preferred for reasons that are explained below.

2.3.1 Characteristics of Traditionality

Assimeng offers useful information about traditionality in general and its concrete meaning in relation to two West African societies, namely the Akans and Igbos.[63] He observes that the concept of tradition is beset with controversies in the field of sociology. However, common to all traditional societies is the element of 'some actual or symbolic past', whose definition the people of a given society accept as collectively binding. Tradition therefore defines collective identity, exercises social control, permits and delineates the nature and scope of social change.[64] It might be useful to repeat Assimeng's quotation of Eisenstadt.

> "However different they may be, traditional societies all share in common the acceptance of tradition, the givenness of some actual or symbolic past event, order or figure as the major focus of their collective identity; as the delineator of the scope and nature of their social and cultural order, and as ultimate legitimator of change and of the limits of innovation. Tradition not only serves as a symbol of continuity, it delineates the legitimate limits of creativity and innovation and is the major symbol of the legitimate past. ... The essence of traditionality is in the cultural acceptance of these cultural definitions of tradition as a basic criterion of social activity, as the basic referent of collective identity, and as defining the societal and cultural orders and the degrees of variability among them."[65]

Tradition, Assimeng continues, is sometimes "contrasted with modernity" by evolutionists. In other cases it is associated with "primordial modes of existence" or with contemporary existence founded on the inspiration of the past. Max Weber views tradition as an authoritative instance in the society, which the members of a given society experience as the "eternal yesterday." Tradition in this sense is connected with "solemnity, immemoriality, gravity and sacredness." Assimeng himself settles on the notion that tradition is "normally viewed in terms of behaviour [sic] that draws legitimation from a behavioural [sic] pattern of a longer, customary, and chequered standing... a pattern [that] is usually seen in the context of >>days gone by<<, if not in the evaluative tone

---

[63] Assimeng, Religion and Social Change, pp. 48-50. The word 'Igbo' is sometimes written 'Ibo' and refers to one of the ethnic groups of Nigeria in West Africa. Akan is one of largest ethnic groups in Ghana.

[64] Assimeng Religion and Social Change, 1989, p. 48.

[65] S. N. Eisenstadt, 'Some Observations on the Dynamics of Traditions' in Comparative Studies in Society and History IX (4), 1969: 451-475, cited in Assimeng, Religion and Social Change, p. 48.

of >>good old days<<."[66] The author is writing as a sociologist, and his interest lies in investigating the extent to which traditionality determines and controls social behavior in a given group of people. Hence Assimeng aptly talks of 'dimensions of traditionality.' Etymologically the word dimension connotes the idea of 'measuring [something] out'[67] and is here presumably used to imply the empirical interest of sociology to investigate the phenomenon under study through empirical observation of the overt actions, material objects, symbols and structures associated with the phenomena in a society. It is probably in this sense that Assimeng explains traditionality with reference to African communities (summarized below). He seeks to establish and assess the area of behavior covered by, or the scope of traditionality in Africa on the bases of empirically observable social data.

In ethics, however, scholars try (in addition to explaining how tradtionality regulates behavior) also to estimate the extent to which traditionality can be considered as a mark of distinction with which a given society defines itself or is defined by others. *Characteristics* of traditionality (instead of Assimeng's '*dimensions* of') was chosen as sub-title above in order to emphasize this second nuance of meaning in the explanation of traditionality with regard to African communities. It is possible to say that in relation to Africans, traditionality has often been used to imply a characteristic feature of Africanness. Below is a summary of Assimeng's explanation, which provides a starting point for expanding the discussion on the ontologization of tradition that seems to identify the African with the traditionalist.

2.3.2 Traditionality and African Communities

With particular reference to West African societies, specifically the Akans and Igbos, Assimeng admits that 'they were essentially traditional until recently' and proceeds to delineate some characteristic features of traditionality in these societies. His views may be summarized as follows:[68]
- Scientific and technological simplicity characterised usually by "immediacy and pragmatism"
- Techno-scientific simplicity binds such societies to nature, making them submit often to nature's seemingly uncompromising conditions.

---

[66] Assimeng, Religion and Social Change, p. 48.
[67] See Webster's New Encyclopedic Dictionary, revised Edition (New York: Black Dog & Leventhal Publishers, 1993), p. 282.
[68] Assimeng, Religion and Social Change, pp. 49-50. On the last point about 'closed knowledge', Assimeng is citing R. Horton, 'African Traditional Thought and Western Science' in B. R. Wilson (ed.), Rationality, (Oxford: Blackwell, 1974), pp. 131-171. Other parts of the summary put in quotation marks are formulations of Assimeng himself.

- Precarious and fear evoking conditions of nature, in the face of struggle for survival, in turn evoke feelings of fear and tremendous fascination, yielding in religious responses and processes.
- Homogeneity due to the relatively small population with little or no room for anonymity. Assimeng calls this "face to face interaction."
- Small population further implies "a corresponding social structure and organization" where the basic muster of social activity rests on myths and "immemorial custom."
- Presumably, such societies have a "limited sense of time as lineal, historical phenomenon." Their geographical and mental mobility is also minimal, so that the society operates "within the framework of a cyclological metaphysic."
- In such societies tradition is an unquestionable authority, closed to doubt and modern intellectual apparatus of evaluation. Knowledge about tradition is 'closed knowledge'.

2.3.3 Tradition and Traditionalism

The demarcating line between Tradition and Traditionalism is at first sight rather thin, and yet it makes a difference of great import in African cultural history. [69] On the semantic level, one may think in the Aristotelian sense and

---

[69] Traditionalism is used here to mean the same as Assimeng's traditionality.
One of the recent works in Ghana on the question of 'tradition and modernity' with respect to African peoples and their cultures is Kwame Gyekye's book entitled, Tradition and Modernity: Philosophical Reflections on the African Experience (Oxford: Oxford University Press, 1997). Especially in chapter eight, Gyekye discusses at length and more systematically many of the issues I have been trying to address in this section of the study. Beginning with a general explanation of tradition, he shows how a static understanding of the phenomenon yields false assumptions. Gyekye also addresses issues of acculturation, in his own terms "cultural borrowing", and goes on to reflect on the different attitudes Africans adopt towards tradition in contemporary times. He classifies these attitudes into two major categories -the revivalists and the antirevivalists. He studies the arguments deployed by both camps to buttress their respective convictions and concludes that both extreme positions do not provide a fruitful solution to the problem. In their place, Gyekye advocates for an appropriate philosophical investigation that will help to decide the normative import of tradition in our times. The section on the positive and negative aspects of tradition or African culture as a whole is very informative, especially in its relation to technological advancement in Africa.

In short, Gyekye has provided a philosopher's diagnosis of the problem. At the same time it is important to point out the basic difference in my direction, even if my topic happens to relate to Gyekye's. My idea is to subject some of the popularly accepted views about the *conditio Africana* to critical questioning. My first concern has not been the treatment of the phenomenon –tradition – as such, as would seem to be the case with Gyekye.

say that tradition, traditional, and traditionalism are only grammatically variant forms of the same word, so that the different meanings conveyed remain systematically related.[70] This argument is true but incomplete, because it forgets to say that the shared meaning, or what Owen[71] calls *'focal meaning'* stems from tradition. We may understand traditionalism as a state of being handicapped by tradition due to excessive adherence to tradition. It is a handicap that contains the three evils, anachronism, authoritarianism and supernaturalism, against which some African scholars complain.[72] It is traditionalism that causes cultural staticism and underdevelopment.[73]

Traditionalism occurs in a society for several reasons of which we mention a few similar to the list provided by Assimeng above, but looked at from the another perspective:

- by way of imposition of homogeneity for the purposes of social control
- by way of theoretical (ideological) and factual *imputation* of traditional identity to a society by external manipulation from another cultural group
- by the crystallizing of ideas, thought and behavioral forms into systems, in which subjective innovation is minimal
- drawing on past instances of humiliation (cultural or otherwise) by manipulating the emotional and subconscious states of individuals or groups as sources of power and domination.

My treatment of tradition in relation to African communities is meant to be an indirect anthropology, serving as a foil for examining the discourse through which African cultural identity has been defined, and for that matter, how the African as an agent of morality has been evaluated. The question I have been proposing for consideration is the extent to which we can define Africanness by way of tradition, especially where tradition is understood as the contrast to modernization. Despite these differences of emphases, the ideas in this part of the study have been positively influenced by Gyekye's work.

[70] See J. Bogen, 'Focal meaning', in Ted Honderich (ed.), The Oxford Companion to Philosophy (Oxford: University Press, 1994), pp.282/3.

[71] G. E. L. Owen, Logic, Science, and Dialectic: Collected Papers in Greek Philosophy, in M. Nussbaum, ed., (London, 1986), p. 184ff. This source was acquired from the article in Ted Honderich, The Oxford Companion to Philosophy.

[72] K. Wiredu, Philosophy and an African Culture (Cambridge: Cambridge University Press, 1980), p. 1. Wiredu attributes these three evils to tradition and does not make the semantic distinction undertaken here. However Wiredu's argument gives cause to understand these evils in connection with traditionalism, since Wiredu does not seem to reject tradition as such. Compare, Masolo, African Philosophy, pp. 204-225. For Wiredu's discussion on 'Tradition', 'the traditional' and the scientific or modern: same book; here, pp. 37-50.

[73] In general the way tradition is understood in contemporary times is traceable to the European experience of modernity. This aspect of the question is taken up later in the discussion.

The points listed above enable us to see traditionalism from two sides. First, as an internal handicap, observable through the material developmental stand of a people, and second, as an external construction through processes of attribution and conceptual manipulation. In the latter instance the people concerned are made objects of traditionalism. They are subjected to a categorical traditionalism, where they remain traditional irrespective of what they do. Traditionalism becomes the hermeneutic tool for understanding their way of life, and the instrument of their subjection. From this perspective, traditionalism as used of Africans has more to do with a "politics of recognition"[74] than with the phenomenon of tradition *per se*.

The sociological factors listed by Assimeng in explaining traditionalism as well as the factors of a politics of recognition listed above are all operative in and real to the African situation. The African suffers both from 'internal' and 'external' traditionalism. Both forms feed on each other and strengthen each other, always leaving the African as the loser.[75]

Tradition on the other hand contains those categories of culture which permit interactive relationship between individuals in a given society, such as custom, mores, usage, thus providing the ambience for the functioning of ideational communication in a given culture. In relation to individuals, therefore, tradition is a *deposit* and the members of the given group form the *depository*

---

[74] Compare A. Gutmann, (ed.), C. Taylor, K. A. Appiah, et. al., Multiculturalism: Examining the Politics of Recognition (Princeton, New Jersey: Princeton University Press, 1994).

[75] The importance of conducting a cultural assessment by having in mind both the intra- and extra-cultural conditions at work in Africa must be considered unavoidable in contemporary times. Any attempt to proceed on a uni-dimensional analysis of the African situation is bound to remain within the parameters of a dichotomous narrative which is no longer suitable for addressing the questions of concern in Africa. In this regard Onoge has made the following observation. In current studies in social science in Africa attention is given mainly to three themes, namely, social change, modernization and economic development. Behind these themes, however, lies a basic presumption that has its roots in the colonial psycho-cultural analysis. It is presumed that African cultures are a hindrance to modernization in Africa. Onoge argues that such a presumption forgets the contradiction African peoples and cultures experience in view of the fact that colonialism and its effects must be accepted as basically given in the existence of Africans. He considers an inner criticism that ends up condemning African cultures to be ahistorical and synchronistic.

As a solution he suggests that we stop seeing African culture as being guilty for the woes of Africans. African culture, he claims, is not more mystical nor less rational than other cultures. The present condition of Africa has much to do with the past traumatic experiences of Africans. He proposes therefore that "Für diejenigen von uns, die [die] niederschmetternde intellektuelle und existentielle Armut kennen, ist es an der Zeit, die überlieferten Theorien, deren Diagnosen und Ratschläge, in Frage zu stellen. ... Das auseinandergefallene Weltbild des gegenwärtigen Afrika ist keine Folge unserer traditionellen Kulturen, sondern im Gegenteil das Resultat unserer bereitwilligen Übernahme der Kolonialmentalität" (Onoge, 'Revolutionäre Forderung', pp. 91-92; his reference to F. Fanon, Studies in a Dying Colonialism, New York: 1970).

thereof.[76] It is necessary to add that in relation to culture, however, tradition is the *depository* and cultural categories form the *deposit*.

Historically, it was Roman civil practice that gave tradition a relatively fixed meaning. In the Roman law of inheritance tradition was used to describe the 'handing on' of property from one generation to the other. Whoever inherited property had the duty of keeping it in trust, of protecting and nurturing what was entrusted to them.[77] In medieval times and thereafter, there was no general concept of tradition, and two to three centuries ago, the word tradition in its current usage was not common. Instead of the word or notion of tradition, there existed the day to day practices and conventions of peoples and communities.[78]

The way tradition is understood today, namely, as outmoded, never-changing way of life anchored on the authority of the 'eternal yesterday' is a development of the past two centuries. One may say the way we understand tradition today is a creation of modernity.[79] In 19th Century Europe, Christian religion, especially in the form of Roman Catholicism was rejected because of its claim of universality. Modernists rejected the absolutist claims of the church and sought for alternatives in their search for the truths which religion claimed to possess. The wise men (theologians and clergymen) were rejected in favor of the expert. The unquestionable framework for decision making and for action founded on religious tradition was called to question. In short modernity sought to destroy the authority of tradition in Europe. Pre-modern forms of life were seen as folly and the shadow of development and progress.[80]

Paradoxically, however, the church became the modernizing agent in her mission in Africa. The bulk of African traditions were seen as the shadow side of development and backwardness. The institutions that had supported community life and social organization were rejected. The indigenous priests, the sages and the chiefs were dismissed and their place taken by catechists, teachers and clerics.

On the one hand, tradition is anthropological, i.e. it belongs to human nature as *homo socius*. Tradition is valid and effective in all human communities. Traditionalism, on the other hand, is an infraction of tradition, indicative of the fact that tradition stands in constant danger of degeneration if it is not constantly accompanied by renewed reflection. Yet even such renewed reflection could be arrested, as is often the case in Africa, by a fore-programmed

---

[76] N. P. Williams, "Tradition" in: Encyclopaedia of Religion and Ethics, Vol. 12, p. 411.
[77] A. Giddens, 'Tradition', 1999 Reith Lectures (BBC Radio 4 Homepage).
[78] Giddens, 'Tradition'.
[79] Giddens, 'Tradition'.
[80] By 1899 modernism was condemned by Leo XIII as heretical and in 1907 the works of Loisy and Tyrrell were censured by Pius X shortly after which followed the Encyclical, *Pascendi Dominici Gregis*, which declared all movements and currents described with the word Modernism as heretical. See Brockhaus Enzyklopädie, Bd. 14, p. 711-712.

mental frame of traditionalism. When that happens we could speak of a vicious circle of traditionalism. In this connection there is cause to question whether Assimeng, and for that matter the Eisenstadt school to which he seems to subscribe, has not passed tradition off to traditionalism too quickly.[81]

In view of the actual danger for Africans of moving in a vicious circle of traditionalism, even if African scholars' "definition of reason and knowledge as propaedeutic therapy for African cultural alienation and backwardness"[82] is correct, the actual therapy would necessarily consist of a method of distilling African tradition from its external and/or self imposed categories of traditionalism. This need to distil African traditions from traditionalism is especially important because of the subconscious and multifarious nature of the conceptual categories at work in Africa. Herein lies the validity of Hountondji's dialectical philosophy which aims at explaining how consciousness relates to reality.[83]

In an ethic of inculturation it would seem proper to relate African traditions to other areas of African life, such as cultural and moral Psychology. An inculturation ethic would therefore go beyond the mere description of the so-called traditional morality of African peoples. Such descriptive methodology fails to *'reflect tradition'*[84] since it lacks the principles of mediation between African traditions and cultural development on one hand, and between cultural development in Africa and the Christian faith on the other hand. In order to *reflect [on] tradition*, one needs appropriate modes of interpreting. The need to understand better calls for a hermeneutic that breaks through the limits and boundaries of conventional knowing, experiencing and conception of reality – a hermeneutic of suspicion.

---

[81] See: Jack Goody, The Domestication of the Savage Mind (Cambridge, 1977), pp. 1-18; and two other works by the same author which could be of interest here are his Literacy in Traditional Societies (Cambridge, 1968) and The Interface Between the Written and the Oral (Cambridge, 1987).
[82] Wiredu, cited in Masolo, African Philosophy, p. 203. This point of view would seem to be the central thesis of O'Donohue's argument.
[83] Masolo, African Philosophy, p.203; also D. Masolo, New Perspectives in African Philosophy, (Rome, 1995), pp. 59-68.
[84] The imagery used here should be understood in two ways. First in the physicist sense of giving back an image or likeness as in a mirror. Secondly in the epistemological sense of working out a system of truth by means of objective and logical reflection.

2.3.4 Cultural Crisis: Crisis of Interpretation

> To be human is to act reflectively, to decide deliberately, to understand intelligently, to experience fully. Whether we know it or not, to be human is to be a skilled interpreter.
>
> [David Tracy]*

Whenever the given modes of experiencing, understanding, interpretation and action cease to carry meaning for a given society, that society experiences a crisis of interpretation.[85] The society's traditions, language and other cultural modes of existence must then be given a new outlet -a reinterpretation- to prevent the culture concerned from collapse. In order to achieve such a reinterpretation, the conventional modes of apprehension, consideration, knowing and understanding must be called to question, and their boundaries and limits traversed in a process that reflects on the society's modes of interpretation and search for meaning. In Tracy's own words, "A crisis of interpretation within any tradition eventually becomes a demand to interpret this very process of interpretation."[86]

In the course of history cultures have usually found people who usher in processes that call for new ways of understanding reality. Euripides bridged a new era in Greek antiquity by rejecting the tradition of Tragedy as the means of interpreting the order of life in his day. At the beginning of the classical era of Christian antiquity are people like Philo and Augustine (the latter is sometimes accredited with the word hermeneutics). The period of Enlightenment had Descartes and Spinoza among others, and the Reformation, initiated by Luther, was equally a challenge to reconsider the conventional interpretation of religious traditions of the day. Modernism needed people like Hegel, Schleiermacher, Pierce and others to take off.[87] In contemporary times the current of post-modernism is felt in all areas of study because of its forceful reinterpretation of the interpretation process carried over from the enlightenment

---

[85] Tracy, Plurality and Ambiguity, p. 8.
* D. Tracy, Plurality and Ambiguity: Hermeneutics, Religion, Hope (San Francisco: Harper & Row, 1987), p. 9. "Menschsein heißt, reflektierend zu handeln, überlegt zu entscheiden, intelligent zu verstehen und umfassend zu erfahren. Ob wir uns dessen bewußt sind oder nicht, Menschsein heißt, ein geschickter Interpret zu sein." Translated into German by S. Klinger under the title, Theologie als Gespräch: Eine Postmoderne Hermeneutik (Mainz: Matthias-Grünewald Verlag, 1993), p. 21.
[86] Tracy, Plurality and Ambiguity, p. 8. "Jede Interpretationskrise innerhalb einer Tradition entwickelt sich schließlich zu dem Anspruch, genau diesen Interpretationsprozeß selbst zu interpretieren", in: Theologie als Gespräch, p. 20.
[87] These examples are taken from Tracy, Plurality and Ambiguity, p. 20ff.

and from modernism.[88] The effects of these crises of interpretation have been theoretically as well as practically complex. Crises of interpretation have resulted in serious political, economic, industrial, religious and moral consequences. People were motivated to know and understand themselves and life as a whole differently through new ways of interpretation.

At the roots of the current African cultural crisis is also a crisis of interpretation. Here however the crisis is double headed. First, there are many African traditions which no longer fit. Second, there is also the load of three centuries of the conventional narrative that complicates the search for a way out of the crisis. Africans who attempt to lead the way in extricating African cultures and traditions from their conceptual stalemate can find themselves uprooting the weeds together with the millet. On the one hand, breaking through the conventional narrative ends up in drawing on African traditions already mutilated by the conventional narrative. On the other hand, the discourse on African traditions (whether as censure or apologetic) culminates in the use of the very conceptual patterns from which Africans seek to liberate themselves. One might say the search for freedom itself bewilders Africans.[89] But this is

---

[88] Post-modern hermeneutics has several shades and may not be easily reduced to any particular form of interpretation. However underlying the various forms is the common rejection of the overly rational and idealistic conception of things based on a causal and totalitarian epistemology, the fruits of the enlightenment and of modernism. Post modernists are suspicious of this classical epistemology and argue that reality is too heterogeneous and pluralistic to be confined to totalistic and universal constructions of truth. See J.-F. Leotard, Das postmoderne Wissen (1982); W. Welsch, Unsere postmoderne Moderne (Weinheim: VCH Verlagsgesellschaft, 1991), pp. 4-8; J.-F. Lyotard, Die Moderne redigieren (Bern: Benteli Verlag, 1988).

[89] In his evaluation of Nkrumah's Consciencism, Diallo Telli observes that in order to establish its intellectual equality with the West, Africa has to master Western versions of intellectual skills (in: Mazrui, The Africans: A Triple Heritage [London: 1978], p. 85.
A good example of this double-binding could be found in the debate on African ethics and religion. J. B. Danquah, a pioneer of Western trained Ghanaian scholars, devoted himself to the articulation of indigenous culture and way of life in his popularly known work, *The Akan Doctrine of God* (originally part of a three-volume work entitled *Gold Coast Ethics and Religion*). In an appraisal of the methods various African scholars have applied to study African ethics, C. A. Ackah criticizes Danquah because "he adopts rather disreputable and unsupported theories about the origins of some Akan words. Secondly, he tends to reproduce Akan thought in the dress of English philosophy of the 1920s and 1930s which he learnt as a student from Professor G. Dawes Hicks. It is difficult at times to see how far what Danquah writes is truly Akan, and how far it is merely the genius of Danquah" (C. A. Ackah, Akan Ethics, Accra: Ghana Universities Press, 1988, pp. 3-4). In contrast to Danquah is Mbiti who uses his first hand knowledge of the indigenous culture and tries to find similarities in African cultures and so establish a general theory concerning certain aspects of religion and ethics in Africa. All the same, Ackah makes the following assessment: "The desire to emphasise [sic] the cultural identity of different African groupings is highly desirable provided it is based on scholarly research. Unfortunately, however, Professor Mbiti's research methods seem to be highly questionable. For example, in his study of the Akamba

only one way, perhaps the pessimistic way, of considering the matter. A more positive approach might be to take the seemingly confounding nature of the situation as the impetus for a radical -reaching to the roots- hermeneutic.[90] To be radical such a hermeneutic must also be double headed. It must question not only the interpretations of the conventional narrative, but also the very notions of Africanness in a theology of inculturation.[91] It must question whether the image of African authenticity proposed in inculturation is not itself the fruit of a conventional way of understanding the African.

A radical hermeneutic would therefore be suspect of the gamut of paradigms used in the attempt to define the authentic African. Elements which are held to be specifically African -such as intuitiveness, spontaneity, communalism, deep religiosity, race and tradition- need a vigorous reinterpretation in contemporary times.[92] In the context of such "re-reading" of the African identity the work of Kwame Appiah, *In My Father's House: Africa in the Philosophy of Culture*, is seminal. In the field of theology J. M. Ela, M. Towa, and S. K. Adotevi have raised their voices against the shallowness of the conventional paradigms for defining Africanness.[93]

---

people of Kenya, Professor Mbiti, who is a member of the tribe, seems to rely entirely on his personal knowledge and memory of traditional beliefs... There is little evidence...that [he] took the trouble to interview the fellow members of his tribe and systematically gave him" (Ackah 1988: 4).

[90] Tracy (Plurality and Ambiguity, pp.8-9) makes the point clearer when he observes that "Interpretation is a lifelong project for any individual in any culture. But only in times of cultural crisis does the question of interpretation itself become central. At such times ... we need to reflect on what none of us can finally evade: the need to interpret in order to understand at all." For the German translation, see Theologie als Gespräch, p. 21.

[91] In this connection African theology has much to learn from feminist theologians like E. Schüssler Fiorenza, with regard to her methodology for the practical application of a hermeneutic of suspicion. See, Schüssler Fiorenza, Brot statt Steine. Die Herausforderung einer feministischen Interpretation der Bibel (Freiburg, 1988); C. Schaumberger, M. Maaßen (eds.), Handbuch Feministische Theologie (Münster, 1986). For the specific context of Africa see: M. A. Oduyoye, M. R. A. Kanyoro (eds.), The Will To Arise: Women, tradition, and the Church in Africa (Maryknoll: Orbis Books, 1992).

[92] Ela does not mince his words in articulating the issue. He writes, "the important blackness (Négritude) movement, born in 1930 and marking an entire generation of black intellectuals and writers, must be singled out for special notice. Everything that was said in *Des prêtres noir s'interrogent* years ago bears the mark of this movement. For years, African Christians have reflected on the problems of faith and its language through the questions raised by Blackness. Today, however, the principles of this movement are being contested by the new generations. For a large number of today's black intellectuals, not only is Blackness outmoded, it constitutes an obstacle to the liberation of Africa. It is beginning to be looked upon as an ideological disguise for African alienation." See Ela, African Cry, p. 122.

[93] M. Towa, Léopold Sédar Senghor: négritude ou servitude (Yaoundé: cle, 1971);S. Adotevi, Négritude et négrologues (Paris: Plon, 1972); others are E. Mveng, ‚Récents développements de la théologie africaine', in Bulletin of African Theology vol. 5, no.9

2.3.5 Crisis of Interpretation: Crisis of Identity

> The self finds itself by risking an interpretation of all the signs, symbols, and texts of its own and other cultures. The ego continually constructs a self only by deconstructing all false notions of... identity.
> [David Tracy]*

A crisis of interpretation is also a crisis of identity. Seeing ethics as narrative and stressing the need for a hermeneutic that yields an adequate consideration of the human person together underscore the fact that "morality is always a consequence of the conception we have of man."[94] The conception we have of a good person constitutes the bias with which we interpret a person's behavior in a given community. In a stoic tradition (say) a good mother may not show remorse for the death of a child she could not prevent from dying. One who does not belong to the same tradition can only appreciate such action if the one realizes that in the stoic tradition a virtuous person is conceived as someone who would accept all misfortune without feeling distress or pity. Because of this bias, a people's actions do not lend themselves easily to interpretation and comprehension. We could compare a people's way of life to 'texts' that cannot be interpreted light handedly. For Tracy the best example of such texts are the classics found in literate cultures.

Like the classics, so are the customs and traditions of peoples good test cases for a theory of interpretation.[95] Classics do not lend themselves easily to interpretation because they possess abundance and permanence of meaning. They are however not open to definitive interpretation.[96] Customs and traditions are also comparable to classics in the extent to which they command meaning beyond their local boundaries. For classics are culturally specific, but they still have the possibility of being meaningful beyond the boundaries of the culture in which they are produced. In their reception customs and traditions also reveal their resemblance to classics. They have the ability of surviv-

---

(1983); B. Muzorewa, The Origins and Development of African Theology (New York: Orbis Books, 1985).

* Tracy, Plurality and Ambiguity, p. 16. "Das selbst findet vielmehr zu sich selbst, indem es wagt alle Zeichen, Symbole und Texte seiner eigenen Kultur wie auch anderer Kulturen zu interpretieren. Nur indem es immer wieder alle falschen Vorstellungen von Identität dekonstruiert, konstruiert das Ich (ego) fortwährend ein Selbst." In, Theologie als Gespräch, p. 31.

[94] B. Häring, 'Morality', in K. Rahner (ed.) The Concise Sacramentum Mundi (Kent: Burns & Oates, paperback ed. 1993), p. 981.

[95] Tracy, Plurality and Ambiguity, p. 12.

[96] Tracy, Plurality and Ambiguity, p. 12.

ing the instability of cultures by paradoxically depending on the "instability of the particular culture's shifting canons of the [conventional]."[97] This capacity to survive by adapting to the changing canons of conventionality makes classics, and similarly customs and traditions more flexible than they are often considered to be.[98]

A people's tradition is always a tradition of tradition because tradition carries its own history. As Tracy puts it "Scholars do not own the classics any more than traditionalists own the traditions that form our cultural lives."[99] The continuous exploration of the *traditional* and the *traditionalists* for the meaning of Africanness is an operation that at times does not take the complex nature of interpretation seriously. This is probably the core of the problem in African-Western communication over the years. It is possible to speak of centuries of unsuccessful dialogue between the West and Africa, and as a result, among Africans themselves. Difficulties in communication arising from biased interpretation is characteristic of the missionary venture in Africa.

As a result of their biased interpretations missionaries and anthropologists were immune to the otherness of Africans. They fell into the temptation of reducing reality to that which they already knew.[100] This bias also worked as a barrier that prevented missionaries and anthropologists from accepting the challenge of the claim to truth that some of the important traditions and customs of African communities possessed.[101] It was therefore difficult for these missionaries and anthropologists to resist the temptation of forcing African traditions and customs into the Procrustean bed,[102] and imposing a domestication on these traditions without first seeking to understand.

The resulting effect of this deficit in the process of interpreting African traditions has been discussed in the sections above and some of the points taken up here are bound to overlap with those previously discussed.

The basic effect of this deficit of interpreting the African way of life was an emptiness of selfhood on the basis of wholesale rejection of tradition.[103] For example, unlike the Stoic mother in the Stoic tradition, a Ghanaian

---

[97] Tracy, Plurality and Ambiguity, pp. 12ff

[98] As an example of the point, Tracy observes that "the biblical texts have exercised a similar role throughout Western history. On the whole, the Scriptures have served, as Northrop Frye insists, as a kind of great code for Western culture. And yet this code has functioned with extraordinary flexibility. Consider, for example, the role of Paul's letter to the Romans before and after Luther or, more recently, before and after the belated twentieth-century exegesis." Tracy, Plurality and Ambiguity, p. 13.

[99] Tracy, Plurality and Ambiguity, p. 14.

[100] Compare, Tracy, Plurality and Ambiguity, p. 15.

[101] Compare, Tracy, Plurality and Ambiguity, p. 15.

[102] See Tracy, Plurality and Ambiguity, p. 15. For the story of Procrustes, see L. Petzoldt, Kleines Lexikon der Dämonen und Elementargeister (München: Verlag C.H.Beck, 1990), pp.101-102.

[103] See E. B. Idowu, The Selfhood of the Church in Africa, in Ministry 3(4) (1963), pp.151-

mother who fails to show sorrow openly for her deceased child would be suspected by many Ghanaians for causing the child's death. She would be considered a witch, an evil person. Many Africans perceive the virtuous person as someone who is able to show pity and sorrow. Yet in the wake of evangelization funeral ceremonies were among the indigenous forms of life that were quickly dismissed as pagan practices. A typical case is found in the *Gemeindeordnung* of Bremen Mission for the local church among the Ewes of Ghana. Article 6, §110 states:

> "Bei Todesfällen und Beerdigungen muß alles <u>heidnische Wesen</u>, Totenopfer, Totengesang, Lautes Geschrei, aufgelöstes Haar, ungewaschene Kleider ... vermieden werden. Dagegen ist es <u>christliche Art</u>, durch Gesang, Gebet und Zuspruch die Leidtragenden zu trösten. Insbesondere sollen Witwen und Waisen nicht nach Art der Heiden trauern, sondern durch Gottes Wort und in der Gemeinschaft Trost suchen."[104]

It is clear that this injunction aims at challenging certain aspects of funeral customs among the Ewes of the time.[105] However this injunction was based on a dichotomous interpretation of funeral customs that forced the indigenous people to form a rather strange understanding of themselves. This crisis of identity is certified in many church documents in Africa. In 1932, one E. Y. Botsoe (who must have been in charge of one of the Christian communities in the absence of the German missionaries) reported on a funeral of a Christian woman in a letter he wrote to the missionaries in Bremen. His purpose was to show, as the heading of the letter states, "the pitiable state of the *Akposso* people and the Enlightenment taking place among them." The letter makes the strong impression that the *Akposso* people who still held to indigenous funeral

---

158; cited in Assimeng, Religion and Social Change, p. 209.

[104] Bremer Staatsarchiv, Stab 7, 1025-43/4, p. 22 "In cases of death and funeral, everything that is of pagan nature – offerings to the dead, lamentations, weeping, unkempt hair, unwashed clothes – must be avoided. In contrast to these, the Christian way is to console the bereaved through singing, prayer and words of encouragement. Widows and orphans especially should not moan in the pagan manner. They should rather seek comfort from the word of God and in the community" (my translation of the German text).

[105] Funeral rites and ceremonies in Ghana used to be and are to a great extent still very elaborate. They involve the whole community. There is drumming and dancing, people (especially women) weep openly to express their sorrow. Lamentations, shaving of the hair, food-offerings and other religious rituals form important parts of leave taking from the deceased. The cost involved and some of the ordeals which bereaved relatives (especially as spouse or child) are made to go through are aspects which must be considered on their own merit and rejected for what they are. This however does not immediately make a dualistic canon of pagan and Christian applicable to Ghanaian funeral ceremonies as a whole. Such an interpretation is simplistic.

customs represented the 'pitiable state', while those who as a result of their conversion to Christianity showed no external signs of sorrow represented the 'state of Enlightenment'.

Botsoe sounds euphoric for being able to inform the missionaries that "through the influence of the deceased woman, her husband had converted to Christianity.... It gives me great joy to note that the man comported himself greatly at the death of his wife. So calm was he that one could hardly believe he was bereaved."[106] In many other church documents and records it is not difficult to find descriptions of indigenous African church leaders which demonstrate how negatively many Africans had come to conceive themselves. Parsons cites a joint statement of African Churches to congratulate missionaries for their work in which the writers expressed themselves as follows: "These kind people [the missionaries] carried our Church from her infancy to almost manhood. They sacrificed their money, knowledge, and even their lives to bring our *benighted race* (my emphasis) the light of the Gospel and civilization." [107]

There is also another illustration of the perpetuation of this negative self-identification by many Africans (with specific reference to Ghana). In a random sample study of the personal records of patients admitted to a catholic hospital in Ghana covering the period January, 1993 to October, 1996, the impression that many Ghanaians still understand themselves in the categories that base on a negative self-understanding was reconfirmed. In these records, all patients who were either not baptized or belonged to an indigenous African religion were entered in the records with the description "*pagan*". It must be noticed that none of the staff of the hospital in question was at this time expatriate.[108]

---

[106] Bremen Staatsarchiv, Stab 7, 1025-77/6. Botsoe's letter was written in Ewe, dated April 30, 1932.

[107] T. Parsons, The Churches and Ghana Society 1918-1955 (Leiden: Brill, 1963), p. 18.

[108] Because of the confidential nature of the records, it is not possible to give any information about the health institution that offered me the chance to have a look in their data bank. But the fact that people freely apply such descriptions to themselves says much about the complex and unconscious nature of the crisis of self-interpretation in Africa. The irony is clearer when one attempts to translate the term pagan into the local Ewe language. The popular Ewe equivalent used daily is *dzimaxoseto* (unbeliever). Often however, the people described as 'unbelievers' (pagans) are people of unrelenting faith in one or the other religious object of worship, and an ultimate belief in God. So even though books have been written on misnomers, Africans still use many of them anyway. Their use may even be found in the offices and documents of the very scholars who protest their application. On the contrary, nowhere in the Western world does one find the use of a religious identification such as "pagan" or even "atheist" in official records. This, notwithstanding the fact that not a few people in the West openly express their disbelief in God, or reject baptism and religion in general.

In a sense the dichotomous narrative did not only deny the African of moments of civilization in the past. It also made the African become the most deprived of himself or herself. In the wake of European expansion, the Indians were allowed to keep their Ashokas in full splendor, and Asians as a whole were not only culturally respected, they were also seen as a civilizing factor in North Africa –the theory of the Hamits. China was respected for its culture. But the African experience was such that the way to African self-identification was closed at one end leaving only the Western-Christian outlet.[109]

In order to liberate Africans from this closed-endedness, it is suggested that in addition to studying the customs and traditions of African cultures, inculturation must yield a theory that extricates the African from the either *African-traditional* or *African-Western-Christian* paradigm of self interpretation. Inculturation must broaden the horizon of the African's self definition by returning to an organic pattern of history and locate the African in this organic history of peoples and cultures.

2.4 African Ethos: Which African? In Search of Other Paradigms

Unless we think statically, an *a priori* definition of cultural identity looks problematic. In Africa, for instance, such a definition would overlook the complex processes of cultural exchanges and the resulting culture change. When the processes relating one culture to, and differentiating it form, the other are ignored in defining African cultural identity, Africanness is forced into one non-recurrent given, based on the principle of negation -the non-African.[110] Such an approach is difficult because Africa has been and still is a watershed of cultures and the African personality is influenced by multiple conditions within and outside Africa.[111] Cultural pluralism is not a mental creation in Africa. It is a fact of life and a daily experience for many people. Language, religious attitudes and creeds, food habits and forms of dress, traditions and institutional structures vary greatly from one group to the other.

At the same time, when one begins to search for the unifying factor in African cultures one cannot refuse to see the complex net of resemblance and relationship that brings the various African cultures together. Such similarities

---

[109] See A. Mazrui, The Africans, pp. 83ff.
[110] See A. Diemer, 'Kulturidentität, interkulturelles Verstehen, Philosophie als transkultureller Dialog', in: A. Diemer (ed.), Africa and the Problem of ist Identity, International Philosophical Symposium on Culture and Identity of Africa (Frankfurt: Verlag Peter Lang, 1985), pp. 51-63.
[111] See Akoi, Religion in African Social Heritage (Rome: 1970), R. Dixon, The Building of Cultures, (New York: 1928).

have led some scholars to suggest that: "when one examines the rather complicated process of African history back into the past ... the sequence of events tends to converge into a common point of origin. Tribes appear to narrow their origins into a common cradle. And cultures seem to rally into a common source of diffusion."[112] In an organic consideration of history, it might even be more fitting to say African cultures have 'common *sources* of diffusion.'[113] In that case the unifying factor, it would seem, is more easily worked out *a fortiori*, by locating those essential aspects of African cultures that create consciousness of Africanness in a person. [114]

One person who explains African identity from a pluralistic perspective is Ali Mazrui.[115] In what he calls the "triple heritage", Mazrui works out three basic components of the African heritage. He explains that these components issue in two forms. In the modern form the triple heritage consists of the indigenous, the Arabic and the Western components. The second is the ancient form which has the indigenous, the Semitic and Graeco-Roman aspects.[116]

---

[112] P. Akoi, Religion in African Social Heritage, p. 57.

[113] It has been remarked elsewhere that in Africa, specific anthropological terminology, and in this case diffusion, must be applied with a lot of care. Diffusion for instance has its own history, beginning from nineteenth century evolutionary thought through to Boasian historicity. Its use refers to the transfer of cultural traits from one group of persons to another as a result of migration, trade, war or other contact (See Winthrop, Dictionary of Concepts, pp. 82ff). It is very likely that Akoi uses diffusion in this sense of transfer of cultural elements from one group to the other in view of the complex history of migrations that are known to have taken place on the continent. In current studies in anthropology, diffusion has been largely replaced with acculturation and the relation between personality and culture, because these latter concepts are held to offer more holistic and psychological insights for understanding culture. Aspects of acculturation in relation to inculturation are take up later in the study. The citation of Akoi here is to accentuate the complex relations and processes of culture that occur in Africa by virtue of the direct contact between members of different groups of persons.

[114] Compare Diemer, 'Kulturidentität', pp. 51-52.

[115] See A. Mazrui, The Africans, 1986; Mudimbe, The Invention of Africa, pp. 59ff.

[116] Mazrui's contribution is very useful for widening the horizons for defining African identity, and much of what follows draws heavily on Mazrui's ideas. At the same time, there is reason to think that even Mazrui would seem to explain 'indigenous' as being essentially the 'traditional' (in a rather static or traditionalistic sense) element in the composite of what he calls African heritage. One gains this impression not just because Mazrui finds examples for the indigenous heritage among the traditional Masai of Kenya and their neighbors the Kikuyu (See Mazrui, The Africans, p. 64), but because the explanation he gives tends to emphasize the traditionalistic aspect of life found among such communities. For instance he notes that the Masai are herdsmen and the Kikuyu agriculturists. It is also striking, according to Mazrui's explanation, that in both the ancient and modern forms of the triple heritage, the indigenous component remains constant, whereas the Graeco-Roman and the Semitic evolve into the Western and Arabic components respectively. Since in acculturation the cultural values exchanged are processed into community-specific values by the respective groups involved, it is legitimate for Mazrui to want to identify specific cultural ele-

There is a sense in which Mazrui's triple heritage sheds new light on African sources of identity. In this paradigm Africanness translates into a composite identity born of multiple cultural traits and world views. These cultural traits and world views are exhibited with varying intensity of combination by different African peoples. The paradigm is particularly relevant to this study because whenever the question of African ethos is raised, it is found to be closely bound up with the need to specify which African, which time and in which context. An elaboration of this paradigm may provide an understanding of the complex nature of the issues involved in trying to specify African identity.

2.4.1 Qualifications and Differentials of African Personalities

For the sake of clarity the main components of Mazrui's triple heritage will be described here as qualifications in order to depict the generic import of the terms indigenous, Semitic/Arabic and Western. Concretely these qualifications subdivide into specific forms which will be described here as differentials. Presuming some amount of liberty in reading the explanation Mazrui gives to the triple heritage, it is possible to identify at least two differentials under each qualification which will be discussed in the following sequence:

- The traditional indigenous and
- modernised indigenous personalities.[117]
- The Arabized but not Islamized and
- Islamized but not Arabized Africans.

---

ments with which African peoples mount the stage of acculturation. It is also valid for him to go after those elements which become 'African-specific' as a result of the process of acculturation by way of localization. Such cultural elements could genuinely be called indigenous African cultural elements, and depend mainly on the historical, geo-physical, scientific, and other context bound situations of the given community. But I fail to see how these indigenous aspects equate to the traditional aspects of life in Africa. Elsewhere, Mazrui presents a different perspective that perhaps helps us to interpret the present text differently. See A. Mazrui and M. Tidy, Nationalism and New States in Africa (London: Heinemann, 1984), p. 298. In this latter work, Mazrui and Tidy observe: "Another obstacle to cultural liberation has been the confusion of the concept of modernization with Westernization....Retraditionalization does not mean returning Africa to what it was before the Europeans came. In hard assessment, it would be suicidal for Africa to attempt such a backward leap. But a move towards renewed respect for indigenous ways and the conquest of cultural self contempt may be the minimal conditions for cultural decolonization."

[117] Mazrui himself does not distinguish between the traditional and modernized indigenous African. The difficulty that arises when this distinction is not made has been discussed at length above.

- Westernized Africans conscious of their bondage to western culture,[118]
- Westernized Africans unconscious of their bondage to Western culture.

2.4.2 The Indigenous Personality

The term *indigenous* describes the original inhabitants of an area, i.e. those living in or belonging naturally to a particular region or environment.[119] Nearest in meaning to indigenous is "native", which translates the late Latin word *'indigena'*, derived from *'gignere'* meaning *to beget*.[120] An indigenous African would imply simply someone who by birth or otherwise has his or her origins in the geographical region called Africa. Obviously such a theoretical definition creates difficulties in its denotative application. But it is at least agreeable that people who consider themselves indigenous Africans would also trace their origins geographically and/or culturally to Africa.[121] The indigenous personality can be used inclusively, therefore to describe different African personalities. Two groups of the indigenous personality are discussed below.

2.4.2.1 The Indigenous Traditional African

Among indigenous Africans, there are those who are traditional. They are communities or groups of persons who live under simple conditions with little scientific and technological influence. Many of them are often illiterate. Their way of life is similar to that of other traditional communities wherever one is found. Their standard of living is, in relation to modern standards, in many respects poor and limited. We could find many examples that properly fit this differential since large sections of African communities are still traditional.[122]

---

[118] This group also sub-divides into the group of Africans strongly attracted towards the West and the group of Africans in search of their roots in the form of a return to 'traditional' Africa. For a good discussion on the arguments of both groups, see Gyekye, Tradition and Modernity, pp. 232-242.

[119] See A. S. Hornby, Oxford Advanced Learner's Dictionary (Berlin: Cornelsen & Oxford University Press, 1974), p. 433.

[120] The proper meaning of the term native is here implied and not the term's pejorative connotations in relation to Africans. It is also not within the limits of this work to discuss the question of which specific geographical area is originally Africa. For the issue of Maps see Mazrui, The Africans, pp. 23-40.

[121] This implies that the term is used here making allowance also for Africans in Diaspora and even other peoples who might trace their culture to the continent of Africa, although such peoples may be located outside the current geographical boundaries of the continent.

[122] For obvious reasons Mazrui makes an exception of the BaMbuti (so-called Pygmies) of

Besides Mazrui's own examples of the Masai and the Kikuyu, one could add the Fulani, found in many West African countries. We could also mention the Dowayos of Cameroon or the Tiv of Nigeria. And considerable portions of Ashanti and Ewe communities in Ghana are still traditional.

There are indications that many of these people find life under traditional conditions oppressive and burdensome. To the extent that they wish to have their life differently organized, it is difficult to argue that such communities define themselves as indigenous because they are traditional.

2.4.2.2 The Modernized Indigenous African

This second differential of the indigenous identity depicts that group of Africans, who while still strongly connected to the indigenous traditions and way of life, enjoy the benefits of modern science and technology. Such people may or may not have western education. Besides being vested in the traditions of the clan or community of origin, they are also well informed about other peoples and widely traveled. Their daily life is organized with the help of modern amenities such as running water and electricity, Western medicine and modern means of communication. Good examples in Ghana could be found among the women who control the daily business on the major Ghanaian markets. Some of these women have no formal education, but many Ghanaians would admit that these women enjoy a relatively modern style of life. At the same time it is observable in many respects that such 'market mummies' (as they are popularly called in Ghana) are not westernized.

On the other hand there are Ghanaians who by every count could be described as westernized. Nonetheless they strongly represent and live by indigenous African traditions and yet are not traditional in their manner of life. For example no Ghanaian would claim to be a better custodian of the traditions, religious beliefs, and moral philosophy of the Ashantis than the Asantehene, who is regarded as the symbol of the collective identity of the Ashantis. Yet Otumfuo Nana Opoku Ware II (the King of Ashanti until February 1999) was a British trained lawyer.[123]

This latter differential introduces an important nuance in the search for an African cultural and moral identity. The close connection between mod-

---

Zaire who live in the Ituri forest, or the Khoisan (so-called Bushmen) of the Kalahari in South Africa.

[123] See. K. Appiah, In My Father's House, p. 185. In many villages and towns in Ashanti and Eweland, the indigenous chiefs are intellectuals, working in bigger towns or in the cities. They have regents who perform many of the ritual functions and do the day to day administration for them. And yet many of such chiefs still consider themselves and are generally accepted as symbols of indigenous identity for their communities.

ernization and the West is undeniable. But the tendency to equate the two when dealing with African cultures is an unfortunate accident of history, because of the double bond situation in which it leaves the African. It is like being told 'you are either African and, for that matter pre-modern, or you are modern and therefore not authentically African.'[124] There is another way in which this double binding effect reveals itself. Instead of condemning the negative aspects of African cultures for what they are, it is rather African culture as such that is often criticized for being essentially traditional.[125] Such criticism creates the impression that moral problems in Africa such as political oppression, corruption, nepotism, exclusionist attitudes towards non-family or non-clan members, and injustice towards widows, to mention but a few random examples, would have been solved when African cultures have been modernized.

2.4.3 The Arabized Personality

According to Mazrui, the Arabic embodiment of the African heritage could be considered as the modernized form of the ancient Semitic heritage. The ancient Semitic connections to Africa are established in the historic presence of Jews of Maghreb in Algeria, dating 2000 years back. Most of them acquired French citizenship as a result of the Cremieux Decree of 1870.[126] In contemporary times there are Jews in Ethiopia, even if their number has reduced to only a few thousands after their mass transfer to Israel in the massive airlift operations code named 'Operation Moses' between 1983-85.[127] The Jews in South Africa present a much larger Jewish presence (numerically) in contemporary Africa.

In contrast to the Falasha of Ethiopia who are economically poor and politically not influential, the Jews of South Africa are by many standards richer than the influential Dutch speaking Afrikaners (even while the latter

---

[124] This is how I understand on one side, Westermann when he says "all that the African wants is to become like the European", and on the other side, the simplistic reactionary type of inculturation and Africanization that usually consists of a negation in which Africans, as it were, respond to Westermann and say: no, thank you, Africans do not wish to become European.

[125] See the earlier reference to O. Onoge, and his suggestions for a revolutionary consideration of African cultures that could be of help in the search for liberation in Africa. It is in this vein that we have expressed our difficulties with the critique of African cultures undertaken by O'Donohue and other Africanists like him. While much of African culture stands in urgent need of renewal, the integral liberation of the African will depend on the discovery of a methodology that avoids further isolation of African cultures from world history.

[126] Mazrui, The Africans, p. 82.

[127] Mazrui, The Africans, p. 82.

still possessed political power). South African Jews could be counted "among the richest of all Jews of the world."[128] The most striking point about both groups of Jews, however, is the question of their identity in relation to Africa. Mazrui captures the paradox of it all when he says:

> "The Falasha were indigenous by every appearance, but they insisted that they were immigrant. They were the 'Lost Tribe of Israel' [Beta Israel]. On the other hand, South African Jews are immigrant by every appearance, but increasingly claim that they are no less indigenous to South African soil than blacks claim to be."[129]

Whatever the case may be, Jewish presence in Africa does not only "[pose] problems about the definition of an African", but also compels Africans to look beyond the usual for their roots.[130] At first sight, it might look quite exaggerated for the sub-Saharan African of today to want to trace his cultural origins partly to some Semitic source. Yet it is precisely because such aspects of cultural history are quickly dismissed from African traditions that one ends up filling the emptiness with traditionalism in an attempt to establish what is authentically African. And there is a sense in which cultures all over the world have found reason to trace a relationship to some other culture which at first sight is difficult to justify on geographical and historical grounds. Why, for instance, do we find the statement "we Germans are the Greeks" in the wake of German nationalistic philosophy?[131] The ancient Semitic-African connections are not mere imagination. Much of this tradition is documented by historians of Arabic (rather than European) origins[132] and is well entrenched in the

---

[128] Mazrui, The Africans, p. 85.

[129] Mazrui, The Africans, p. 85.

[130] We have mentioned that a narrow definition of African identity creates difficulties. This is clear in this context. Mazrui asks "how can we accept Muslim Arabs as Africans if we reject the Jews, who were in Africa before the Muslim conquest of north Africa?" A more intricate question is how to accept South African Jews as Africans and reject the Dutch speaking Afrikaners. This raises the question both on the subjective and temporal levels. Should we define a person as African by sheer durability through time in Africa, or must the person feel and claim Africanness or should we use the 'native' criterion?

[131] See Tracy, Plurality and Ambiguity. In the German translation of the same book, Tracy writes: "In der deutschen Kultur beachte man die Bedeutung der römischen Klassiker bei Kant mit dem Refrain von Hegel bis hin zu Heidegger, daß wir Deutschen die Griechen *sind*" (Tracy, Theologie als Gespräch, p. 26, author's italics).

[132] P. Akoi, Religion in African Social Heritage, pp. 57ff, here p. 60:footnote 3. Akoi points out how well the Arabic scholars were acquainted with African history. He refers to such documents as the records of the first Expedition of *Hakam Ibn Abdel* to the Sudan, *Khwarizsmi*'s linguistic and historic account of names around the old Ghana empire, and the records of *El Mas'Udi* about his travels through African countries between India and

oral traditions of many African peoples. Interestingly enough such tradition is known more to the illiterate custodians of African history and legends of migration and not to many a western schooled African.

In a research work based mainly on interviews and oral tradition, Mamattah elaborates on the claims of the Ewes of West Africa about their Semitic origins.[133] In doing so he also succeeds in mapping the close resemblance in the cultures of the Yorubas in Nigeria and the Ewes in Ghana drawing on the complex networks of migrations that must have taken place in the development of cultures on the African continent. The similarities in the findings of Mamattah and the historical documentation of Akoi (earlier referred to) are striking.

Certainly much of the tradition on which Mamattah and his informants depend in ascribing Semitic connections to Africa is a medley of legends including overtones of Jewish sacred history and oral tradition about the migration of various African peoples in the ancient past. It would therefore be a misplaced emphasis should one begin to attribute some scientific historical importance to such stories or even claim an actual historically supported Semitic ancestry for sub-Saharan Africa.

What these traditions about African-Semitic connections do, however, is arouse our curiosity about the *history of African history*. They are traditions that raise questions about many of the similarities between some African cultural and religious practices and Old Testament practices. For instance, what is the source of male circumcision found among many peoples in West Africa? Why are many indigenous religious rituals accompanied by the sacrifice of animals? How far can we probe the indigenous religious value of setting days aside where tilling the soil is taboo, in order to give rest to *"asase yaa" (mother earth)*?[134] Or is it just sufficient to say it is an *Ashanti traditional* be-

---

Spain. *Abu Ubeid El Bekri*, using travel accounts on Africa, wrote on the state of pre-Islamic Ghana, Northern Africa, and the Almoravids. More popularly known is *Ibn Batuta Abu Abdallah Mohamed Ibn Ibrahim*, who documented his travels (around 1325) to Mecca and Egypt. He also visited many other countries including Mali (Timbuktu) and Niger. More importantly, Akoi reminds us that Europe owes a lot of its knowledge of medieval Africa to *Leo Africanus*. This man was born in Grenade and his real name was *Al Hassan Ibn Mohammed el Wazan es Zayatti*. He was a respected scholar who had been influential in the Morrocan jihad against Portugal. He also traveled extensively. It was on one of such journeys in 1515 that he was picked up at sea by Sicilian pirates and taken to Pope Leo X. His excellence of learning made him a favorite in the papal palace, being christened later under the name *John Leo Africanus*. He lectured on Arabic culture and language in many Universities in Italy and Spain and translated his "Description of Africa" in 1526.

[133] C. M. K. Mamattah, History of the Ewes of West Africa (Keta: Volta Research Publications, 1978), pp. 31ff.

[134] See P. A. Sarpong, Ghana in Retrospect (Tema: Ghana Publishing Corporation: 1974), pp. 116ff.

lief? Why is the belief in metaphysical punishment for moral evil so strong among many African peoples?

In contemporary West Africa however, this direct Jewish presence is rather insignificant. Instead there is the indirect and modern form of the Semitic heritage, i.e. the Arabic/Islamic embodiment. The Arabic factor has been more influential in Africa's history on account of the Arab conquest of North Africa in the 7th and 8th centuries.[135]

There are in contemporary times conditions that still propel the "making of new Arabs" in Africa. There are various Islamic movements, which aim at planting Islam in Africa, using all means available. They may use education (by way of offering scholarships and study opportunities for young people in Islamic countries), or economics, by offering assistance to poorer nations in Africa, or the use of political cohesion, through the imposition of *Sharia* as state law, to mention a few examples.[136] Egypt illustrates well how total the process of cultural and religious Arabization has been in some parts of Africa. But whereas North Africa was Arabized through a biological (in the sense of intermarriage) and cultural process, Africa south of the Sahara, and especially, West Africa is being speedily Arabized through a religio-cultural process, though the biological aspect cannot be completely ruled out.[137]

Apart from East Africa where colonial rule succeeded in halting the growth of Islam, the Islamic population of North Africa, the Horn of Africa and West Africa stands mountain high[138]. As Mazrui puts it, the heartland of Black Africa's Muslims is definitely in West Africa. Nigeria presents clearly the weight of the Islamic factor in Africa. It is estimated that there are more Muslims in Nigeria than there are in any one Arabic country.[139] The Yorubas and Hausa-Fulanis are predominantly Muslim. This is interesting because Nigeria also represents quite well the other two components of the triple heritage. The Christian/Western factor is dominant among the Ibos. Smaller groupings such as the Tiv represent the indigenous cultural and religious factor.[140] In view of the current situation in Sudan, we can say that Mazrui was prophetic in his thinking when he asked:

"Are the Southern Sudanese the next target of the conquering wave of Arabization within the next 100 to 200 years? Will the

---

[135] Mazrui, The Africans, p. 90.
[136] P. F. Stamer, Islam in Sub-Saharan Africa (Estella: Verbo Divino, 1995), pp. 60ff.
[137] Stamer, Islam in Sub-Saharan Africa, 1995, p. 154.
[138] See statistics given in Stamer, Islam in Sub-Saharan Africa, 1995, p. 28ff. Since then the numbers have increased considerably. In Ghana for instance the Muslim numerical strength has gained about 3%.
[139] Mazrui, The Africans, p. 92.
[140] Mazrui, The Africans, p. 92.

twin forces of biological mixture ... and cultural assimilation transform the Dinkas and Nuers of today into the Black Arabs of tomorrow?"[141] Today we might put the question a bit differently. Has the military option replaced the bio-cultural process towards the Arabization of South Sudan? From a historical – cultural point of view, we could say that the brutalities and atrocities of war being experienced in Sudan over the years have their roots to some extent in the historical crisis of African identity. The ugly nature of this identity rupture which takes various forms all over the continent is presented in its bare and most extreme form in the Sudan nightmare.[142]

Ghana has about 16% of its total population being Muslims. Among the Ashantis, there is quite a good number of indigenous Ashantis converted to Islam – the so-called *'Asante Krambo',* and big portions of Muslims are dotted all over Eweland. But the intensity of Islam is felt more in the North of Ghana, among the Dagomba, for instance. Here the effect of Islam on the way of life of the people is open to observation. The Islamic factor is superimposed on Dagomba political institutions, titles of prestige, marriage ceremonies and other occasions of import which may not even be directly linked to Islam.[143]

The length of time in which Islam has more or less peacefully cohabited with African traditions, persuades us to think that some of the traditions marked out today as 'traditional' African traditions actually have their roots in the Arabic heritage of Africa. It might for instance be revealing to study thoroughly the relationship between polygamy in African traditions and polygamy in Islam, and in relation to its ancient near Eastern parallels.

---

[141] Mazrui, The Africans, p. 92.

[142] It is import to remark that it is not our intention to portray the war in Sudan as a religious conflict. Nor would such a view be a proper interpretation of Mazrui's analysis. What we are underscoring is the fact that identity crisis in Africa has deep-set historical roots, and that such a crisis can have very serious and far reaching consequences on the continent. Of course this three-faced personality of Africa could be manipulated into a religious ideology, creating tension between the indigenous religion, Islam and Christianity. It could also be politically manipulated and culturally stratified in order to maintain the status quo.

[143] See C. Oppong, Growing up in Dagbon (Tema: Ghana Publishing Corporation, 1973), pp. 14ff. Oppong informs us that even though the Islamization of the Dagomba was not achieved overnight, "Muslim migration and conversion have continued till the present day with the result that observers now write of the >>Muslimized Dagomba<<" (Oppong, Growing up in Dagbon, citing, D. Tait, The Konkomba of Northern Ghana, Oxford University Press, 1960). Oppong further observes that "an influential factor resulting in the increased number of converts,... is the high prestige value of Muslim insignia, clothes, names, rituals and learning" (Oppong, Growing up, p. 14, with reference to J. S. Trimingham, Islam in West Africa. Oxford: Claredon Press, 1959, p. 75).

2.4.3.1 The Arabized but not Islamized African

The first differential of the Arabic heritage is represented by those who have been culturally and linguistically Arabized without becoming Muslims. Once again South Sudan and Nigeria are good examples. South Sudanese increasingly speak Arabic but many of them resist Islam.[144] In the same vein the Copts of Egypt in the Horn of Africa exhibit a profound linguistic and cultural Arabization. They are however not Muslims by religion.[145]

The Arabic language plays an especially important role in the Arabic influence on the African identity. Besides the vast majority of Africans who speak Arabic directly (as a first or second and official language), the language has a great indirect effect all over Africa. Many Arabic nouns are found in the Hausa language, spoken both by the Hausa and Fulani, besides the indigenous Fulfude language of Hausaland. In Nigeria the Hausa and Fulani peoples form quite a considerable percentage of the total population. In addition to the fact that Hausa is directly spoken in most, if not all of West Africa, it has influenced many other West African languages.[146] In East Africa, the Kiswahili language vastly used across tribal and national boundaries is even more directly influenced by the Arabic language.

Considering the role language plays in personality formation and in the transmission of cultural values and traditions,[147] it becomes difficult to cling to only certain traditional aspects when elucidating African identity. Mazrui's alertness enables him to bring to light some of the assumptions that are taken for granted in this regard. For example, Nyerere's experiment of *'Ujamaa'* is seen in many circles only as an attempt to use indigenous African spirit of solidarity as a basis for political socialism in an African context. Mazrui studies the same phenomenon and makes an analysis that immediately broadens our horizons about the reality involved. He writes: "Indeed, the term ujamaa in Tanzanian Kiswahili is a fusion of the triple heritage. The word itself is Arabic-derived. It refers to the indigenous phenomenon of ethnic solidarity or the solidarity of the extended family.... The word ujamaa is Islamic, the ancestral phenomenon of solidarity is indigenous, and the conceptual metaphor equates African familyhood with European socialist fellowship."[148]

---

[144] Mazrui, The Africans, p. 90.
[145] Mazrui, The Africans, p. 90.
[146] Mazrui, The Africans, pp. 88ff.
[147] Compare M. M. Lewis, Language, Thought and Personality (London: George G. Harrap & Co. Ltd.,1963).
[148] Mazrui, The Africans, p. 97.

2.4.3.2 The Islamized but not Arabized African

There are on the other hand, Africans who have been (or are being) Islamized, but are not culturally Arabized. Mazrui gives the example of the Wollof of West Africa. The *Asante Krambo* also hardly speaks any Arabic, and does not particularly portray the Arabic culture as such. One must however add that a change in manner of dress is increasingly observable among both men and women of Ashanti and Eweland who have been converted to Islam. Besides, the Arabic influence in its religious expression does not remain only with people who convert to Islam. The intricate similarity between some of the practices of Islam and indigenous religion ripples the Arabic/Islamic influence into the broader circle of indigenous African communities. The indigenous Ashanti religionist sometimes does not discriminate between the divination conducted by a Muslim cleric and that of an indigenous diviner. People go to these diviners as it is opportune for them under the circumstance. Thus whereas the former differential gains expression through specific cultural categories, the latter is expressed in religious elements.

2.4.4 The Westernized Personality

> One of the greatest ironies of modern African history is that it took European colonialism to inform Africans that they were Africans.
> [Ali Mazrui]

Mazrui begins his exploration of the Western impact on the African identity with the statement quoted above, and ends the discussion by specifying the same statement as follows:

> "When we say that Europe Africanised the identity of the inhabitants of the continent, we mean that this was in spite of the wishes of Europe.... Europe's supreme gift was the gift of African Identity, bequeathed without grace and without design, but a reality all the same."[149]

Between these two statements lies the vast sea of the effects of the African-European contact for centuries. One drags one's feet, staggering through the sandy beach into this sea. And when one successfully sails across it and comes out at the other end, walking further remains as difficult as before. This imagery portrays the difficulty involved in properly working out the effects of

---
[149] Mazrui, The Africans, p. 99.

the West on the African personality. In contrast to Mazrui's tone of victory is the other side of the coin, which for our purposes is represented by the Bremen missionary, Westermann. He worked many years among the Ewes of West Africa and traveled through a greater part of the continent towards the end of the 19th century and the first decades of the 20th. He summarized his idea about Africans in the following observation. "All that the African wants is to become like the European."[150]

Mazrui's triumphalism and Westermann's militantism are both symptomatic of the African—Western dialectic. Accuse Africans of Westernization and they will find excuse in the fact that they are compelled to be so. Find fault with Westerners for Westernizing Africans and the Westerners will find justification in the fact that Africans are only receiving what they earnestly desire.

Look at it one way or the other, it remains true that the effect of the contact with the West sits deep in many an African. The Western way of being and of interpreting reality became normative in Africa. In matters so banal as of dress, food and drink, to more serious issues concerning African tradition and moral standards, such effects are observable. For example, an African dressed in an impeccable suit is more likely to receive polite attention from a civil servant than someone indigenously dressed.[151] Against the background of

---

[150] Westermann, Afrika als europäische Aufgabe, (Berlin: Dt. Verlag, 1941).

[151] The irony of this attitude is depicted with literary imagination in many of the works of the African Writes Series. See for instance, C. Achebe, No Longer at Ease (New York: Anchor Books, reprinted 1994); T. M. Aluko, Chief the Honorable Minister (London: Heinemann, 1985). The issue of dress is only one example of the general displacement of things African: aesthetics, ethics, language, literature, art, politics, education and technology, and culture in general. The fact that many Africans, who can afford it, consume more of European products than those produced in their countries of origin does not always depend on preference or better quality. It is an attitude arising from what Kwesi Appiah calls "asymmetries of cultural power" (K. Appiah, 'Topologies of Nativism' in D. LaCapra (ed.), The Bounds of Race: Perspectives on Hegemony and Resistance [London: Cornell University Press, 1991], p. 159). Such patterns of behaviour imply a subconscious pre-selection of goods, and probably of the good as such. In Appiah's essay cited above, he concentrates on the literary works of Sub-Saharan African writers and illustrates this phenomenon of pre-selection in which many Africans have to operate. He writes:
"The African teacher of literature teaches students who are, overwhelmingly, the products of an educational system that enforces a system of values that ensures that, in the realm of cultural production, the West in which they do not live is *the* term of value. The American teacher of literature, by contrast, has students for whom the very same West is the term of value, but for whom that West is, of course, fully conceived of as their own. While American students have largely internalized a system of values that prohibits them from seeing the cultures of Africa as sources of value for them—despite ritualized celebrations of the richness of the life of savages, ... African students, raised without relativism, expect Americans to value their own cultural products because they are, by some objective standard, superior" (Appiah, 'Topologies of Nativism', p. 159; the same essay is reworked in

African egalitarian communalism, one may rashly judge the civil servant for acting unethically. But the situation becomes different when we remember that the suit may only be evoking a subconscious connection to the colonial master who always had preference before the African.

A suit is aesthetically admired the world over, and in some cases preferable for its practicability. But to the extent that this suit assumes such importance as to determine a person's worth, it raises fundamental questions about African cultural identity. So is the Western aspect of the African personality in many respects subtle. It influences thought patterns, judgements, and worldview. We might say that the Western factor is represented by those whose Africanness is itself sieved through the Western muster of interpretation of things. This qualification will apply in the first place to the African western trained scholar, characterised by long years of school education. The best illustration might be found among African elite, including politicians as well as clerics.

Whereas we may not generally classify all African urban dwellers as candidates of the Westernized personality, many will be found in urban centers. The speed of urbanization in Africa today is occurring at a high rate. Many of these city-dwellers are indigenous Africans, but not so far as to prefer an evening of moral formation from an old lady who tells a story around the evening fire in the compound of the house to watching a TV program under the comfort of a ventilator.

2.4.4.1 Self-conscious Westernized African

Among Westernized Africans there are those who are conscious of their state of cultural bondage. Mazrui says of the late Senghor of Mali that he was one of "the most deeply westernized of all African intellectuals. In many ways he [was] a black Frenchman.... Indeed I have never seen a single photograph of President Senghor in anything but an impeccable Western suit, in spite of all his homage to Negritude."[152] Yet on the subjective side, he was so conscious of the dangers of Westernization that he channeled much of his energy towards rejuvenating African cultural identity by way of Negritude.

Appiah's own book, In My Father's House, 1992, pp. 47-72). See also N. Wa Thiongo, Moving the Centre, 1993; V. Y. Mudimbe (ed.), The Surreptitious Speech, 1992.

[152] Mazrui, The Africans, pp. 13 and 14. A similar situation is observable in some independent churches in Ghana. Many of these churches are praised for their bold Africanization of the Christian religion. One such church is the Deeper Life Church, which has made major inroads into Ghana from its Nigerian habitat. This church does not spare the Catholic Church in Africa criticism for her extreme Westernization. Ironically, however, one hardly sees the pastors of this church ministering without a suit.

More interesting is the issue of names. Many outspoken African scholars who plead the cause of Africanization bear names that show the lasting impact of the West on the African personality. Anthony Kwame Appiah explains in his book, *In my Father's House*, how his name *Anthony* is a corruption of the Ashanti name *Antorey*.[153] The list of such English corruption of Ashanti and Ewe names is unending. One influential name in Ghanaian history is *Aggrey*, corrupted from the Fante name *Agyir*. The name *Turkson*, used by many Fantes, is also explained to have come originally from the Akan *Takyi* or *Tekyi*. *Amissah* (and its variant form *Menson*) stem from the Akan name *Mensah*. On the Ewe side similar examples are the Ewe names *Gbokle*, *Haga* and *Klu* corrupted into *Beckley*, *Hagan* and *Ocloo* respectively.[154] Many of those who bear such names however are also active in the search for and rejuvenation of an authentic African identity. They are aware of their attachment to Western ways of life. At the same time, they look beyond the external trappings of names and tastes of dress or food habits, and seek for positive indigenous African traditions and genuinely acculturated African-Western values.

---

[153] See Appiah, In My Father's House, p. 182. Kwame Appiah has a rather attractive style and has successfully applied it in the explanation he gives to his names. The explanation is woven into his family history, or perhaps better to say history of families. This allows the reader to obtain a quick insight into the intricate constellation of a typical Ashanti family and its network of relationships.

[154] In each case the first is the indigenous form of the name and the second its corruption respectively. There are several sources in which the study of the corruption of African names (in Ghana) mainly during the colonial times and after is recorded. One common source known to nearly all second and third cycle students who are interested in African studies is J. Loglo, West African Traditional Religion for A Level Religious Studies (Accra, 1984, enlarged 1988), here pp. 19ff. The Ghanaian Film, 'The Road to Kukurantumi', produced by King Ampaw in the 1980s has elaborate scenes in which the irony of these "new names" is depicted. The producer attempts to show how this change of names affected not only the external self identification of the people concerned, but how such names also inculcated a whole new value and cultural system based on the colonial mentality. Thus the individuals (probably representative of whole communities) did not only take on new names, they also took on a new self image – an identity – that had deep effects on their perception of the good person. See K. Ampaw, (producer), The Road to Kokurantumi, Accra: Ghana Film Industry, 1988. The possibility that such people developed fragmented attitudes toward the question 'who must I be', cannot be completely ruled out. Thus care must be taken to select genuine forms of modernization in Africa (be they Western, Arabic or Indigenous) and what sociology of knowledge describes as "false consciousness." The idea of false consciousness is traced to Marx and is understood to mean a thought pattern that is alienated from the real social being of the thinker. In our context the same phenomenon could be described as *'de-culturation'*. With regard to moral identity we could talk of *false conscientization*, i.e. alienation from the cultural and social categories of value of the cultural actor.

2.4.4.2 Westernized Africans unconscious of their Westernization

There are on the other hand, Westernized Africans who remain to a great extent unconscious of their cultural bondage. Such people are not necessarily different from those who are conscious about their Westernization, except that in the case of the former the pose of Africanness often turns out to be a subtle caricature of self-alienation. As Mazrui puts it:

> "the differences among educated Africans do not lie in whether we are cultural captives but in the extent to which we are. We vary in degrees of bondage but not in the actual state of being enslaved."[155]

Some Africans choose to forget about their African roots because of the continuous political and economic instability on the continent. In their frustration they accept cultural bondage as a lesser evil to the insecurity and poverty of Africa. And yet this very choice continues the spiral of identity crisis, which in turn influences the social, moral, political and economic conditions of Africa. In this connection Mazrui recommends Mobutu of Zaire for making "a brilliant distinction between authenticity and ... negritude. [For Mobutu] negritude was a rebellion against the arrogance of others; Authenticity was the rebellion against one's own dependency and imitativeness."[156]

Unfortunately, it could hardly be said that Mobutu himself engaged in this *rebellion-against-self*. In deed one wonders whether the catastrophic end of Mobutu's political career and the deplorable state in which his period of office left the country could not be traced to this lack of consciousness of his cultural dependency (expressed perhaps through his villas in France and Belgium and huge accounts in Swiss banks). Despite his reaction against European names and dress, he failed to come to terms with the essences of Westernization, which were carried in the external trappings of names and dress.[157] Does this Mobutu episode itself provide a possible diagnosis of the general state of the Westernized African? Is it not possible that the very Africans who complain about Westernization do so only to hide their own cancerous wounds? Should we continue to trace the unethical acts in politics all over Africa (corruption, autocracy, brutality and unrestrained force, militarization of power, etc.) to only the *traditional* aspect of the African heritage?

---

[155] Mazrui, The Africans, p. 13.
[156] Mazrui, The Africans, pp. 13, 14.
[157] Mobutu, like Eyadema of Togo, is known to have ruled against the use of Christian names and European style of dress.

Chapter Three

3 African Theology and Inculturation Ethics

African Theology is growing out of a situation in which the old patterns of meaning are found to be heavy and burdensome, because the African Christian finds it difficult to identify himself in the conventional patterns. African theology is therefore very much concerned with learning to understand in new ways, in the sense of obtaining an awareness of the self and of one's history in relation to God and to his saving action in Jesus. In this context one can speak properly of historical consciousness in the Lonerganian sense.[1] It is in this context that inculturation obtains its proper meaning.

The suspicion African theology has for conventional ways of understanding the African makes the need "for a relevant theological hermeneutic ... not only necessary for African Christian self-understanding and maturity, [but] ... also a legitimate theological pursuit. Africans want to appropriate the riches of African insights into the human condition and the divine life, so as to enrich and enhance Christian life and thought."[2]

The historical situation also makes African theology closely related to political-cultural movements such as Pan-Africanism and especially African nationalism. African theologians have had much to learn from political and cultural analysts, whose diagnosis of the 'African condition' provides relevant material for theological reflection in the African struggle to redress the relegation of Africa to the 'underside of history'.

To the extent that African theology challenges the place of Africans in the world order of cultures, politics, economics and values, it could be said to be 'political'. On such issues African Christians experience Western theology as being Euro-centric in its interpretation of the Jesus event as the ultimate intervention of God in human history. By overlooking the oppressive situations of Africans Western theology fails to communicate with African Christians. It is, for instance, striking that even in the wake of Western political theology as shown for instance in the works of Metz, Moltmann and Sölle, the parallel experiences of slavery, racism, colonialism and neocolonialism in Africa were overlooked.[3] In view of such experiences African theology begins to

---

[1] See Lonergan, Method, 175-196.

[2] Martey, African Theology, p. 55.

[3] Against this background of long years of silence in Western theology on important life experiences of African Christians and Africans in general, the bold step taken by some European Christian men and women in connection with the *Initiative Kindugu*, on the occasion of the African Synod becomes all the more laudable. These men and women signed a statement in which they "acknowledge the countless wrongs inflicted on African people. ... It seems impossible to assess the extent of such sin or even to redress it. We dare ask for forgiveness...God alone can bring about the healing. With you we beseech Him for

understand Western theology as a 'local theology' that seeks first and foremost to answer questions peculiar to the European experience. In chapters one and two of this study attempts have been made to show how this conventional approach to world events has led to the isolation of Africa from history, helping to create a state of alienation on the part of the African.

What is the role of ethics in a theology such as African theology? How exactly are we to understand ethics in the context of inculturation and how do we formulate the Christian religious foundations of an inculturation ethic? In chapter one the parameters of the question of an inculturation ethic were sketched. It was opined that since inculturation in Africa cannot presume to begin with a neutral cultural history,[4] or rather that since the robbing of Africa of its history is part of the reason for inculturation, an existentialist approach is imperative.[5] The effects of inculturation, it was argued, will remain peripheral if inculturation is considered only in its formal and essential perspectives. On account of the historical and existential reality of Africans, inculturation takes on an unavoidable moral import that cannot be overemphasized. This moral perspective on inculturation emerges from the people and from their existential history.[6]

---

it." Such a move makes the Christian witness of these men and women more honest, expressive of a genuine desire and openness to enter into dialogue with African Christnans. It is an action that derserves reciprocal recognition and opennes from African Christians. For the full text see: The African Synod. Documents, Reflections, Perspectives (Maryknoll: Orbis Books, 1996), p. 71. The statement was signed by many scholars, lay people and religious, including Pedro Casaldiliga, Erwin Krautler, Bernhard Häring, Notker Wolf, Peter Hünermann, Wolfgang Hoffmann, Guiseppe Alberigo, Norbert Greinacher, Walbert Bühlmann, Hans Küng (African Synod, note on p. 71).

With regard to the silence of European political theology on the African situation, B. Bujo has a different opinion (See. Bujo, Die ethische Dimension der Gemeinschaft. Studien zur Theologischen Ethik, Freiburg Schweiz, 1993, pp. 130ff). In view of the radical insights of Metz (See J. B. Metz, Glaube in Geschichte und Gesellschaft. Studien zu einer praktischen Fundamentaltheologie, Mainz, 1992) on the importance of anamnesis in any genuine theology, Bujo reads Metz as implying that it is imperative to avoid a partial application of the Jesus event (memoria passionis et resurrectionis Christi) to certain specific moments of human suffering, such as the holocust of World War II, as if these had no relation to other and similar experiences in Asia, Africa and elswhere. The theology of Metz has contributed fundamentally to the development of contextual theologies, such as Liberation Theology in Latin America, and its parallel of Black Theology in South Africa. Still, we may argue that political theology in Europe did not have the same eye for experiences of the indigenous peoples of North and South America, Asia and Africa, as it had for the experience of Auschwitz.

[4] See chapter one of this study, footnote 88.
[5] See chapter one of this study.
[6] See chapter one of this study.

From the background of an existentialist frame of reference arises the thesis that doing inculturation ethics is not, in the first place, the justification of norms or of African moral systems. More important is the anthropological question: 'who is the actor?' In other words, how African must Africans be if their morality should be at once Christian and authentically African? The paragraphs that follow attempt an articulation of some of the relevant aspects of the Christian religious foundations of inculturation ethics in view of this pertinent question of Africanness.

3.1 Africanness, Christian Theology and Inculturation Ethics

The question of Africanness has a number of presuppositions that create difficulties for theologizing about African Christian morality. First it presumes knowledge of a certain state of being African, which alone makes Africans authentic. Underlying this presumption is another one: Africans are not (yet) as African as they should be.[7] But what makes the question of Africanness as a starting point for theological reflection most difficult is its propensity to a certain form of ethno-theology that inadvertently services the *either-or* paradigm for analyzing the African situation. The difficulty lies in the fact that this type of ethno-theology has a dead end.[8]

A possible means of overcoming this paradox is for the ethic we are seeking to establish on two central theological elements, namely, incarnation and awareness. The incarnation is vital because without it inculturation loses its meaning. In the same way, a theology of African Christian morality cannot avoid being Christological. Christian theological reflection as such centers on the Jesus event as its basic purpose and theme. Other issues of the Christian faith are illuminated on the basis of this one motif.[9]

---

[7] In a situation of identity crisis, this paradox is unavoidable. By calling one's identity to question, one presumes knowledge of what one's proper identity should be. The paradox lies in the fact that one doubts precisely what one presumes. See Alwin Diemer, "Kulturidentität, interkulturelles Verstehen, Philosophie als transkultureller Dialog", in: A. Diemer (ed.), Cooperation with J. Paulin Hountondji, Africa and the Problem of its Identity (Frankfurt am Main: Verlag Peter Lang, 1985), pp. 51-63, here p. 51. See also Kwesi Wiredu, "Problems in Africa's Self-definition in the Contemporary World", in: G. F. McLean (ed.), Person and Community. Cultural Heritage and Contemporary Change, Series II. Africa, Vol. 1 (Washington: CIPSH/UNESCO, 1992), pp. 59-70, here p. 59.

[8] J.-M. Ela, "The Memory of the African People and the Cross of Christ", in: Y. Tesfai (ed.), The Scandal of a Crucified World (Maryknoll: Orbis Books, 1994), pp.17-35, here p. 19.

[9] Ela, 'The Memory', p. 17, referring to Walter Kasper, Jesus the Christ (New York: Paulist Press, 1977), p. 15.

Awareness, many philosophers would agree, is based on the ultimate datum on which knowledge starts – experience.[10] Experience is not a state of mind, and it is itself not open to more prior acts of cognition. Experience is at once cognitive and affective. I feel, or see, or taste, or smell. Since it is difficult to get behind experience, awareness is a state of consciousness that properly constitutes a primary act of knowledge. We might say being aware is knowing concretely because it produces a state of consciousness that has an object.[11] In order to emphasize the importance of the element of awareness in a theology of African Christian morality we shall call it a theology of awareness. How, then, do the incarnation of Jesus and awareness help to formulate the Christian religious foundations of an inculturation ethics?

Awareness in the context of an integral African theological hermeneutic implies a consciousness of the concrete experiences of Africans, of their concrete history, and of the Africans themselves. In this way inculturation ethics must begin with what the question of Africanness presumes, i.e. this African, of flesh and blood, of today, and all that this embodied African concretely implies: historical isolation and destitution, illiteracy, poverty, hunger, disease, homelessness, humiliation, pain, torture, anguish and death. The concrete African also implies the African who experiences joy, who shows grave strength of endurance, peace, magnanimity and friendship.

African Christian morality would seek to establish an authentic African narrative in which Africans not only relate to the Jesus event, but participate in it. Such a theology would show how the African situation concretely reveals the very ambivalence of the cross of Christ. "Jesus is ours through the depth of

---

[10] It is true that the subject of awareness is rather contentious in Western epistemology, and it is not our intention to follow the debate between empiricists and idealists that characterizes the Western moral philosophical tradition. Should one decide to take a quick look into this tradition however, there is enough proof that both schools of thought—Kant as well as Locke—agree in principle that knowledge is founded on experience. The list of literature to the topic is long. For our purposes see, James Iverach, "Epistemology", in: J. Hastings (ed.), Encyclopaedia of Religion and Ethics, vol. 5 (Edinburgh: T & T clark, 1926-1976), pp. 337-356, here pp.339-340. See also Annemarie Pieper (Hrsg.), Geschichte der neueren Ethik 2 Bde. (Tübingen und Basel: A. Francke Verlag, 1992).

[11] Pastoral experience with rural communities in Ghana, among whom the European thought pattern based on abstraction is unfamiliar taught me this basic truth. After months of enthusiastic *dissemination* of seminary theology among these communities, it became clear to me that questions about the people's 'knowledge' of God have to be conceived differently if one wished to communicate successfully with them. I was always embarrassed that my question 'who is God?' usually found a dead end. Accidentally I asked on an occasion, 'How have you experienced God?' (this question would translate into some of the indigenous languages as: 'What has God been doing for you'?). To this question, I found not only interlocutors, but teachers, people convinced of their knowledge -primary knowledge of God.

his humiliation. ... [Africans] are related to Christ in humiliation."[12] This Christological foundation for a theology of awareness in the African context means pausing for a moment in our search for a presumed African to be found in the romantically described traditions, take a second look and become conscious of this man, this woman, this African. The concrete African must be the subject of an inculturated African ethic.

3.1.1 Inculturation ethics, Incarnation and the Paschal Mystery

African theology concerned as it is with liberation, cannot avoid the theme of the cross. We cannot look for an 'African of the resurrection', risen in the form of traditional African moral systems without first becoming conscious and accepting the challenge of 'the African of the cross.' Commensurate with the motif of liberation, inculturation ethics must make clear that the state of the African has much to do with humanly designed and sustained structures and systems.[13] Ela is straightforward in his observation: "We know today that the suffering of people is not natural; it does not result from any human limitations. Instead it is produced by people, by groups in power, and by models of society and culture." [14]

A theology of awareness establishes the important relationship between the incarnation and the passion of Christ. A good hermeneutic, however, will avoid emptying the Jesus event into the African experience. It is rather the African story that empties into the story of Jesus. Inculturation ethics "will have to give back to the man Jesus his full integrity as a human being, and give his death the historical and political meaning that in fact it possessed."[15]

Shorter is right, therefore, in observing that basing inculturation on the incarnation without relating it to the paschal mystery (especially when understood only in terms of Jesus' *enculturation* into his particular Jewish culture) is of little value.[16]

---

[12] Ela, 'The Memory' p. 29.
[13] Ela, 'The Memory', pp. 18ff.
[14] J.-M. Ela, My Faith as an African,(Maryknoll: Orbis Books, 1988), p. 111, cited by Tesfai, 'Introduction', p. 12. That human agency is behind human suffering is a fact known all too well to Africans. Evil has a bearer, an architect whom many African communities call a witch or a wizard. The metaphysical aspects of this phenomenon (of witchcraft) are open to debate or even to skepticism. But the fundamental issue which African ideas about witchcraft underscore is true the world over. The cure for the evil in the world needs good people, witch-doctors!
[15] H. Assmann, Theology for a Nomad Church (Maryknoll: Orbis Books, 1976), p. 86, cited by Yacob Tesfai, 'Introduction', in: Tesfai, (ed.), The Scandal of the Crucified, pp. 1-16, here p. 6.
[16] Shorter, Toward a Theology, p. 81.

The dangers of such an incomplete consideration of incarnation include limiting the meaning of inculturation by analogy to "the first insertion of the Gospel into a culture", building on a Christology that is far removed from the historicity of the incarnation, and the danger of submitting to culturalism by forgetting to submit specific cultures to the challenge posed by the Gospel.[17]

Shorter's application of the passion and resurrection of Jesus as an analogy of inculturation, however, seems to have missed the slant it requires in the African context. Having worked out the disadvantages of the model of inculturation based on an incarnation separated from the paschal mystery, Shorter ends up applying the paschal mystery only to culture and not to persons in their concrete situation. The conclusion of such an application is obvious: there is need for "Cultures ... to be evangelized and to undergo *metanoia* or conversion at their profoundest level. ... [C]ultures are called upon by Christ to 'die' to everything that is opposed to the ultimate good of humanity."[18]

The need to work towards the conversion of culture may not be downplayed. But there remains a pertinent question that African theology cannot overlook. Why, one may ask, could Shorter not see the people who bear the culture and their relation to the paschal mystery? Why the silence about the question that is so pertinent to Africans, which Bujo so candidly poses:

> "Liegt, anthropologisch gesehen, der afrikanische Mensch nicht schon im Sarg? Bräuchten wir nicht einen neuen Ezechiel, der über ausgetrocknete Gebeine Afrikas sprechen kann, um sie durch den Geist Gottes wieder lebendig zu machen (Ez 37)?"[19]

In this connection the criticism made of Shorter and Schineller earlier is better understood.[20] Although they see the urgent need of liberation as an integral approach to inculturation, there is every reason to believe that for them and many other theologians, including some indigenous Africans, the motive of liberation is understood in a way that retains the skirmishes of a conventional missionary activity.

In contrast to this approach Latin American liberation theology (probably because it arises directly from the daily experience of suffering and death rather than from a theoretical reflection about a people's reality) explains that

---

[17] Shorter, Toward a Theology, pp. 81-82.

[18] Shorter, Toward a Theology, p. 84.

[19] "Is the African, anthropologically considered, not already buried? Do we not need an Ezechiel, who is able to speak to the dry bones of Africa so as to revive them through the Spirit of God (Ez 37)?" [My translation of the german]. B. Bujo, Die ethische Dimension der Gemeinschaft (Freiburg: Universitätsverlag Freiburg Schweiz, 1993), p. 129, quoting E. Mveng, L'Afrique dans l'Eglise. Paroles d'un croyant (Paris: 1985), pp. 203-213.

[20] See chapter one of this study.

there is no way in which we can talk about the cross of Christ without talking about concrete people who die. Liberation theology insists that since many people die today as a result of similar structures and systems that led to the tragedy of Jesus, the cross finds its place in the suffering of the people of today. Tesfai poignantly expresses the point: "God is paradoxically revealed in the powerlessness of the victim. This is the occasion of the ultimate incarnation: God's presence in the weakest and most vulnerable form of suffering. It is the point where >>God becomes genuinely other<<."[21]

3.1.2 Africans: Moral Agents in an Inculturation Ethic

A theology of awareness presents a point of departure for addressing the question of agency in African Christian morality. In doing ethics as an aspect of inculturation, "It is impossible for us [Africans] to throw a veil of shame over our real condition in history, ... because [it] is the place where the "great black cry" springs, the cry that joins the anguished appeal of the crucified of Golgotha."[22]

More directly, the "great black cry" can be said to relate to "the great black narrative", the African-story. This narrative is different from the conventional narrative in several ways. It drowns the chorus of a romantic narrative that abstractly praises the goodness of African moral traditions. These traditions are the very traditions which the dichotomous narrative had declared to have no place in the "world community". An authentic African story, however stands out in relief against both the romantic and dichotomous narratives, because it neither placates the conscience of the status quo nor gives warmth to the African. A theology of awareness gives light, not warmth, and by virtue of this light, we are compelled to renew our conception of being African and Christian.[23]

Rather than use a presumed form of Africanness that was, a theology of awareness brings us face to face with the experience of Africanness today, of refugees, asylum seekers, of politically brutalized people, terrified and held to ransom by their own kin and kith, a clumsy mixture of peoples and tribes (on account of artificial boundaries), faceless faces, whose place in world history

---

[21] Tesfai, 'Introduction', p. 14. The last statement is Tesfai's citation of Leonardo Boff, Passion of Christ, Passion of the World: The Facts, Their Interpretation, and Their Meaning Yesterday and Today (Maryknoll: Orbis Books, 1987), p. 52.

[22] Ela, 'The Memory', p. 28.

[23] The idea expressed here certainly echoes Lonergan's analysis of the subject of morality, where he emphasizes the baffling nature of self-consciousness arising from a processes of immanent self-experience. See Lonergan, Second Collection (London: Darton Longmann & Todd, 1967).

is charted according to statistics of wars and tragedies, an Africanness of no beauty, so as to deserve the looks of other people (Is 53,1-3). This contemporary embodied Africanness, in its historical actuality, constitutes the moral imperative for African Christians and for the community of believers at large. It is implied that if Africans uncritically develop theologies of African Christian morality based on compliments about the beauty and soundness of African moral traditions, they stand the danger of sinking back into the 'delirious frenzy of story upon story,' which however hardly contains an inner connection to Africans. Such theologies would end up leaving the African in his state of retrograde amnesia.[24]

3.2 The Question of Method in Ethics

Engaging meaningfully in ethics depends on the ability to work out an appropriate method that allows for fruitful reflection on moral issues. Regarding the centrality that the problem of moral pluralism has rapidly achieved in the life of the Church in recent times, the need for a commensurate method that is theologically fruitful has become particularly compelling. Insofar as inculturation ethics relates to the question of moral pluralism in the church,[25] it requires a theological method that adequately supports systematic reflection on African Christian morality, in relation to the universal church. Two approaches which could be of use (at least by analogy) in developing a method for doing inculturation ethics are the concepts of Janssens (earlier referred to) and Komonchak.[26] In the section that follows I try to sketch both methods and then attempt an application of the two methods to inculturation ethics.

---

[24] A citation from Sacks, The Man who Mistook, in Allen, 'When Narrative Fails', p. 28. See also chapter two of this study.

[25] It is clear that the project of working out a fruitful method which will meet the question of moral pluralism in the Church is a rather difficult task. The sensitive and controversial nature and the gravity of the question cannot be underestimated. The question of moral pluralism is itself important to inculturation ethics. The topic, however, goes beyond the limits of this study.

[26] See Janssens, 'Artificial Insemination'. Part of the essay has already been used in chapter one of this study. The second essay is Joseph Komonchak, "Moral and the Unity of the Church", in:), Concilium 150 (October, 1981), pp. 89-94.

3.2.1 Sample Method I: Komonchak

It is possible to understand the scheme Komonchak proposes for systematic reflection on Christian ethics by reducing it to three major elements, namely: generative principles, mediation and action. These elements co-ordinate to form a structure of complex relations in their concrete application to moral decision and action. At the base of the structure are the 'generative principles'. They serve as "the existential and productive basis of both the process and criteria of moral discernment."[27] In other words generative principles are those criteria which in the first place make the moral process and action at all possible.

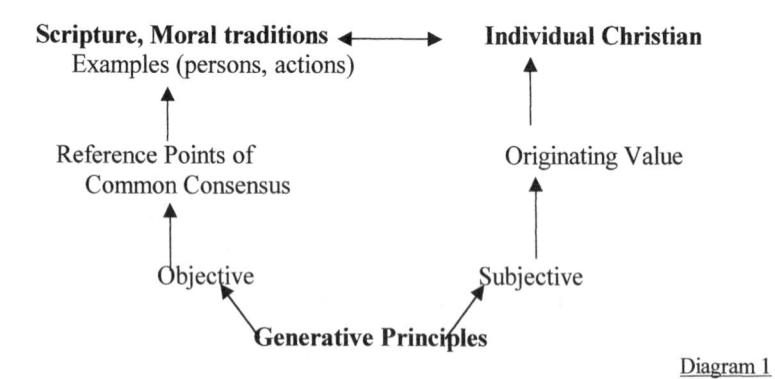

```
Scripture, Moral traditions  ←——→  Individual Christian
  Examples (persons, actions)              ↑
            ↑                               |
    Reference Points of               Originating Value
    Common Consensus                         ↑
            ↑                               |
        Objective                       Subjective
                    ↖            ↗
                  Generative Principles
```
Diagram 1

Generative principles sub-divide into objective and subjective principles. The objective principles are experienced as "reference points of common consensus". Concrete examples are Scripture, moral traditions, examples of person and action in Christian tradition. The subjective principle is experienced as an instance of "originating value." Komonchak explains, "The subjective principle of Christian moral activity is the Christian himself as an >>originating value<<, the existential subject of a moral sensitivity become >>connatural<<."[28]

Generative principles however are not the end point of morality. They are only the basis, the beginning of a process that ends in action. Secondly, generative principles do not issue directly into concrete action. Since generative principles function in given concrete situations and in the day to day experiences of people which demand Christian moral responsibility they are me-

---

[27] Komonchak, 'Moral', p.90.
[28] Komonchak, 'Moral', p. 90. He acknowledges that the idea of "originating value" is a reference to Lonergan who worked out the concept in his analysis of 'the structure of the human good'. See Lonergan, Method, pp. 42-57.

diated through "interpretation, discovery and application." Mediation is necessary because the day to day experiences of people are so dynamic and varied that no objective principle summarily covers all possible situations. On the other hand the subjective principle is no "substitute for knowledge."[29] This is why traditional moral theology insists on the obligation on the part of each individual Christian to cultivate an adequately informed conscience.[30]

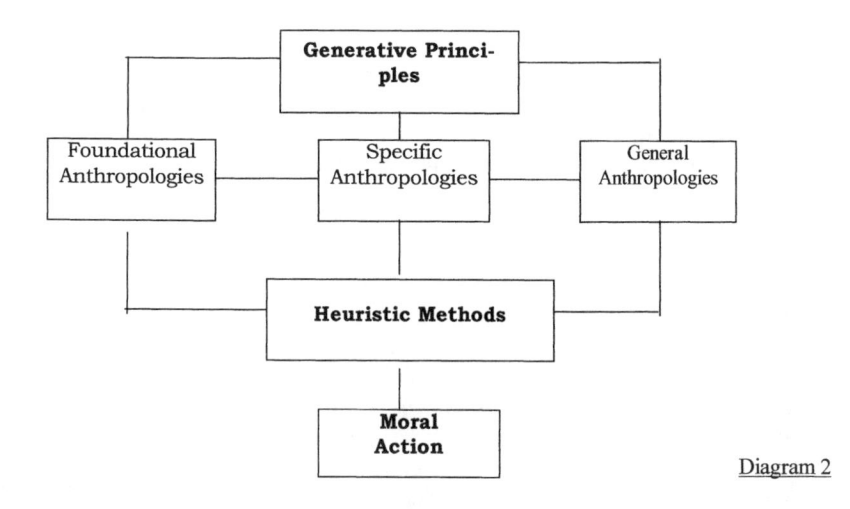

```
                    ┌─────────────────────┐
         ┌──────────│ Generative Princi-  │──────────┐
         │          │       ples          │          │
         │          └─────────────────────┘          │
┌────────┴───────┐  ┌─────────────────────┐  ┌───────┴────────┐
│  Foundational  │──│      Specific       │──│    General     │
│ Anthropologies │  │   Anthropologies    │  │ Anthropologies │
└────────┬───────┘  └──────────┬──────────┘  └───────┬────────┘
         │                     │                     │
         │          ┌──────────┴──────────┐          │
         └──────────│  Heuristic Methods  │──────────┘
                    └──────────┬──────────┘
                               │
                         ┌─────┴─────┐
                         │   Moral   │
                         │   Action  │
                         └───────────┘
```
Diagram 2

According to Komonchak the four main elements which mediate generative principles are: foundational anthropology, general anthropologies, cultural and historically specific anthropologies and heuristic methods for concrete moral action[31] Foundational anthropologies "attempt to define the basic

---

[29] Komonchak, 'Moral', p. 90.
[30] See G. W. Hunold, 'Verantwortung. Von den Baugesetzlichkeiten der menschlichen Handlung', Unpublished Lectures, Sommersemester, Tübingen, 1996. See also 'Gewissen und Verantwortung', in A. Hertz, W. Korff, et al. (Hrsg.), Handbuch der christlichen Ethik, Bd. 3 (Freiburg: Herder, 1993), pp. 19ff; Karl H. Peschke, Christian Ethics: Moral Theology in the Light of Vatican II, vol. 1 (Alcester and Dublin: C. Goodliffe Neale, 1985), pp. 203-230, pp. 222ff explain the traditional concept of "the vincibly erroneous conscience"; Bernard Häring, Free and Faithful in Christ. Moral Theology for Priests and Laity, vol. 1 (Middlegreen: St. Paul Publications, 1978), pp. 246ff; Terence Kennedy, Doers of the Word. Moral Theology for Humanity in the third Millennium, vol. 1 (Middlegreen: St. Paul Publications, 1996), pp. 168-198; B. Bujo, African Christian Morality, pp. 45-46.
[31] Komonchak, 'Moral', pp. 90-91.

situation of every person before God and other persons in the world."[32] These anthropologies have the highest claims of universalizability. Foundational anthropologies are bound, by virtue of their universal validity, to be abstract and metaphysical. General anthropologies are accretions of knowledge about humanness arising from many different realizations in time, place and culture. Their universality remains within those limits. Specific anthropologies by definition cannot be universalized, though they still have relevance for the larger community. They are "cultural and historical realizations."[33]

Heuristic methods refer to the concrete application of these various anthropologies in evaluating and discerning the course of action in a given situation. Such methods must be able to reflect the moral constants of the foundational and general anthropologies. At the same time they must properly apply the specific anthropologies of a given place and time by critically relating them to the foundational and general anthropologies.[34]

Developing a fruitful method for ethical reflection, then, depends greatly on the ability to distinguish the various forms of anthropologies while simultaneously discovering their dynamic correlation. Such a methodological enterprise would enable a person to avoid a number of snares. One such pitfall is an ethnocentric interpretation of reality, where "'civilization' is contrasted with 'barbarism'", or a classicist interpretation where "natural is opposed to the aberrant or unnatural."[35] Another pitfall is the tendency of seeing theology as a 'first science' which alone says the last word about all areas of study. This attitude results in the inability to accept the competence of the human sciences which study human persons and their cultural differences empirically. As Komonchak observes, "The critical introduction of these sciences into the theological task is...still very difficult because of the fundamental methodological controversies that bedevil both theology and the human sciences."[36]

---

[32] Komonchak, 'Moral', p. 91.
[33] Komonchak, 'Moral', p. 91.
[34] Komonchak, 'Moral', p. 91. This interplay between the foundational and general anthropologies on the one hand, and the application of the cultural specific anthropologies on the other hand is crucial. We pointed out some of the mistakes that could arise when ethical reflection fails to apply a method that is properly heuristic. This for instance was the case with O'Donohue, which was mentioned in chapter two of this study. O'Donohue, it was argued, proposes a foundational anthropology, in which he concedes a basic anthropological sameness of all human beings,
thereby presupposing a foundational anthropology. He fails, however, to reconcile this foundational anthropology with a specific African cultural anthropology. See chapter two of this study.
[35] Komonchak, 'Moral', p. 91.
[36] Komonchak, 'Moral', p. 91. See also chapter two of this study, where some of the foreprogrammed categories behind the method of the social sciences, especially in their application in Africa was briefly discussed.

A fruitful method for ethical reflection would also have to pay attention to the fact that neither foundational nor general anthropologies exist in a 'culture-free' or pure form. The moral constants that we receive at the generative level are themselves already mediated. The Scriptures, Christian teaching and moral traditions are mediated "by the culturally and historically specific and by the particular. Holy lives including that of Christ, are particular realizations of meaning and value within specific contexts and in response to particular situations."[37] Obviously, as Komonchak further explains, the universal normative import of the life of Christ, say, is undeniable. But there is need for a method that helps to "re-mediate"[38] and locate such universal normative significance in a given context and history.[39]

3.2.2 Sample Method II: Janssens

In order to understand the approach Janssens proposes, we have to keep in mind the eight basic dimensions of the human person (subjectivity, corporeality, being in the world, sociality, institutionality, historicity, spirituality and basic equality) that he worked out in the light of *Gaudium et Spes*.[40] He uses these dimensions to develop what he calls 'the personalist criterion' for evaluating moral actions. Janssens maintains that "In accord with this criterion we say that an act is morally good if it serves the humanum, human dignity, that is, if it in truth -according to reason enlightened by revelation- is beneficial to the human person adequately considered in himself (as personal subject in corporeality) and in his relations (in his openness to the world, to others, to social groups, and to God)."[41]

Conditions to be fulfilled for an appropriate foundation of a personalist method in ethics are based on GS 3, 13, 61, 63, and 66. These paragraphs of Gaudium et Spes, specifically define the integral nature of the human person as body and soul, heart and conscience, mind and will, in relationship to God, to others and to the world. These two perspectives—i.e. the human person in herself or in himself and in his or her relations are of absolute importance for any adequate assessment of a person's integrity. The human person's disharmony with God results in a disharmony with "himself, with others and with all

---

[37] Komonchak, 'Moral', p. 92.
[38] Personal formulation.
[39] Komonchak's application of the implications of this method to the concrete situations of moral action in the church is directly related to the question of moral pluralism in the church. See pp. 92ff of Komonchak's essay.
[40] Cited in chapter one of this study. See pp. 47-55.
[41] Janssens, 'Artificial Insemination', p. 14.

created things" (GS 13).[42] There is therefore an urgent need on the part of each person to "preserve a view of the whole human person, a view in which the values of intellect, will, conscience and fraternity are pre-eminent" (GS 61).

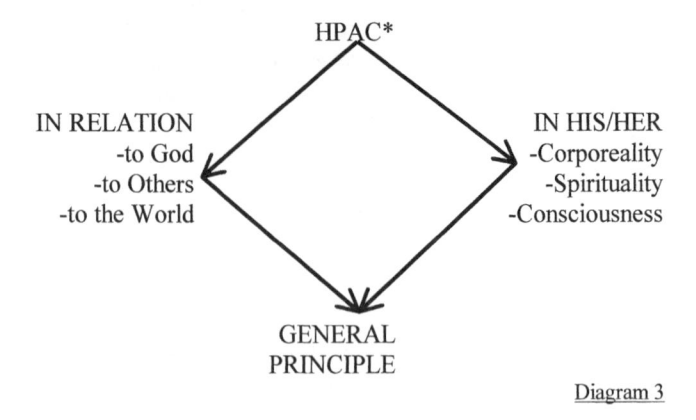

```
                    HPAC*
                   ╱     ╲
                  ╱       ╲
    IN RELATION  ╱         ╲  IN HIS/HER
      -to God   ╱           ╲  -Corporeality
      -to Others             -Spirituality
      -to the World          -Consciousness
                  ╲         ╱
                   ╲       ╱
                    ╲     ╱
                   GENERAL
                   PRINCIPLE
```

Diagram 3

The importance of viewing the whole human person also redounds in the socio-economic realm. Here too "the dignity and total vocation of the human person must be honored and advanced along with the welfare of society as a whole" (GS 63).[43] This view promotes a healthy consideration of culture by emphasizing three important dimensions: society as 'co-existence' (community-living together), society as 'co-operation' (community working together), and society as 'co-participation' (community sharing the fruits of its labor).[44]

As it were an appropriate consideration of the human person achieves an appropriate consideration of society and culture. This appropriate consideration of society and of culture rejects a sporadic history in favor of an organic one. Thus the document proclaims: "The destiny of the human race is viewed as a complete whole, no longer, as it were, in particular histories of various peoples: now it merges into a complete whole" (GS 5).[45] The fact that

---

*HPAC = Human Person Adequately Considered

[42] Janssens, 'Artificial Insemination', p. 13.

[43] The citations of Gaudium et Spes in this paragraph are taken from Janssens, 'Artificial Insemination', p. 13.

[44] Janssens, 'Artificial Insemination', p. 14.

[45] This statement reminds us of the argument of Polybios that was cited earlier (see chapter two, p. 1). It is a statement that assumes uncompromising validity when one uses it as a critical spectacle for revising and correcting the effects of the centuries in which human

an adequate consideration of the human person yields an equally appropriate consideration of culture also reveals the many connections between culture and faith. And the fundamental element that unites both insolubly is the commitment to establishing a world that is more human.

In view of these anthropological constants the criterion of HAPC demands dynamism of method (dynamic ethic),[46] balanced by wisdom that expresses itself in a deep yearning for what is true and good (GS 15).[47] Janssens sees a relationship between the need for wisdom as guide for dynamism and the traditional demand in moral theology for "knowledge through affinity (*cognitio per affinitatem aut connaturalitatem*)."[48]

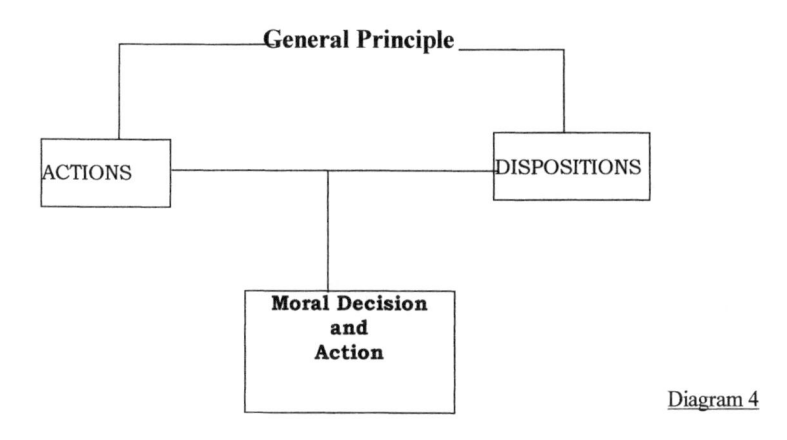

```
                    General Principle
            ┌───────────────┬───────────────┐
            │               │               │
        ACTIONS                          DISPOSITIONS
            
                    ┌───────────────┐
                    │ Moral Decision│
                    │      and      │
                    │    Action     │
                    └───────────────┘
```

Diagram 4

The personalist criterion, then, bases firmly on the concrete human person as a general principle of morality, a value with universal validity. Still the human person does not achieve moral actions automatically. In the daily life of persons, morality is achieved by the concrete effort and openness to a specific

---

history was strategically programmed to progress sporadically.
[46] See earlier reference to Janssens in chapter one, pp. 53-54, also footnote 151 on the need for a dynamic ethic in view of the historicity of the human person.
[47] Janssens, 'Artificial Insemination', p. 14.
[48] Janssens, 'Artificial Insemination', p. 14. The principle, Janssens explains, implies that given a good person, inspired by a good disposition, there is every possibility, *ceteris paribus*, that this person would correctly discern how to apply what is new in a morally responsible way in practice.

operation -disposition- and by the actual completion of a given operation- action.[49] We shall explain first the latter and then the former briefly.

When we act, there ensues an active interchange between us and "*worldly* realities."[50] Because our actions are so bounded to the world, they are characterized by ambiguity by reason of our temporality and our spatiality. Temporality means in choosing to do this and not that, we forego the many other possibilities at a given time. We are thus faced with the question of how to justify our preference for a particular action. Spatiality refers to the fact that our bodies and other things of the world are governed by complex and multiple properties and physical laws. Our actions therefore have an "inseparable connection between negative aspects (disvalues) and positive attributes (values), such that they are simultaneously detrimental to and beneficial for the human person."[51] The question here is how to discover the "proportionate reasons" that allow us to engage in an action that is at once negative and positive.

Besides good actions, there is the morally good disposition. A personalist approach to morality sees a good disposition as "inner attitude" by which a person exhibits a basic readiness to direct his or her actions towards the promotion of the self and of others—of the humanum. The NT view of this inner disposition finds expression in Jesus' double injunction: love of God and neighbor (Mt 22,37-40; Mk 12,29-34; Lk 10,27).[52] Basically, "The good disposition is the source and the dynamic principle of our moral life: it is only real and authentic insofar as it leads us to strive toward its realization and incarnation in concrete acts."[53]

3.2.3 Relationship between Janssens and Komonchak

Both Janssens and Komonchack would seem to have similar underlying ideas about a theologically fruitful method for moral inquiry in contemporary times. Both acknowledge the fundamental importance of a good anthropology which allows for an integral consideration of the human person, of society and of

---

[49] Janssens, 'Artificial Insemination', p. 15.
[50] Janssens, 'Artificial Insemination', p. 15. In the author's own words, actions are defined as "active commerce with *worldly* reality" (author's italics).
[51] Janssens, 'Artificial Insemination', p. 16. He gives the example of a therapeutic amputation which can be shown to give life. At the same time the amputation involves a mutilation that is burdensome for the subject. There is also the example of traffic on our roads which enhances mobilization and at the same time causes damage to the environment. The problem is experienced more intensively with regard to the social dimensions of the person. How do we achieve a personal benefit without depriving the rest of society of the same benefit?
[52] Janssens, 'Artificial Insemination', p. 15.
[53] Janssens, 'Artificial Insemination', p. 15; see also the author's footnote 22.

culture. By so doing both underscore the fact that the concrete form of morality is greatly determined by our conception of the human person. They also underline the fact that the human person constitutes for himself or herself a "generative principle" (Komonchak) or "general principle" (Janssens) of morality.

In addition, Komonchak and Janssens insist that the social aspects of humanness be taken seriously in moral inquiry. What we know about ourselves and about others is ultimately a complex combination of personal, cultural and historical mediations. The knowledge we are able to generate by our own inner judgements of fact and value is just a small part of our general knowledge and of our self-definition. The greater part of our knowledge is community mediated and is relational. Human societies are also subject to geographical, historical and cultural boundaries. For that matter even the foundational knowledge about ourselves which claims universal validity is still tainted by culturally specific limitations.

The methods of Komonchak and Janssens are for our purposes useful because they foster a good sense of Christian anthropology. They are firmly based in scripture and Christian tradition and are concerned with theological fruitfulness. Komonchak and Janssens differ, however, in their emphasis. While Komonchak was immediately concerned with the question of moral pluralism in the church, Janssens developed his method in search of a new criterion for doing Christian ethics. He concretized his search on the moral implications of artificial insemination. Komonchak, it would seem, tends to be more structural, while Janssens seems to adopt a more personal approach. The former shows how necessary it is to find a proportionate measure for combining the human person as a moral principle with objective social, cultural and historically given principles in the process of moral decision. The latter works out how the human person adequately considered already combines in himself or herself the subjective and objective principles for moral decision and action. The structuralist and personalist approaches however do not present a contradiction. They rather strongly complement and highlight each other.

3.2.4 Relevance of Komonchak and Janssens for Doing Inculturation Ethics

Conventional approaches to the study of African morality in general, and in relation to the Christian faith in particular, have been shaped to a large extent by centuries of an outlook in which African institutions and way of life in general were denied moral value. It was mentioned earlier in this study that conventional approaches tend for that reason to be descriptive and apologetic. Depending on the thinker's position, such 'apologies' have taken one of two forms: traditionalism (a kind of anti-Westernism), cultural revivalism, or cultural synthesis.[54] Conventional methods have therefore not given specific attention to the question of the African as moral agent in the process of moral decision and action.

The thesis of this study is that in the context of African cultural identity crisis, a fruitful method for doing inculturation ethics must emphasize the individual African as a fundamental principle for generating African Christian morality. In this regard the criteria proposed by Komonchak and Janssens are relevant. If there is any point on which the majority of scholars who study African morality agree, then it is the point of the personal and humanist foundations of African moral systems. Wiredu remarks:

> "Traditional thinking about the foundations of morality is refreshingly non-supernaturalist. Not that one can find in traditional sources elaborate theories of humanism. But anyone who reflects on our traditional ways of speaking about morality is bound to be struck by the preoccupation with human welfare: What is morally good is what befits a human being; it is what is decent for man—what brings dignity, respect, contentment, prosperity, joy, to man and his community. And what is morally bad is what brings misery, misfortune, and disgrace."[55]

This humanist and personalist approach to morality does not deny that many African communities see a direct relationship between morality and religion.[56] Immoral behavior is hateful to God and to other supernatural beings (lesser gods?)[57] and to the ancestors. In contemporary times, we can speak of a litany of the values of the African way of life, especially in connection with the ancestors.[58] The fact that the African world view has no platonic divisions be-

---

[54] See the introduction of this study.
[55] Wiredu, Philosophy and an African Culture, p. 6.
[56] Wiredu, Philosophy and an African Culture, p. 6.
[57] In contemporary African studies, the use of the word 'god' to qualify the supernatural beings and/or powers that abound in indigenous African religions is open to debate. From the point of view of what indigenous religionists say and do there is cause to question how far the word gods adequately translates the spiritual beings of indigenous religions. Among the Ewes of Ghana for instance, *Mawu* (the Supreme Being) is considered as a class of its own that does not relate to the supernatural beings and powers in the sense of *Primus inter Pares*. Thus *Mawu* among the Ewe does not readily translate into the **Great God** above the **lesser gods**. Compare K. Wiredu, "Formulating Modern Thought in African Languages: Some theoretical Considerations", in: Mudimbe, The Surreptitious Speech, pp. 301-332.
[58] There are observable connections between religion and morality in many African communities. In view of this connection, the ancestors would seem to play a vital role in the way many Africans conceive and actualize the good way of life. However, there is no reason why the religious foundations of African moral systems should be understood as the

tween profane and holy, body and soul, the integral relation between the human being and his/her immediate surrounding, the sacredness of forests and wild life (while still depending on them for livelihood), the spirituality and inviolable nature of human life that extends not only to the living but also to the 'living-dead' (and more) are topics that have assumed increasing significance. Thus many studies have tried to show the intensity with which African moral systems command the improvement and maximization of the humanum.[59]

Yet the duty of an African Christian morality begins precisely at this point of convergence between African moral systems and a personalist approach to ethics. It is in the midst of the chorus of this litany about the humanist orientation of African morality that inculturation ethics raises its voice. It makes the 'beautiful' end its irritating beginning by asking important questions: If African morality is so humanist, why do Africans find themselves so often reduced to limits less than human? Could it be that Africans themselves ignore this morality just as much as it is ignored by the outsider? Where are the important values of life, of human welfare, of hospitality to be found in the Sudan nightmare, in Sierra Leon and Liberia? Where has the humanist orientation remained in the never-ending crisis in Angola and where was the humanism in the Rwandan massacre?

These are but a few examples of the many questions that the African can no longer afford to answer from a distance nor from the stage of a romantic drama.[60] When African Christians attempt to answer these questions critically and practically from the background of their faith in Jesus who reveals *par excellence* the fullness of humanness, they engage in African Christian morality. A personalist approach to inculturation ethics thus enhances self dis-

---

rod that makes Africans behave morally as a result of fear (see Chapter two). As Wiredu reminds us, the question of the role of the 'gods' in morality is neither new nor restricted to African cultures. The tendency to *religionize* ethics has been equally strong in many other cultures. Yet, despite this strong similarity of the experience in various cultures and at different times in history, in the case of cultures that have had the freedom to speak and think of themselves autonomously, the question has not been answered the way Kudajie or many Western anthropologists have answered it in Africa. Wiredu reminds us that the linking of morality to religion "is not that something is good because God approves of it but rather that God approves of it because it is good in the first place – a distinction which, as Socrates noted in the context of a different culture, does not come easily to every pious mind" (Wiredu, Philosophy and an African Culture, p. 6).
[59] The list of literature about these topics is rather long. One can say that such conceptions about the African way of life is almost commonplace today. For two recent works that take up these topics, see L. Magesa, African Religion: The Moral Traditions of Abundant Life (Maryknoll: Orbis Books, 1997); K. Gyekye, African Cultural Values: An Introduction (Philadelphia/Accra: Sankofa Publication Company, 1996).
[60] See Chapter One, where it was argued that if inculturation is based on the paradigm of the incarnation, then it demands more reality and less drama.

covery and exposes Africans to the resources available for organizing and maximizing their own humanness. This conception of inculturation ethics happens to be the definition Bujo gives to autonomy, an expression that is highly prized in ethics today. According to Bujo, "In modern theology, autonomy means the fact that human beings by reason of their intelligence can interpret the happenings they are faced with, and arrange their own moral life."[61] As it were, if African Christian morality succeeds in becoming authentic it would also be autonomous and *vice versa*.

Briefly put the relevance of a personalist method in doing African Christian ethics is crucial. The crux of the discussion in this study until now has concentrated on pointing out the inappropriate consideration of Africans in history. It is therefore necessary for African Christian morality to adopt a method that exposes the subtle forms in which the inadequate consideration of the African is masked in contemporary times, and reconstitute Christian faith and African culture as necessary ingredients of awakening to self, and of becoming true subjects.

On the structural level (that is in her relation to other communities of faith) the African church is reminded that Christian morality is not a concern limited to Africans. Hence the responsibility of African Christian morality would be to re-mediate the significance and role of the Christian religion within the African cultural matrix.[62] On the personal level African Christian morality must witness to "a Christ who is as close to [Africans] as he can possibly be and who is interested in their traditional culture, to the extent that this culture contributes to the development of the whole human being."[63]

3.3 Ethics and other Terms relating to Inculturation

Inculturation is associated with two important concepts in sociology and anthropology. These concepts are enculturation and acculturation. An understanding of these concepts could enhance our understanding of the anthropological constants at play in the process of humanization as such and in morality in particular. In discussing these concepts, the paragraphs that follow at-

---

[61] Bujo, African Christian Morality, p. 16. Bujo quotes Mieth who also defines autonomy as "the methodic independence of moral reason and…the finality that the human person possesses in itself, …the conjunction of the two principles *secundum rationem agere* and *secundum personam agere*". D. Mieth, "Autonomie. Emploi du terme en morale chrétienne fondamentale", in: Autonomie. Dimensions éthiques de la liberté (Freiburg, 1978), p. 94.
[62] Lonergan, Method in Theology, p. ix.
[63] Bujo, African Christian Morality, p. 39.

tempt to offer some social scientific perspectives of the elements Janssens and Komonchak emphasize for an adequate consideration of the human person. We shall conclude the chapter by illustrating that the morality of the people of the Old and New Testaments is itself subject to concrete anthropological conditions. Morality, as it were, is itself a process of humanization (incarnation) and is therefore intricately connected to human sociality.

3.3.1 Acculturation

Acculturation as a concept belongs properly speaking to anthropology. It is used generally to refer to culture change that results from the direct contact of two different cultural groups. Like many other concepts in anthropology, acculturation has not had the same meaning all the time. In the late nineteenth century it was used to describe the betterment of "savage tribes" who as it were copy civilization and in so doing replace old ways with new and civilized ones.[64] Others have paraphrased the idea to imply a broader notion of intercultural learning for mutual improvement through intermarriage, trading, lending and borrowing.[65] Used in this sense, one is reminded of the anthropological concept of diffusion which acculturation has come to replace. Unlike diffusion which concentrates on the transfer of culture traits from one culture to the other through culture contact, acculturation has had the tendency to emphasize culture change "through the involvement of an alien, politically dominant society."[66]

In Boasian anthropology the concept of acculturation received other nuances, and came to be used basically to describe the operations involved in culture contact, the consequences arising thereof and conditions under which culture contact occurred. Such conditions include the balance of power between the two societies, the way the dominated culture responds, and the cultural premises used to explain the culture contact as such.[67] The Social Science Research Council defines acculturation as "those phenomena which result when groups of individuals having different cultures come into continuous,

---

[64] Winthrop, Dictionary of Concepts, p. 3, referring to J. W. Powell, cited in F. De Laguna, "[Introduction to Section VII] Method and Theory of Ethnology." F. De Laguna (ed.), Selected Papers from the American Anthropologist, 1888-1920 (Washington, D. C.: American Anthropological Association, 1960), pp. 787-788.
[65] Winthrop, Dictionary of Concepts, p. 3, citing De Laguna, in: De Laguna (ed.), "[Introduction]", p. 788.
[66] Winthrop, Dictionary of Concepts, p. 83.
[67] Winthrop, Dictionary of Concepts, p. 4.

first-hand contact, with subsequent changes in the original culture patterns of either or both groups."[68]

Simply put acculturation deals with the encounter between two different cultures and works as the principal cause for cultural change. It is cultural learning that occurs on the collective rather than on the individual level. Acculturation is not readily open to individual choices and as Shorter explains, "its consequences can be discerned *post factum* at the conscious level, but many of the conflicts it engenders are worked out at the subconscious level."[69]

Since acculturation is so strongly concerned with what occurs when two different cultures meet, there are connections with the concept of inculturation. Shorter observes that acculturation is sometimes so closely associated with inculturation that one is mislead to think the two terms are interchangeable.[70] Inculturation necessarily involves acculturation, but both concepts are distinct from each other. Acculturation and enculturation (to be discussed presently), explain the anthropological dynamic and intricate connection between sociality and humanness. Inculturation on the other hand explains that God takes these anthropological constants seriously and places them at the disposal of humans to help them work towards the fullness of humanness as revealed in Jesus.

As a cultural phenomenon, acculturation is dynamic, historical, and diachronic.[71] It is dynamic because inter-cultural communication is an on-going process that does not happen on occasion or in a given and predetermined measure. It is historical because the conditions under which cultural contact occurs vary through time and the consequences of such contacts are open to ambiguity and limitation. Acculturation is diachronic because unless it is understood as cultural domination,[72] where one culture lords it over the other and declares the dominated culture taboo for the members of the dominating culture, culture contact always issues in consequences that seriously effect a change in both cultures concerned. The intensity may vary, but none of the cultures involved leaves the stage of acculturation unscathed from a change of attitudes, of reality construction and of values. Shorter reminds us that "Acculturation, the communication between cultures on a footing of mutual respect and tolerance, is a necessary condition of Catholicism, of a Church that claims to be universal."[73]

Just as no individual can become human without being part of a given society, so cultures must be open to other cultures in order to survive and con-

---

[68] R. Redfield, et. al. "Memorandum for the Study of Acculturation." (1936), p. 149, cited in Winthrop, Dictionary of Concepts, p. 5.
[69] Shorter, Toward a Theology, p. 7, author's italics.
[70] Shorter, Toward a Theology, p. 6.
[71] Shorter. Toward a Theology, p. 7.
[72] See Shorter, Toward a Theology, pp. 8-9.
[73] Shorter, Toward a Theology, p. 8.

tribute meaningfully towards increasing humanness. Acculturation thus connects us back to an organic consideration of reality in which "the destiny of the human race is viewed as a complete whole."[74]

3.3.2 Enculturation

Another parallel concept from which inculturation stems[75] is the anthropological concept known as *enculturation*. The term enculturation is used in sociology and anthropology to describe the intricate connection between humanness and sociality. Luckmann and Berger observe that "solitary human being is being on the animal level (which, of course, man shares with other animals). As soon as one observes phenomena that are specifically human, one enters the realm of the social. Man's specific humanity and his sociality are inextricably intertwined. Homo sapiens is always, and in the same measure, homo socius."[76]

For Harris enculturation is a concept that finds its origins in the period of Enlightenment. Against the background of the Enlightenment, enculturation helps us to understand the tremendous significance of cultural education in the life of each human person. A person's recognition of himself or herself as human and the gamut of operations undertaken by a person which are recognized to be human or moral depend on the cumulative heritage of a given culture, which constitutes "an individual's entire history of sense experience."[77] It is the source of the composite of ideas or knowledge which an individual can claim to have. The Enlightenment professed a strong belief in the effect of enculturation on individuals. One of the persons who strongly represented this belief was Turgot who explains the differences in human behavior as:

> "A lucky arrangement of the fibers in the brain, a greater or lesser quickness of the blood, these are probably the only differences which nature establishes among men. Their spirits, or the power and capacity or their minds, display real inequality, the causes of which we shall never know and never be able to reason about. All the rest is the effect of education, and that education is

---

[74] Gaudium et Spes, 5, earlier referred to on p. 20 above.
[75] See Shorter, Toward a Theology, pp. 5-6.
[76] P. L. Berger, T. Luckmann, The Social Construction of Knowledge (New York: Doubleday, 1966), p. 51. See also our reference (this manuscript, p. 40) to Janssens' treatment of the elements needed for an adequate consideration of the human person as worked out by Vatican II in Gaudium et Spes.
[77] Harris, The Rise of Anthropological theory, pp. 14-15.

the result of all our sense experience, of all the ideas we have been able to acquire from the cradle onward. All the objects which surround us contribute to that education; the instructions of our parents and teachers are only a small part of it."[78]

Locke was even more radical in surmising that it was possible that some people could have so little exposure to culture that they might behave exactly like animals.[79] In his *An Essay Concerning Human Understanding*, Locke stressed the relationship between the conditioning environment and human thought and actions. The human mind, for Locke, was comparable to an "empty cabinet" at birth. The ideas or the knowledge that the mind later acquires was due to a learning process that is today called enculturation.[80]

Contemporary anthropology similarly understands enculturation as the process by which a person learns to become an *actor* of his or her culture.[81] The concept establishes the fact that value is to a great extent a social construct, and that a human being is very much a product of his or her culture, as much as human beings produce their culture. Culture is here understood as a network of interactions between specific individuals who possess shared knowledge, which is at the same time socially distributed. These individuals benefit subjectively by abstracting a world of meaning for themselves through direct participation in the network of interactions.[82]

Besides the fact that our physical survival is dependent on how we share the possibilities and opportunities of life with others, we also depend heavily on the immediate society and culture for our patterns of behavior. This process of humanization however is possible for each person insofar as the person is directly involved. There is no humanization by proxy, i.e. one does not become human passively. This direct involvement in the processes of inter-human commerce as a means for the attainment of humanness is the crux of enculturation.

---

[78] A. R. J. Turgot, Plan de Deux Discours sur l'Histoire Universelle. Oeuvres de Turgot (Paris: Guillaumin, 1844, org. 1750), p. 645, in: Harris, The Rise of Anthropological Theory, pp. 14-15.
[79] Harris, The Rise of Anthropological Theory, pp. 15 and 16.
[80] Harris, The Rise, p. 11, paraphrasing J. Locke, An Essay Concerning Human Understanding (Oxford: Clarendon Press, 1894 [orig. 1690]), I: 48. Harris does not forget to add that Locke's main concern was with the epistemological knowledge than with how individuals and whole tribes come to possess their customs and cultural knowledge.
[81] See F. J. Porter Poole, 'Socialization, Enculturation and the Development of Personal Identity", in T. Ingold (ed.), Companion Encyclopedia of Anthropology (New York, NY: Routledge, 1994), pp. 831-854.
[82] E. Sapir, Selected Writings of Edward Sapir in Language, Culture and Personality, ed. D. G. Mandelbaum (Berkeley: University of California Press, 1949), p. 515, cited in Poter Poole, 'Enculturation', p. 381.

There is a close connection between socialization and enculturation,[83] but scholars analytically distinguish the one from the other. Whereas socialization is a demand on the individual who wishes to be counted as a member of a given society to fulfil certain conditions and requirements, enculturation is "the process of learning a culture in all its uniqueness and particularity."[84] In order words enculturation results in a person's ability to display the mastery that identifies him or her as an "insider" of a particular culture.[85] Studying enculturation therefore involves an investigation into the complex and dynamic processes that enable individuals "to develop more or less adaptive interpretations, representations, expectations, evaluations, feelings, intentions and so on, concerning their socio-cultural milieu and their positions within it from perspectives that are both socio-centric and personal."[86]

3.4 Ethics, Enculturation and Acculturation

One may not reduce ethical questions to a purely social scientific methodology. Still the knowledge provided by the the social and human sciences on the personal and social development of human beings can no longer be ignored in the study of ethics. To do so would be to postulate "an ethical anthropology [founded on] a purely imperative morality, where everything is based on abstract principles [and therefore] culturally sterile."[87]

For the purposes of this study we could say that acculturation and enculturation help us to understand that the material content of morality always depends on the concrete situation or context in which people live. Christian mo-

---

[83] See M. J. Herskovits, Man and His Works, (New York: Alfred A. Knopf, 1948), p. 38; M. Mead "Socialization and Enculturation", in: Current Anthropology 4, 1963, p. 185. Poole intimates that in anthropology the studies done by Whiting and Whiting (1975) have provided probably the most influential model for studying socialization. The weakness of the model however lies in its portrayal of the children studied as passive recipients of social knowledge. In many African communities such a passive acquisition of social knowledge is all the more implausible if we remember the many structures put in place to help children acquire social knowledge by actively participating in social life, for example through games, song and dance, beginning at a relatively early age to train in the economic activities of their parents and so on. For more information see Egblewogbe, Games and Songs, pp. 21, 27ff.
[84] Mead 1963:185, cited in Porter Poole, 'Enculturation'
[85] I. Weber-Kellermann, Saure Wochen, frohe Feste: Fest und Alltag in der Sprache der Bräuche (München: Verlag C. J. Bücher GmbH, 1985), pp. 14-18.
[86] Porter Poole, 'Enculturation', p. 834. For further explanation on the actual process of enculturation, i.e. the acquisition of cultural modes for processing information which Poole calls "the acquisition and use of cultural schemata", see the Essay from Poole, pp.833-835. On his ideas about "Rethinking socialization and enculturation", see pp. 836-841.
[87] B. Häring, Free and Faithful in Christ, vol. 3 (Middlegreen: St. Paul, 1981), p. 213.

rality is not exempted from this basic anthropological norm. Cultural authenticity, moral autonomy and morality itself are illusory should one affirm them "independently of the social conditions of their formation."[88] The relevance of these social scientific perspectives for Christian ethics has been properly worked out by various scholars. I shall depend on a few of such works and attempt to illustrate the socio-cultural foundations of morality, using the examples of the Old and New Testaments, and the example of the North African Church in Christian antiquity.

3.4.1 Illustration 1: Old Testament

There are many laws, precepts, commands, prohibitions and liturgical directives in the OT. For example, Ex 19 – Num 10, 10 is replete with such laws and prescriptions. But the body of laws that usually occupies the attention of scholars in the study of TO morality is the decalogue (Ex 20; Dt 5). Opinions vary on many aspects of the decalogue-- its sources, date, context, totality and universalizability and its priority of importance in comparison to other individual prescription that compose the Torah.[89] By virtue of new findings and of the information available in recent times on biblical traditions, scholars insist that it is no longer possible to see the decalogue as a summary of OT ethics or of biblical ethics as a whole.[90] It is also argued that one may not play the developmental history of the decalogue against its final application and reception in the institutions of Israel so as to establish the autonomous ethical element in the decalogue.[91]

Despite these and many other differences between the way the decalogue is understood today in contrast to its understanding in the past, still many scholars agree that the formation and maturation of the decalogue and the individual norms of the Torah as a whole did not descend from heaven.

---

[88] Mieth, 'Autonomie', p. 100, cited in Bujo, African Christian Morality, p. 16.

[89] For the important aspects of the discussion on the decalogue in connection with OT ethics, see F. Crüsemann, Bewahrung der Freiheit. Das Thema des Kekalogs in sozialgeschichtlicher Perspektive (KT 87) München, 1983; Crüssemann, Die Tora. Theologie und Sozialgeschichte des alttestamentlichen Gesetzes (München: 1992); W. H. Schmidt, Die Zehn Gebote im Rahmen der alttestamentlichen Ethik (Damstadt: 1993); C. Dohmen, Um unserer Freiheit willen. Ursprung und Ziel biblischer Ethik im >>Hauptgebot<< des Dekalogs, IKaZ (1992), pp. 7-24; N. Lohfink, Kennt das Alte Testament einen Unterschied von >>Gebot<< und >>Gesetzt<<? Zur bibeltheologischen Einstufung des Dekalogs, in: >>Gesetz<< als thema Biblischer Theologie (JBTh 4) Neukirchen-Vluyn 1989, pp. 63-89; W. Groß, Wandelbares Gesetz – unwandelbarer Dekalog? ThQ 175 (1995), pp. 161-170, the literature cited here was acquired from Groß.

[90] See Crüsemann, Bewahrung der Freiheit, p. 8.

[91] See Groß, Wandelbares Gesetz, pp. 161-162.

These laws have a socio-historical, contextual and cultural background to their concrete content.[92] It is true that in Israel's religious experience, these laws were understood not only as the will of God, but also and especially as his presence and self-revelation. For the people of Israel, morality resulted from their close and personal experiences of God in their history as a people.[93] Hence it is no longer tenable to postulate a dualistic developmental history with the claim that the decalogue first existed as a purely "profane" ethos which was only later elevated to a sacred ethic in the decalogue.[94] Morality in the OT was a constant call directed not to an unidentified group of persons, but specifically to a people whose self-definition was inextricably linked to God [Yahweh].

The theonomous nature of morality in the OT notwithstanding, it is still remains true that the concrete form and content of the laws were influenced by factors of cultural fission and fusion. Such elements are illustrated for example through the similarity found between the decalogue and the famous Hammurabi's stele and the attribution of morality to deities by other Mesopotamian cultures.[95] Besides, one must consider the fact that Israel had constantly to define and maintain its identity in the midst of neighboring peoples and cultures. This self-definition of Israel sometimes found expression in Israel's domination over others as war Lords who captured land from their neighbors.[96] At other times it was as captives and landless exiles at the mercy of their neighbors. This fact suggests that Israel's history presents a watershed of cultural communication, a classical example of acculturation, which must have greatly influenced the ethos of Israel.

Significant events in the history of Israel also played an equally important role in the formation of a theonomous ethos. This is shown, for example,

---

[92] Compare F. Böckle, "Die kulturgeschichtliche Bedingtheit theologisch-ethischer Normen", in: H. Trümpy (Hrg.), Kontinuität und Diskontinuität in den Geisteswissenschaften, (Darmstadt: Wissenschaftliche Buchgesellschaft, 1973), pp. 115-132; See G. W. Hunold, Wider den Konkurs der Freiheit: Vom bleibenden Zeitgespräch des Dekalogs zwischen Vernunft und Sittlichkeit, ThQ 175 (1995), 173, 175-176.
[93] See R. Mack, "Morality in the OT", in: Ghana Bulletin of Theology, Vol. 4, No. 3 (1972), pp.2ff; T. Kennedy, Doers of the Word: Moral Theology for humanity in the third Millennium, vol. 1 (Middlegreen: St. Pauls, 1989), pp. 93-102.
[94] See Groß, Wandelbares Gesetz, pp. 160-161.
[95] See J. Bright, History of Israel, pp. 134ff; C. Curran & R. A. McCormick, Readings in Moral Theology, (New York: Ramsey, 1984), pp. 178ff; McKenzie, A Theology of the OT, 1974, pp.192ff – he speaks of "cosmic protological constant" in describing the specific difference of Israelite morality.
[96] Crüsemann (Bewahrung der Freiheit, pp. 80ff) argues that considering the context in which the decalogue developed, and because of its omission of a list of laws for social justice and solidarity with the poor (and many others), there is reason to believe that the decalogue was more a kind of "class-ethic" which sought to protect the freedom of landlords. See also Groß, Wandelbares Gesetz, pp. 162-163.

in the transition of the ethos of Israel from clan specific ethos, to a more generally binding moral order, following the coming into being of a confederation of the twelve tribes, around 1200 BC.[97] The most significant event, however, unique to the historical, social and political saga of Israel was the liberation from Egypt. It was the event that constituted Israel into a people, specially chosen, through this liberating initiative of God and on account of God's covenant relationship with Israel. From this point on all life was seen as a response to God's call and covenant, a call to be lived as part of the daily experiences of the people. Morality was therefore "walking in the presence of God" (Gen 17, 1; Deut 10, 12; 13, 4; Is 2, 3),[98] and every moment of moral transaction was not just a fulfillment of laws but an act of worship.[99] In this way Israelite morality became in itself a type of "creed" and the canon for the foundation and establishment of a binding moral system.

A critical consideration of some of the laws organizing biblical marriage and sexual morality also offers some grounds for proposing that on the material level, it was the concrete realities of life that engendered the Israelite ethical system. Within the context of the biblical faith, however, it was the principle of covenantal love that was fundamental to the ethical process, making the 'Yahweh religion' become in a way the selective principle for moral norms in the society. Its effect on the factual situation was that it compelled Israel to confront the morality of its neighbors, and so reject the influence of their sexual cults and morality in favor of a personal relationship with Yahweh. No wonder Israel came to understand and express this relationship metaphorically with a language full of marital imagery.[100]

The relevance of paying attention to cultural and socio-historical circumstances underlying the morality found in the OT (based on the example of the Decalogue) for the study of theological ethics today can be summarized as follows: The decalogue neither begins the history of Israel, nor can the decalogue be understood without the history and social history within which the decalogue obtains its historical setting ("Ort"). This socio-historical setting delineates and defines the limits of the decalogue's validity.[101] The decalogue does not postulate a timeless morality and it makes no attempt to cover generally everybody's moral needs at all times. Considered within its cultural and socio-historical context, it is also historically and theologically difficult to

---

[97] Böckle, 'Die kulturgeschichtliche Bedingtheit', p. 117.
[98] Böckle, 'Die kulturgeschichtliche Bedingtheit', p. 118.
[99] Peschke, Christian Ethics, vol. 1, p. 23.
[100] Böckle, 'Die kulturgeschichtliche Bedingtheit', p. 119.
[101] Hunold, Wider den Konkurs der Freiheit, pp. 175-176; also his references to J. M. Lochmann, Wegweisung der Freiheit. Abriß der Ethik der Perspektive des Dekalogs (Gütersloh: 1979); F.- L. Hossfeld, Der Dekalog. Seine späten Fassungen, die originale Komposition und seine Vorstufen (Götingen: 1982).

generalize the decalogue into a summary of OT morality as a whole,[102] forgetting thereby the relevance of the other laws of the Torah.

3.4.2 Illustration 2: The New Testament

Many scholars would admit that it is difficult to trace any particular concrete moral norm as stemming directly from Jesus or Paul, or any of the other authors of the NT.[103] In discussing the moral challenges of Jesus as shown in the Gospel of Mark, Matera observes: "The Markan Jesus does not offer a new ethical code, much less abolish the old."[104] NT morality like that of the OT can be shown to have remained in its concrete content, very closely a part of the given context, much the product of the anthropological constants of humans just as any other human ethos.[105] Bujo explains that "On close inspection, Jesus proposes no programme [sic] of social reform, and one would look in vain to Jesus for concrete norms that could govern the ethics of economy. There is no call to social revolution, and slaves remain slaves."[106] Jesus drew on the day to day experiences of his people and their cultural heritage to challenge them to a radical morality.

NT morality is nonetheless distinct because it bases on the person of Jesus and his proclamation of the Kingdom of God.[107] Hence in speaking on the

---

[102] See Crüsemann, Bewahrung der Freiheit, p. 80.
[103] See J. Blank, Unity and Plurality in New Testament Ethics, in: Concilium 150 (10/1981), pp. 65-70, especially the conclusion on p. 70, where he says: "If we were to draw a general conclusion, ... we could say that basically there is no such thing, according to the New Testament, as a >>Christian ethics<< as a firmly established >>system<<." See also Bujo, African Christian Morality, p. 27, who also refers to the French edition of Blank's Essay. An additional reference from Bujo is A. Auer, Autonome Moral und christilicher Glaube (Düsseldorf: 1971), pp. 80f. See also N. P. Harvey, The Morals of Jesus (London: Darton, Longman & Todd, 1991).
[104] F. J. Matera, New Testament Ethics: Legacies of Jesus and Paul (Louisville, Ky.: Westminster John Knox Press, 1996), p. 34.
[105] For relevant information on the social background of the New Testatment, see: R. E. Brown and J. P. Meier, Antioch and Rome: New Testament Cradles of Catholic Christianity (New York: Paulist Press, 1982); D. L. Balch (ed.), Social History of the Matthean Community: Cross-Disciplinary Approaches (Minneapolis: Fortress, 1991). Matera (New Testament Ethics) also mentions this sources.
[106] Bujo, African Christian Morality, pp. 27-28. Here Bujo makes two references to Blank's French version of the Essay in Concilium referred to above and to K. H. Schelkle, Theologie des Neuen Testaments III, Ethos, (Düsseldorf: 1970).
[107] One may ask, what about the law of love, as the characteristic difference of NT morality? This question is justified, but in recent studies, the theory that bases the difference of NT morality solely on the law of love has not gone unquestioned, precisely because of the material contextuality of morality. See Bujo, African Christian Morality, pp. 25ff, especially his reference to N. Lohfink, Altes Testament-Ethos der Weltgestaltung, in N. Lofink

moral challenge posed by the NT today scholars concentrate on the radical shift from the law to the person as moral imperative. In the words of Bujo, "it may be said that Jesus' ethics consists not in the number of norms but rather in their quality. ... It is a matter of a new horizon where everything centres [sic] on the reign of God."[108]

The radical nature of Jesus' moral challenge also lies in the integrity and wholeness he envisages. This is illustrated by the fact that Jesus does not see the social, cultural and historical aspects of the person as elements that bind a person to his or her given group or place or time. Based on his proclamation of the universal reign of God Jesus challenged his contemporaries to look beyond their own socio-cultural barriers.[109] For example Jesus spoke about pagans entering the Kingdom of God (Mt 8, 11ff), the tax collector -and not the Pharisee- being heard in prayer by God (Lk 18, 9ff), and the Samaritan as an example for the Jew (Lk 10, 35).[110] Jesus also made a radical demand for the love of one's enemies, nonresistance, refusing no who asks and giving more than is demanded (Lk 6, 27-36).[111] These challenges consisted in a provocation of the social, religious and political traditions of his people. The importance of the law, the temple and even the identity of Israel as a chosen people of God, whose way of life constituted the standard for all other peoples was challenged.[112] For example gentile Christians questioned practices such as circumcision and food habits, which were essentially jewish-specific customs and traditions.[113]

---

und R. Pesch, Weltgestaltung und Gewaltlosigkeit. Etische Aspeckte des Alten und Neuen Testaments in Einheit und Gegensatz (Düsseldorf: 1978). Bujo reminds us of Lohfink's rejection of too strict a differentiation between the law of love in the NT and in the OT, even if the OT does not use the word 'love' directly (See Bujo, African Christian Morality, p. 28).

[108] Bujo, African Christian Morality, p. 29. The idea Bujo expresses here has been reiterated in more recent studies on New Testament ethics as shown for example by Matera when he concludes his discussion on the moral message of Jesus in Mark's Gospel by noting that "To know [the] story [of Jesus] is to be shaped by a new ethical vision whose horizon is none other than the in-breaking kingdom of God. (Matera, New Testament Ethics, p. 35). See also J. D. G. Dunn, Jesus' Call to Discipleship: Understanding Jesus Today (Cambridge: Cambridge University Press, 1992).

[109] J. Becker, 'Vermittlungsinstanzen christlicher Ethik', in A. Hertz et. al. (Hrg.), Handbuch der christlichen Ethik, Bd. 1 (Freiburg: Herder, ²1993), pp. 248-249; also Matera, New Testament Ethics, p. 31ff.

[110] Becker, 'Vermittlungsinstanzen', p.248.

[111] See A. E. Harvey, Strenuous Commands: The Ethics of Jesus (Philadelphia: Trinity Press International, 1990), pp. 90ff.

[112] See E. P. Sanders, Jesus and Judaism (SCM Press. 1985). The book presents a discussion on what in the reported sayings of Jesus would have been offensive or not to first century Jews.

[113] See Matera, New Testament Ethics, p. 25.

The relevance of these insights into NT morality is the fact that Jesus uses the cultural and historical material moral content of his people as a tool to challenge them to new levels of ethical awareness and behavior. Their cultural and historical self understanding became itself a moral challenge demanding that they go beyond the boundaries of group specific classifications of morality, of prejudices and limitations.[114] Jesus challenged his people to transcend these limitations by means of creative spontaneity of love. The implication for us is the truth that what we learn from the social sciences to be our "conditio-humana" is at the same time our moral vocation, rather than an excuse from moral responsibility.[115] The Bible for that matter is not being used as a proof text for a social scientific premise. Rather it provides a hermeneutic category for understanding the subject of Christian morality. In the view of Jesus the anthropological constants of our humanness must be subject to an organic consideration of reality by crossing personal and group specific boundaries and prejudices. In the Gospels, Jesus commanded his disciples to be zealous about obtaining in their own actions a righteousness that surpasses that of the scribes and Pharisees (Mt 5, 20).

The paradox we are faced with almost begs the question. For one cannot do without one's own social group, one's own context and history if one should act morally. At the same time, a person's morality obtains its Christian quality by going beyond the group specific ethos and joining in the general destiny of humanity in view of the Kingdom of God. It is possible to say therefore that whereas Jesus challenges a *ghetto* morality, it is also clear that he does not propose a morality *ex nihilo*.[116]

3.4.3 Illustration 3: Early North African Christianity

The fact that there can be no morality *ex nihilo* is also illustrated by the example of the early Christians in North Africa, in their development of what we might today call inculturation ethics. Egyptian Coptic theology, especially its ethics and spirituality, developed in the 4th and 5th centuries from the back-

---

[114] Becker, 'Vermittlungsinstanzen', p. 249.

[115] This ties in well with the view earlier expressed that African Christian ethics cannot be something developed from outside, as if there were an Africanness external to the African we now know. At the same time what the African is makes him or her responsible for what he or she desires to be and even challenges him or her to go beyond the limits of his or her dreams of authenticity.

[116] For more information on the ideas expressed here concerning New Testament morality in recent studies, see: T. Kennedy, Doers of the Word, pp. 93-111; W. Schrage, The Ethics of the New Testament (Philadelphia: Fortress, 1988, translated from the original German under the title, Ethik des Neuen Testaments, Vandenhoeck & Rprecht, 1982); R. Schnakenburg, Die sittliche Botschaft des Neuen Testaments, 2 vols. (Freiburg: Herder, ³1988).

ground of the indigenous religion of the Hellenistic provinces of the time.[117] This development is said to have taken place as part of Egyptian nationalism against Byzantine imperialism in the time of Constantine and thereafter. This North African example could thus be considered as an interesting parallel to the experience of many African churches of our time.[118]

Around the time under consideration, there were imperial prohibitions of religions other than Christianity which had gained state recognition. Constantine had moved his capital from Nicomedeia to Byzantium (which henceforth bore his name, Constantinople) and was taking steps to consolidate his power in the Empire. This had initiated a process that together with other factors induced a rapid decay of the native Hellenistic religion in the region.[119] Despite this decay of the native religion, however, certain aspects of it remained intact. One of such aspects, which was strongly held to, was the belief and hope in a 'life after death'. This belief was originally a strong religious attitude in the worship of the *man-god* Osiris. Osiris had been slain out of jealousy and evil. He rose again, however, and lived as the king of the dead, having been brought back to life through the action of his sister and wife Isis.[120] It was believed that the dead would obtain eternal happiness through the god Osiris. This belief in life after death was nonetheless strongly based on elevated notions of morality and justice. Moral austerity was held to be a necessary condition for the attainment of eternal felicity. "The weighing of a person's good and evil deeds [were]…thought to be necessary before a person could pass the judgement hall of Osiris."[121]

In the Alexandrian community this 'Osiris-theology' was assumed into the platonic Christian doctrines of the time. The combination yielded the practice of strict asceticism and meditation.[122] It is said therefore that two important things which would seem to have influenced the theology of early Christian communities in and around Egypt were the strong belief in a future life

---

[117] See K. Baus, "Der Weg in die Heidenwelt", in: H. Jedin (Hrsg.), Handbuch der Kirchengeschichte, Bd. 1, (Freiburg: Herder, 1962), pp. 107-111; P. D. Scott-Moncrieff, "Coptic Church", in J. Hastings, Encyclopedia of Religion and Ethics, vol. 4 (Edinburgh: T&T Clark, 1926-1976), p. 113.

[118] See Martey, African Theology, p. 4;. F. Hobbhouse, The Church and the World in Idea and in: History (London: 1910).

[119] Baus, 'Der Weg in die Heidenwelt'.

[120] See A. T. Mann, J. Lyle, Sacred Sexuality (Shaftesbury: Element Books Ltd., 1995), pp. 46-59; S. Quirke, Ancient Egyptian Religion (London: British Museum 1992); G. Haart, Egyptian Myths (London: British Museum, 1990).

[121] Baus, 'Der Weg in die Heidenwelt', p. 108. It might be interesting to note that this idea of "weighing" the dead is not strange to the indigenous religions of some African peoples, as shown by some ethnic groups in Ghana for instance. Here however, the "weighing" is done to investigate whether a person had been a witch or wizard. Compare E. E. Evans-Pritchard, Witchcraft Oracles, and Magic among the Azande (Oxford: Clrendon, 1976).

[122] See Baus, 'Der Weg in die Heidenwelt', pp. 108ff.

and the transcendentalized ('inculturated'?) forms of the Osiris-Isis worship with its strict moral implications.[123]

Thus this example also illustrates a transition from the concrete moral attitudes and philosophy of life of native Hellenistic religion into Christian theology and practice. The ensuing austerity of life arising from the theology and spirituality of this time must have been a tool for safeguarding the little that had remained of the indigenous religion and must also have served as an attitude of defiance in the face of imperial domination.

That the ensuing theology was not only a matter of religious and cultural authenticity, but also of political and social emancipation are interesting aspects of 4th and 5th century Coptic theology, which when properly investigated might yield important contributions for the development of African theology today. Such an investigation, however, is not within the limits of this study. The three illustrations from the Old and New Testaments, and from early North African Christianity, are meant to help end this chapter by deducing some general conclusions about African traditions and inculturation ethics in contemporary African theology.

3.4 The role of African traditions in Inculturation Ethics

Inculturation ethics, it has been noted, has to found on a theology of awareness. Such a theology should sensitize Africans on the fact that an African Christian ethic cannot be written from the perspective of paradise. But this should not be interpreted to mean a rejection of positive African traditions. In view of the correlation between humanness and sociality, African traditions remain important insofar as they can be harnessed to provide strength for a concrete and historical self-awareness about the 'is-condition' of the African. Only out of this 'is-condition' can we begin to develop towards the ought-condition. It is in place to repeat a passage from Ela which penetratingly explains this relation between African traditions and awareness.

> "It cannot be denied that, since the meeting of Africa with the West, a tradition has arisen about ourselves, about our African experience in history, in the midst of the tensions and conflicts that have marked our imagination. Life histories, songs and worship, myths and symbols, forms of struggle and resistance belong to this imagination that constitutes the privileged context where Africans recognize themselves and their condition. Whenever so-

---

[123] Baus, 'Der Weg in die Heidenwelt', pp. 108ff.

ciety is gripped by the crises and challenges of the day, it goes back to its imagination to construct a specific identity. Reconstructed each time, "the tradition" becomes a resource to update the materials used in art and music, languages belonging to the popular culture, the written and oral stories, the religious and political life. All these areas that the memory takes hold of lead us to the center of our historical consciousness. Taking into consideration the importance of the places where the profound imagination of a people is shaped, we ought to rediscover the African across these places where memory is invested. Our society never ceases maintaining its relationship with these stations. It finds there the ground for its own comprehension; it draws from them materials through which it makes sense of itself. African theologians cannot therefore spare the memory if they want to hear the narrative of the Passion of Jesus Christ in the specific places where the concrete and historical dimensions of the African imagination are rooted."[124]

African traditions constitute an important reference point if Africans really wish to become aware of themselves. No one can dialogue who cannot remember. Narrative rests fundamentally on a person's capacity to remember. But each time we narrate, we reconstruct our memory. In the same way, whenever tradition serves as a resource for the reconstruction of identity, that tradition itself undergoes a renewed construction. So there is no memory without a self, and there is no tradition without a bearer. Tradition, like memory is useful when it remains directly connected to its bearer and when it is admissive of changes in time and context.

Whereas Africans need their indigenous traditions by all means in order to be authentic, they cannot afford to be traditionalistic, since in doing so they would be separating memory from the self. In a situation of identity crisis such as in Africa, the attempt to postulate some original form of tradition which must be rejuvenated, in order to achieve the authentic traditional African is to propose an unproductive and burdensome undertaking. Bujo sounds this caution: "It seems to me that we simply have missed the opportunity to save many of our black traditions from disappearance. If now we are not ready and honest enough to face this deplorable fact, I am afraid that we shall be wasting our time trying to produce an artificial theology of *Paradise Lost*."[125]

Rather than engage in such a restorative theology, it is more important for inculturation ethics to investigate the complex cultural experiences of Africans, the flux, and even sometimes conflicting nature of the socio-cultural

---

[124] Ela, 'The Memory', p. 21.
[125] Bujo, African Christian Morality, p. 122. Author's italics.

forces with which Africans have to construct their reality. Moral inquiry in Africa must seek to understand the struggle of Africans to integrate their plural heritage[126] and the ambivalence Africans are faced with in their process of cultural integration. In this respect acculturation and enculturation point to the complex levels of relations and cultural elements at work in the consciousness of the African, who attempts to live morally. A fruitful analysis of the African response to Christian moral principles is only possible when an attempt is made to reflect on these levels of consciousness and on their implications for the self-definition of the African Christian.

---

[126] See chapter two above, and Mazrui's paradigm of a 'triple heritage'.

Chapter Four

4. Where Theory and Praxis Meet: Inculturation Ethics and Politics in Africa

> All theory of interpretation -like all theory itself- is an interpretation as good or as bad as its ability to illuminate the problems we discover or invent and its ability to increase the possibility of good action. Good theory, after all, is both an abstraction from, and an enrichment of, our concrete experience.
>
> [David Tracy]

This chapter attempts to apply some of the insights worked out in the first three chapters above to the concrete problem of political leadership in Africa. It is important to remark straight away that the chapter promises more than it offers for reasons of limitation. The nature of political problems vary from one African nation to the other and the situations in which African leaders operate are equally different. It will need an interdisciplinary study involving history, linguistics, political science, economics, cultural psychology and sociology, comparative religion and theology, to achieve a reasonable picture of the complex issues involved in African politics. It is not within reach of this study to provide such an analysis.

What is intended here is to test the ability of inculturation ethics, based on the personalist method, to shed light on the fundamental and complicated nature of the problem of leadership all over Africa. Political leadership could be said to be a moral embarrassment that challenges all responsible Africans. Hence the chapter begins by sketching some important elements of a political ethic and leadership as a moral value. We shall then describe aspects of indigenous forms of leadership in Africa in the past in order to highlight the problems in contemporary forms of leadership in modern African states. The effects of contemporary leadership are briefly discussed and the various reactions to the deplorable state of affairs is discussed. The chapter then offers an alternative analysis of the situation, depending on the personalist criterion for doing ethics, based on an adequate consideration of the human person. The chapter ends with suggestions on the contribution of inculturation ethics with regard to the problem of leadership in Africa.

4.1 Sketch of a Political Ethic

Politics has been explained generally to imply the basic social activity in which people struggle for and use power for the realization of the aims of one group against those of another group in a given social situation.[1] In this sense politics is rather broadly understood and does not necessarily imply the existence of a state as precondition. It includes all those instances in which people come together and organize themselves for the attainment of certain communal ends. We may understand politics rather roughly as a social means of organizing and enforcing the right of law for the proper functioning of a given society, for the welfare of its members and for the attainment of the common good. Political leadership could then be understood as that activity which promotes the good of order in a given community, by helping people to enjoy freedom, solidarity, peace and the dignity of their humanness.[2]

The word leadership is usually qualified with the adjective "political" so as to emphasize "the official, public (non-private), or governmental" connotations of the meaning of leadership.[3] We can designate this purely politico-social consideration of leadership as governance based on the rule of law. In the paragraphs that follow the aspects of actual governance (politics), of organization (polity), and of legitimacy (policy) are not separately treated. The complex connection between politics, polity and policy in the day to day experiences of African nations, and the frequently clumsy nature of such connection makes it impossible to attempt a distinguished treatment of each of these aspects in this study. We shall oscillate between these aspects in the treatment that follows.

With regard to political questions, ethics seeks ultimately to assert the human person as the inalienable value in which the good of order that politics pursues in a given community is to be situated.[4] The build up of institutions, the provision and delivery of empirical goods and services such as food, water, communication systems, schools, which people need to live form important aspects of politics. Ethics considers how these goods and their achievement relate to persons, i.e. the leader as well as those being led, and the implications of these arrangements for the maximization of humanness in the community concerned. Besides, there is the problem of how to reconcile the inviolable nature of the individual's freedom of conscience and the

---

[1] Compare Max Weber, Wirtschaft und Gesellschaft (Tübingen: Mohr, 1922), pp. 11ff.
[2] Compare B. Häring, Free and Faithful in Christ (Middlegreen: St. Paul Publications, 1981), vol. 3, p. 326.
[3] K. Gyekye, Political Corruption, pp. 2 & 3. Gyekye shows that this purely socio- political understanding of leadership, especially in Africa has often led scholars to analyze the problems of political leadership in Africa without considering the moral aspects of the question.
[4] See B. Lonergan, Method, pp. 31ff; B. Lonergan, Insight: A Study of Human Understanding (London: Longman, 1961).

communal representative character of political institutions and actions. Since political action is based on the agreement of the members of a community (common consensus), from which political action obtains its legitimacy, how do we achieve this representative power, without sacrificing the value, i.e. the human person and the inviolable freedom of persons, for which political power is necessary in the first place?[5] These and other questions have been central to political philosophy since its beginnings with Plato and Aristotle to the present and mark the close connection between politics and ethics.[6]

In the late 18th and early 19th century Europe when the use of Christian denominational wars as a means for acquiring power had to give way to the formation of modern states based on new political systems, there evolved a new consciousness about the value of the human person in political organization.[7] This new consciousness induced new meanings of authority and of power. Since then it has become necessary for ethics to establish normatively the limits of political power and at the same time to justify the place of political authority in the life of human communities. Political ethics thus spreads over a wide field of issues including the freedom of the human person (autonomy), communality, and the authority of the state, not forgetting the modern context and formulation of fundamental- and human rights.[8]

This classical understanding of the role of ethics in politics is closely associated with the history of the development of the modern state and the idea of democracy in its Western ramifications, where political leadership would seem to be founded primarily on the rule of law. In this wise, the legal structure legitimizes the leader's authority. Since this legitimacy of power is external to the community, there has been the danger of leaders expropriating the law in order to obtain absolute power. This makes it incumbent on political ethics to provide an understanding of politics in which the rule of law (external legitimacy of political power) is reconciled with an internal sanction arising from the value of leadership itself based on the community's good.

There are however (as shown below with the example of African political systems) other systems in which leadership is already based on an inner-community value, whose justification is therefore independent of

---

[5] See T. Koch, "Kriterien einer Ethik des Politischen", in A. Herz, W. Korff, et. al. (ed.), Handbuch der christlichen Ethik, Bd. 2 (Freiburg: Herder, ²1993), pp.244-245. Compare Sindima, Religious and Political Ethics, p. xiii.

[6] See G. Sabine (ed.), A History of Political Theory,. (New York: Holt, Rinehart and Winston, 1961).

[7] See T. Koch, 'Kriterien einer Ethik des Politischen', pp. 244-252.

[8] See T. Koch, 'Kriterien einer Ethik des Politischen', pp. 244-252; B. Häring, Free and Faithful in Christ, vol. 3, pp. 326ff; F. Mordstein, Menschenbild und Gesellschaftsidee. Zur Krisis der politischen Ethik im 19. Jahrhundert (Stuttgart: Kohlhammer, 1966); F. M. Schmölz, Chance und Dilemma der politischen Ethik (Köln: Bachem, 1966); F. E. Oppenheim, Moral Principles in Political Philosophy (New York: Random House, 1968). The last three sources were acquired form Häring.

external legal structures. Here also there is still need for political ethics since this internality of legitimacy does not prevent the abuse of the system itself and/or the abuse of power as such. In this case, however, it seems reasonable to argue that the role of ethics would differ slightly from the classical meaning. Here ethics would be basically concerned with two things. It would seek on the one hand to investigate the conditions that cause the disintegration of the existing inner legitimacy of political authority. On the other hand, ethics would seek to project those elements that enable the preservation and promotion of the immanent control and justification of political power as a community value.

Whatever the political system may be, however, there is a point of convergence established in current studies in political ethics as well as in politics itself. It is also a point of convergence on which both non-Christians and Christians alike agree in one way or the other; namely, that governance has essential moral implications since it is directly related to the inalienable rights of persons. Rendtorff explains this by proposing that we consider a fictive situation in which a good number of people could be found, who neither believe in God, nor have any personal political convictions nor a conscience, nor a meaningful idea about communal life. What import would legal systems and political leadership have in such a situation?[9]

This fictive situation makes it clear that even where the law is seen as an instance of political authorization, the law remains meaningless unless it is also understood as having the duty of providing individuals with an effective formation that allows for the cultivation and development of fundamental values and rights.[10] In other words no legal system can function which is not directly related to the dispositions of concrete human persons, whether as individuals or groups. In the same way African systems of leadership be they as good and internally constituted as possible, would not automatically produce good leaders unless there are people committed to the system. In both ways one thing is emphasized. Irrespective of the extent to which political power may be dependent on the rule of law or otherwise, leadership has essential characteristics of moral value and implies personal responsibility.

4.1.1 Political Leadership as Moral Value

In the flux of world events and rapid globalization, people are becoming more and more aware that something new is taking place, and that humanity finds itself at the dawn of a new society in which the old methods of leadership no

---

[9] T. Rendtorff, "Das Verfassungsprinzip der Neuzeit", in: Handbuch der christlichen Ethik, Bd. 2, p. 231.
[10] Rendtorff, 'Das Verfassungsprinzip', p. 231.

longer answer the questions of our times adequately. Society is becoming more complex and it is difficult to find universal answers that fit in all situations. Hence want to have leaders who act out of personal commitment based on sound moral convictions.[11] In the introduction to the 'Report of the Independent Commission on International Development Issues', Willy Brandt, the president and mentor of the commission, entreated:

> "We expect much of those among the young generations who will soon carry major political responsibility. We hope that their insistence on dealing with human beings rather than bloodless abstractions or self-serving institutions grows stronger. We also hope that they are more concerned with human values than with bureaucratic regulations and technocratic constraints."[12]

The appeal of Willy Brandt is relatively old and may sound rather remote since the work of the commission was unfortunately all too soon forgotten. But the fundamental meaning of the commission's appeal is still relevant. The human family is faced with questions such as taxation, security and pension for the aged, situations of war and natural cataclysms, abortion and genetic manipulation, teeming numbers of refugees and homeless or landless people. In the face of such questions, "One of the crucial things about being a politician, or a public servant, is that deep inside yourself you have to be able to say, as your constituents come to see you, "And you too are divine".[13] In these words Shirley Williams not only represents the many voices making a renewed call for us to take the moral implications of political leadership seriously, she also introduces the fundamentally religious aspects of the value of leadership. In current studies in theology, the term leadership is used by some scholars to emphasize this religious and moral character of authority in distinction to governance.[14]

Writing in connection with leadership among the Ewe of West Africa, Hevi explains the ethical implications or leadership. He defines leadership as "The capacity to initiate, and involve oneself in, ideas and/or actions which

---

[11] See Hevi, Indigenous Leadership, pp. 3ff. He provides a valuable list of literature on the increasing demand for morally rather than (only) legally founded leadership in politics.

[12] W. Brandt, "A Plea for Change: Peace, Justice, Jobs", in: The Independent Commission on International Development Issues, North-South: A Programme for Survival (London: Pan Books Ltd., 1980), p. 11.

[13] S. Williams, "The Faith of a Politician", in: The Tablet (14. August, 1999), p. 1096.

[14] See J. McKenzie, Authority in the Church (London: Chapman, 1966), pp. 21, 48-50, 89ff. Mckenzie argues that the term leadership is more biblical than the term government.

inspire others to do the same, as the realization of fundamental human values of one's immediate community in particular, or the human community in general."[15] Hevi explains that the word 'capacity' denotes the "inner strength" on which the "disposition" of a person who assumes leadership is founded. Such inner strength differentiates a leader's action from "mere ability, or dexterity, to manipulate something". Besides, leadership is to promote and symbolize values by communicating ideas that enable others to achieve value, or by direct "performance of exemplary actions" that challenge others to follow the example in the attainment of value, or by a combination of ideas and action for the same purpose. This is expressed by the terms "ideas and/or actions" in the definition.[16]

Hevi's definition presupposes that leadership is a moral value in the service of the aspirations of human persons to preserve and transform themselves as best as possible. Thus someone invested with authority and charged to influence the attainment of this vocation to humanness must themselves invest a personal response to the values that are held important in the community. The leader cannot defer this personal imperative to some institutional structures of social organization.[17] The paragraphs that follow will investigate briefly how leadership was conceived as a community value in indigenous African communities. Then follows a description of the actual state of affairs socially and politically in many African countries in contemporary times. The bad state of affairs explain why the problem of political leadership in Africa must be considered as an urgent concern in inculturation ethics.

4.2 Indigenous African Systems of Leadership.

Once again we have to remind ourselves that there is "a varied host of very different systems of rule" which flourished in Africa in the past centuries.[18] Kingdoms or chiefdoms as well as the Islamic dynasties of the Sokoto caliphate following the jihad of Uthman dan Fodio, the Songhay empire or the Mandinka empire under Almami (Samori) Toure[19] and feudal systems of

---

[15] Hevi, Indigenous Leadership, p. 82; also his reference to M.-F. P. Jassy, Leadership (Kampala: Gaba Publications, 1974), p. 2. In developing our ideas in this paragraph, we have depended on some of the insights of Hevi (Indigenous Leadership).

[16] For all this, see Hevi, Indigenous Leadership, pp. 82-83.

[17] Compare Hevi, Indigenous Leadership, pp. 60ff.

[18] J. Vansina, "Kings in Tropical Africa", in E. Beumars and H.- J. Koloss (eds.), Kings in Africa. Art and Authority in Central Africa: Collection Museum für Völkerkunde Berlin (Utrecht: Foundation Kings of Africa, 1993), p. 19.

[19] See B. Davidson, et al., The Growth of African Civilisation. A History of West Africa 1000-1800 (London: Longman, 1965); J. B. Webster and A. A. Boahen, The Growth of African Civilisation. The Revolutionary Years: West Africa since 1800 (London:

Norther Nigeria called Emirates or the 'chief' system among the Igbos[20] are but few examples. Secondly, what is known about the chiefdoms has to be purged of the mythology and fairy-tales that surround the information if we should obtain a clear picture of chiefdom as a system of governance in Africa in the past centuries.[21] We shall depend on the specific example of the Ashanti to explore briefly some indigenous ideas about leadership.

It would seem that political organization in its African indigenous structure, in the form of chiefdoms, was closely connected to kinship.[22] Among the Ashanti, for example, belonging to a lineage (matrilineal descent in Ashanti) also implied a person's inclusion in a Chiefdom. Busia describes a chiefdom as "a combination of localized lineages inhabiting a given territory and forming a political community."[23] As a political unit each lineage had a leader, who also fulfilled the function of representative on the council of elders, the overall ruling body, in conciliar collaboration with the chief.[24] One became a lineage head through election by the adult men and women of the lineage. The structural organizations of these kinship units ranged from lineage, to village, through sub-divisional to divisional and tribal levels. There was decentralization of power so that each unit can manage its own affairs which did not affect the whole tribe.

Above all, it is the religious position which the chief occupied that legitimized his political authority. This implies that leadership was essentially a moral responsibility, a value which could not be imposed on the community

---

Longmans, 1967), pages 304-313 of this book offer a chronological table of the transitions and varieties of leadership in Africa from about 4000BC to 1800CE. See also J. Ki-Zerbo and D. T. Niane (eds.), General History of Africa, Vol. 4: Africa from the Twelfth to the Sixteenth Century (Paris: UNESCO Publishing, 1997); B. A. Ogot (ed.), General History of Africa, vol. 5 (Paris: UNESCO Publishing, 1997). P. Diagne introduces his contribution to the African political, economic and social structures during the period covered by the last book cited here as follows: "Largely as a result of internal factors such as demography and ecology or under the impact of external forces such as the slave trade, Christianity, Islam and capitalism, African social, economic and political structures were continuously transformed between 1500 and 1800. ... It will be evident from this analysis that in most parts of the continent the idea of timeless African structures or institutions is a historical myth with no real substance" (Diagne, in General History of Africa, vol. 5, p.23); P. Akoi, Religion in African social Heritage (Rome: 1970).

[20] Pobee, Religion and Politics, p. 24.
[21] Vansina, 'Kings in Tropical Africa', p. 19.
[22] See K. Busia, "The Ashanti", in: D. Ford (ed.), African Worlds. Studies in the cosmological ideas of African Peoples (London: Oxford University Press, 1954), p. 200. For a general description applicable to a wider section of African communities, see the essay of Jan Vansina, 'Kings in Tropical Africa', pp. 19ff. The many similarities which the Ashanti specific example shares with Vansina's wider representation are readily observable.
[23] Busia, 'The Ashanti', p. 200.
[24] Compare Vansina, 'Kings in Tropical Africa', p. 19.

by external structures of power. On the contrary, the leader's role was judged as being good or bad according to the criterion of the leader's ability to initiate the realization of the ultimate aspirations of the community. The leader found his responsibility defined in terms of the realization of the community destiny.[25] Thus leadership was experienced among some African communities as a specific and decisive response to the end goal of peoples in their particular and concrete situation. It was a practical intention directly linked to a given finality.[26] For many African communities, this goal was the ensuring of the continuous flow of life for the community and assuring the quality of that life for the members of the community.[27]

The African community, however, is composed of the living, the dead and the yet unborn. These three are so interconnected that they are seen as dimensions of one and the same community.[28] Mediating the flow of life in proportionate circulation among these three dimensions of the community was the source of the leader's moral and political authority and at the same time the "degree" of responsibility he or she shouldered.

---

[25] Hevi, Indigenous Leadership, p. 28. Referring to Häring (Manipulation: Ethical Boundaries of Medical behavioural, and Genetic Manipulation, St. Paul Publications, Slough, England, 1975, p. 77), Hevi explains that both the community and the leader experience this community destiny as a 'degree of responsibility' because of the ambiguity of human action and the 'situations of conflict' that characterize humanness. In this regard, humans can only make the 'best possible' decisions that are nearest to the totality of their reality (Hevi, Indigenous Leadership. p. 28, footnote 41).

[26] Hevi, Indigenous Leadership, p. 38.

[27] L. Magesa, African Religion (Maryknoll: Orbis Books, 1997); T. Sundermeier, Nur Gemeinsam können wir leben (Gütersloh: Gütersloher Verlaghaus, 1988); J. B. Danquah, The Akan Doctrine of God. A fragment of Gold Goast Ethics and Religion (London and Redhill: Lutterworth Press, 1968).

[28] See below the citation from Busia, 'The Ashanti', p. 202. See also T. Sundermermeier, Nur gemeinsam können wir leben. Das Menschenbild schwarzafrikanischer Religionen (Gütersloh: Verlaghaus Gerd Mohn, 1988), pp. 16-30; G. Parrinder, West African Religion. A Study of Beliefs and Practices of Akan, Ewe, Yoruba, Ibo and Kindred Peoples, (London: 1961), pp. 113ff; Rattray, Religion and Art in Ashanti (London: Oxford University Press, 1927). It might be of interest to note that the idea of a society or community as consisting of the living, the dead and the yet unborn is not a thought completely absent in the thinking of some Western scholars, even if they do not make any metaphysical connections in that regard. F. Tönnies for instance observes: "Dem Worte Volk muß noch ein anderer und besonderer Sinn gegeben werden; ich wage ihn dahin auszudrücken, daß er nicht nur die Lebendigen, sondern auch die Toten und die Nachkommen bedeutet, und zwar gerade die Verbindung und Einheit dieser drei Schichten," in: Tönnies, Die Sitte, (Frankfurt am Main: Rütten & Loening, 1909), p.15.

"The word 'Volk' (a people) must be given another and special meaning; I dare say, the word does not mean only the living, but also the dead and the yet to be born [descendants], and implies the direct relation and union of these dimensions" (my translation of the German).

Busia has illustrated the close link that exists between the world of the living and the world of spirits in the cosmogony of many African peoples using the example of the Ashanti. Busia notes that "The Ashanti believe that there is a world of spirits (*asaman*), where all their ancestors live a life very similar to life on earth, and this conception is implicit in Ashanti funeral rites. The dead are given food and drink and gold-dust to help them on their journey to the world of spirits."[29]

Busia further explains that the idea of leadership was rooted in this close connection between the living and the dead. He notes that because the ancestors are believed to play a rather important and direct role in the lives of the living, "each lineage has its blackened stool which is the shrine of its ancestors. On this shrine the head of the lineage at the appropriate seasons offers food and drink to the ancestors, praying that they may protect the members of the lineage, bless them with health and long life, that the women may bear children, and that their farms may yield food in plenty."[30]

The supreme moment of a chief's authority and function was the moment when he presides over this prayer of sacrifice and supplication on behalf of his people to the ancestors. His authority resulted, therefore, from the mediatory role he played. These sentiments are given regular expression in the various festivals held by the Ashanti in present times. The *Adae* and *Odwera* festivals are especially important in this connection.[31]

Commensurate with this mediatory role, the 'enstoolment' of a chief was not a ceremony which merely entrusted the chief with civil or political authority, but a symbolic religious celebration.[32] The main rite that actually enacted the installation was the gentle lowering and raising of the chief-elect "three times over the blackened stool of the ancestor believed to be the founder of the royal lineage. By this ceremony the chief is believed to have been brought into a peculiarly close relationship with his ancestors. Thereupon his person becomes sacred. ... An Ashanti chief [thus] fills a sacred role as the >>one who sits upon the stool of the ancestors<<."[33]

Form this point on, the personal destiny of the chief became intricately bound up with the communal destiny. This was sometimes explicitly stated in the oath of office (in the case of paramount chiefs) or in the oath of allegiance (in the case of divisional chiefs) which was sworn on the occasion of the 'out-

---

[29] Busia, 'The Ashanti', p. 201.
[30] Busia, 'The Ashanti', p. 201.
[31] Busia, 'The Ashanti', p. 202; also Busia, The Position of the Chief in the Modern Political System in Ashanti: A Study of the Influence of Contemporary Social Change in Ashanti Political Institutions (London: Frank Cass, 1968). Compare also Vansina, 'Kings in Tropical Africa', p. 23.
[32] Compare Vansina, 'Kings in Tropical Africa', pp. 22-23.
[33] Busia, 'The Ashanti', p. 202. This also explains the many rules and prohibitions which the chief had to observe. Compare Vansina, 'Kings in Tropical Africa', p. 23.

dooring' of the newly installed chief. The chief bore and symbolized the community saga, the narrative of the origins, existence, and identity of the lineage or the tribe. His seat of office, the blackened stool, was the soul of the lineage or the tribe; as it were his authority did not arise form a legal constitution, but from the total life and existence of the community. Busia concludes:

> "That stool, the symbol of his power, is what the famous Ashanti priest, Anokye, described as 'the soul of the nation'. It is the sacred emblem of the tribe's permanence and continuity. The chief as the occupant of the stool represents all those who have occupied it before him. He is the link, the intermediary, between the living and the dead; for, according to the conception which the Ashanti share with other Akan tribes, the dead, the living, and those still to be born of the tribe are all members of one family, and it is the stool that binds that family together."[34]

Among the many symbols of office (usually found on the linguist's staff) is the sign of an egg held cautiously with a hand. This sign expresses, among other things, that leadership demands absolute responsibility. Should the egg fall and break, the damage is irreparable. If a leader should failed in discharging his duties, the result was the destruction of the people whose life he bore in his hands. In order to obviate any conflict of interests which the chief might face, i.e. choosing between his own enterprise and that of the community, indigenous practice did not allow the chief to "engage in trade to enrich himself."[35]

This policy concerning chieftancy, which forbade the chief from engaging in enterprises or owning personal property is open today, as it was in the past, to different interpretations and can also create difficulties in its concrete application. There is enough evidence which demonstrates that the

---

[34] Busia, 'The Ashanti', p. 202.
[35] K. A. Busia, The Position of the chief in the Modern Political Systems of Ashanti (London: Frank Cass, 1968), p. 199; also pp. 50-51, cited in Gyekye, Political corruption, p. 21. In order to help the chief live by this principle, however, the system took steps to ensure the comfort of the chief so that in many cases, the chief was actually the wealthiest member of his community. This wealth was derived from the enterprise of his wives and his servants in the form of industrial goods such as textiles. The chief was also entitled to "corvee labour" where members of the community or the army worked for the chief upon request. Besides, some chiefs (true also of the King of Ashanti) collected revenue and taxes from the title holders within their territory. But "the king's wealth was important for making government possible, for furthering the reputation of the king's power, and for making it possible for the king to be generous and use gifts to gain the personal allegiance of major and even minor titleholders" (Vansina, 'Kings in Tropical Africa', p. 21).

policy was often misunderstood by the colonialists in their time[36] and it would seem, as we attempt to show later, that the idea is also grossly misunderstood and/or blatantly abused by current African politicians. Yet the fact that the chief possessed symbolically all the wealth and property of his chiefdom was in no way permissive of tyranny or despotism. Arbitrariness and extravagance on the part of the chief to the detriment of the people was liable to the highest punishment of death. Jan Vansina quotes a report about southeast Africa, written by Al Mas'udi around 916 in which the abhorrence for tyranny is illustrated.

> "The Zanj capital is there and they have a king called *mfalme*. This is the ancient name of their kings, and all the other Zanj kings are subject to him; [...] *wafalme* means son of the Great Lord, since he is chosen to govern them justly. If he is

---

[36] Such misunderstanding is revealed in the case of a certain Prince Mpundo Akwa of Cameroon who was arraigned on eight charges of fraud before the provincial court of Altona (near Hamburg in Germany) in 1905. He had borrowed money at the direction of his father for his upkeep and eventually for commerce. He could not pay his debtors since the money his father had promised to send him never materialized. His father was the famous King Dika Akwa of Duala and his mother was Bekene Akwa, herself a daughter of King Bell. In July 1884 King Akwa signed a trade agreement with two companies represented by Herr Eduard Schmidt for the firm Woermann and Herr Johannes Voss for the firm Jantzen & Thormählen respectively. In the same agreement King Akwa also ceded his kingdom to the protection of the German Kaiser. German flags were hoisted for the first time in Cameroon a day after this agreement was signed. In the years that followed the German governor and representative of the Kaiser in Cameroon subjected King Akwa and his people to the most unbearable oppression and maltreatment. King Akwa no longer had any right to the property and wealth of his kingdom, for example ivory, which belonged to the King by tradition. Besides King Akwa was directly forbidden to collect any money from his people, neither for his own upkeep nor for the daily running of his kingdom. Yet King Akwa was not permitted by tradition to pay even for minor transactions from his personal pocket, because as King he could not own any money or property of his own. The governor's prohibition thus impoverished Akwa absolutely.

Mpundo Akwa explained at court that he was unable to pay because his father had not sent him money as he promised, and that the governor had prevented his father in turn from collecting the money from his people. Ironically, the same governor had himself imposed unbearable taxes on the people in Cameroon. The defendant's lawyer made use of this state of affairs to put up the defense for his client. The interesting aspect of this story is that Mpundo Akwa was acquitted of the charges of fraud and spared prison sentence, not because the German administration itself had been responsible for his inability to pay his debtors by meddling with an important tradition of chieftancy. Rather Akwa was cleared principally on the grounds that he lacked a clear sense of judgement to know that his action was punishable by law. In effect the poor prince Akwa was set free since he was too stupid to be responsible! [I am grateful to the Süd Deutscher Rundfunk (SDR)for the permission to use the Script, "Prinz Mpundo Akwa aus Kamerun und die Kabinettsjustiz im Deutschen Kaiserreich", authored by M. Michelsen, edited by E. Klasse and directed by C. Preuß, Program transmitted on Tuesday, 23. Sept., 1997, from 14.05-14.30 hours CET].

tyrannical or strays from the truth, they kill him and exclude his seed from the throne; for they consider that in acting wrongfully he forfeits his positions as the son of the Lord, the King of Heaven and Earth."[37]

By and large it is possible to conclude that among many African communities the understanding of leadership was based very much on value and differed in many respects from the interpretation it received in Western literature. Let us now consider the current political climate in Africa in order to show why it is urgent for inculturation ethics to study the problem of political leadership and make useful contributions for the church's pastoral praxis.

4.3 The African Political Climate: An Overview

The actual socio-political situation in many African communities today is in many respects different from what it used to be in its indigenous context. Not only have the structures, the institutions and persons of leadership changed, but also the results of current forms of leadership are very different. Unfortunately, the difference is rather negative. The results of leadership in Africa today are in ways rather deplorable. Although political leadership is not the only moral problem facing Africa, a personalist approach to moral problems demands that we prioritize certain areas of life in which the African church needs to make a significant contribution. Priority means, among other things, urgency. Since morality is about increasing the humanum, certain moral issues in Africa which seem to reduce the humanness of the African with greater magnitude deserve attention before others of their kind. One such area of priority is political leadership.

A quick look at the African political scene corroborates the urgency of the problem. In Kenya, Rwanda, the Republic of Congo, Sudan, Nigeria, Togo, Ghana, Liberia, Sierra Leone and Angola, and in the majority of African nations it is impossible to overlook the worrisome, oppressive and embarrassing political climate in which millions of Africans battle for survival, if they are allowed even to live. It is estimated that out of the fifty or more countries in Africa, twenty or more are at war, either internally or with their neighbors. In countries where there are no wars on a large scale, the level of corruption is scarring and national cohesion is but a dream in the face of factionalist attitudes to the political enterprise and administration.[38]

---

[37] Cited in: Vansina, 'Kings in Tropical Africa', p. 19.
[38] Compare H. J. Sindima, Religious and Political Ethics in Africa. A Moral Inquiry (London: Greenwood Press, 1998), pp. 13ff; R. Dowden, "What's Wrong with Africa", in: The Tablet (January 16, 1999), pp. 72-73; K. Gyekye, Political Corruption. A Philosophical

African peoples are sacrificed at the hands of unbearably oppressive dictatorships on the one hand and the bloody brutalities of so-called rebels on the other hand, — rebels who any way are vying for the same autocratic power they claim to be fighting against. The nightmare in Sierra Leone is a revealing example in recent times.

Many African peoples are hemmed in from both ends. Those who take up arms to fight dictatorships in Africa proceed as if it were the voiceless people who were the enemies. The poor and illiterate rural folks, some of whom probably have no idea how the parliament houses of their countries look like, because they may never have seen them, are tortured, brutalized, and massacred in cold blood. These people are used both by autocratic political leaders and so-called liberation fighters to service the international arms trade.[39] It would seem that in Africa, liberators become oppressors and the 'teachers' rob their 'followers' of wisdom, rather than support it.

In the wake of African nationalism and independence, Africans had high hopes of regaining their dignity, and not have to continue "to live like

---

Analysis of a Moral Problem (Accra: Sankofa Publishing Co. Ltd., 1997). In recent times, the most recurrent topics in the pastoral letters of the conferences of bishops and other Church documents in the various parts of Africa are calls for responsibility in view of social and political irresponsibility and/or irregularities, for peace in the face of unending wars, and for an end to corruption. These consistent calls are corroborated in the collection of articles and pastoral letters of bishops and other pastoral workers from Africa, Asia and Latin America in the magazine "Weltkirche", jointly published by Adveniat, Misereor and Missio. In 1996, for instance, the third and fifth issues carried leading articles on peace in Liberia and on the situation in Zaire (now Republic of Congo) and in the Sundan respectively. In the case of Sudan the bishops even demanded the resignation of president Omar Hassan Ahmed al Bashir. In the sixth issue, the bishops of Ghana wrote on the signs of social and political crisis and called for serious responsibility on the part of the leaders and citizens of Ghana. The seventh issue contained a pastoral letter on corruption and social irresponsibility in Kenya and another about war and peace in Liberia. The next issue of the magazine had articles on the death of the Archbishop of Bukavu (of Zaire), war, refugees, and the need for peace in Zaire. The ninth issue contained pastoral letters encouraging the people to say no to war and to work for peace in Zaire and in Zambia. The same trend, and with a higher frequency, is observable in the years that followed. In 1988 all the issues of "Weltkirche" carried articles and pastoral letters from the bishops of one or the other nation in Africa dealing with war, corruption, the rule of force, torture and social disintegration. See Weltkirche: Dokumente aus Afrika, Asien und Lateinamerika, (München: Missio, 1996-1999).

[39] The irony is that apart from South Africa, one can hardly find another African nation that produces arms in any reasonable quantity. Current survey shows the growth in the arms trade and the income accruing to arms producing nations. 'The Council for a Livable World' is said to have intimated that in 1997 U. S. weapons exports throughout the world totaled $10.9 billion, and Egypt was the largest purchaser. See United Methodist News Service, http://cpsa.org.za/news/news214.html. For current information on the arms trade see, Arms Trade News (July 1999), http://www.clw.org/cat/atnmain.html.

some kind of sub-human species in the land of [their] birth."[40] All too soon, the fathers and mothers of African nationalism began to forget the hopes and aspirations of the people for whom they fought to dispense with the colonial authority. They began to impose themselves on their peoples, filling in a way the seats of the colonial masters.

The effect of this state of affairs was poignantly described by Archbishop Sarah of Conakry on the eve of the Synod of African bishops in Rome.[41] On the international scene Africa is seen as the most undeveloped of peoples. Africa is described as a continent of wars, at the verge of collapse, or in the description of John Paul II, "a continent at risk", and in the words of Michel Camdessus, Director General of the International Monetary Fund (IMF), a "continent of damnation".[42]

On the internal African scene, the effects of this rapacious and almost community annihilating forms of leadership find expression in inferiority complexes of all kinds, lack of self-confidence, pessimism and resignation, a belief that the African is condemned to the fatality of his or her fate. As Sarah puts it, "Im tiefsten der afrikanischen Seele gibt es bis heute das seltsame Gefühl, von Gott verdammt zu sein."[43]

Africans have become ever more dependent so that many no longer know where they stand in relation to themselves, to their aspirations and hopes. Many Africans doubt their very abilities as persons with a responsibility for their lives. Sarah strikes the substance of the problem when he observes:

"Es sieht so aus, als seien der afrikanische Mensch und der Mensch in Afrika, der afrikanische Christ und der Christ in Afrika nicht mehr in der Lage, ihren eigenen Gesetzen – Ergebnisse eigener Vorstellungskraft und Intelligenz – zu folgen, und – was noch wichtiger ist – ihres eigenen Willens. Das Risiko ist groß, daß in diesem Spiel der Bilder in der Seele, im Herzen, im Geist der Afrikaner etwas Fundamentales zerbricht."[44]

---

[40] D. Russell, Kenneth Kaunda. Zambia Shall be Free (London: Longman, 1978).

[41] See R. Sarah, "Den aufrechten Gang finden", in Herderkorrespondenz (HK). Monatshefte für Gesellschaft und Religion, 5 (1994), pp.245-251. The essay was originally published in French in the *Dokumentation Catholique*, 4. (1994), pp. 337ff.

[42] The descriptions of John Paul and Camdessus are cited by Sarah, 'Den aufrechten Gang finden', p. 246.

[43] Sarah, 'Den aufrechten Gang finden', p. 246. "There is today, deep in the African soul, a rare feeling of being cursed by God" (my translation of the German). Sarah warns, however, that this picture about Africa can be rather simplistic if it is not located within the overall historical context of Africa. Some of these aspects have been discussed above.

[44] Sarah, 'Den aufrechten Gang finden', p. 248. "It looks like the African and the person in Africa, the African Christian and the Christian in Africa are no longer in the position to follow their own internal constitution –the result of their power of imagination and intelligence, and –what is more important –their will. There is a great risk that through this

The current socio-political situation would thus seem to have fundamental implications for African peoples, than the moral problem of, say, polygamy. If we recall that in the past slave traders (both African and European collaborators) were piously baptized and not polygamists, it becomes clearer that we come close to repeating history should inculturation ethics seek to give priority to and expend energy on inquiring into the moral justification of polygamy and whether polygamists could be baptized or not in the face of serious politico-moral issues that continue to reduce the African beyond the minimum of humanness.[45]

The words of Sarah, that we face the risk of a fundamental mutilation in the internal constitution of Africans, in their soul, in their heart, in their spirit and will, adequately describe the effects of poor political leadership in Africa. Beyond the immediate and observable experiences of poverty, disease, terror and oppression, there is the more sublime and cumulative effect, which ultimately makes it difficult for many Africans to find meaning in life, to believe in the love of God for them and to enjoy and build on the fundamental dignity of their humanness.

4.4 Reactions to the Current Political Climate in Africa

Many people agree that the seriousness of the problem makes it incumbent for us to undertake a conscientious analysis of the situation. We have to seek

---

state of affairs, something fundamental gets destroyed in the soul, in the hearts and in the spirit of Africans." (My translation of the German).

[45] The issue of polygamy has been raised often as one of the moral problems which the African church must tackle. Looking at the trend of life in many African countries, it is possible to say that polygamy has no favorable prognosis (see Bujo, Die ethische Dimension der Gemeinschaft, pp. 109-111). Socio-economic conditions, emancipation of women, education and other factors of cultural change such as urbanization no longer provide a favorable atmosphere for the growth of polygamy. Given that the trend of change continues, polygamy might die out silently in the course of time. On the other hand, Christian churches have often achieved much success in this area than would seem to be the case in the area of political organization and leadership. In Ghana for instance the attempt on the part of Nkrumah's government to propose a bill of law allowing polygamy was strongly resisted by the Churches and the bill was dropped. See Pobee, Religion and Politics, p. 64. Even in this regard, Pobee comments that in this fight against polygamy, the churches failed in their arrogance to respect African institutions and sought to impose a single marriage system on a pluralistic community. In the African Church of today, it would be unwise to propose polygamy as the way for African Christians. But there are still serious questions in pastoral practice about people who had been polygamists before they came into contact with Christianity. This is an area still open to serious, more personal and historical consideration in African Christian morality. Compare Bujo, Die ethische Dimension der Gemeinschaft, pp. 97-111; W. Bühlmann, Afrika. Die Kirche unter den Völkern (Mainz: Matthias-Grünewald-Verlag, 1963), pp. 131-153 passim.

reasons for, and solutions to the problem. How this search for meaning should be done, however, is a question that is answered differently. We can identify two main trends. One trend sees the styling of politics in Africa on concepts foreign to indigenous traditions as the cause of the deplorable state of affairs and suggests that the positive aspects of African systems of leadership should be re-cultivated as a solution to the problem. The second trend considers the problem from the perspective of Africans' own responsibility or irresponsibility in organizing and ordering their social and political life. We shall briefly consider these two approaches and, based on an adequate consideration of the human person, show why both fall short of a suitable solution to the problem. We shall call the former the authenticity and the latter the responsibility approach.

4.4.1 The Authenticity Approach.

This approach recalls portions of chapters one and two of this study, which discussed what might be called the classical way of doing inculturation. Proponents of this approach hold that problems in the various areas of life in Africa are to be blamed in part on the fact that many Africans have lost contact or directly despise their culture. Hard as Africans may try to organize their life on concepts foreign to those indigenous to African peoples, they are bound to meet with failure since such foreign categories lack the potential and direct appeal that indigenous traditions have. It is proposed therefore that engaging in inculturation implies the working out of the positive aspects of African traditions and way of life, subjecting these traditions to and explaining them in the light of biblical and Christian tradition, and suggesting how these traditions could be rediscovered and concretely applied in the daily life of Africans. With particular reference to politics, the authenticity approach attempts to develop an African political ethic along the lines of a return to the good aspects of indigenous forms of leadership, and to how this return to the good old sources can empower Africans as well as their leaders to discharge their civil duties with moral excellence.

Sindima's book, *Religious and Political Ethics in Africa* is a good illustration of this approach in many respects.[46] He argues that Africans tend to despise their culture more than any other group of peoples in the world. This is lamentable since communities result from human ingenuity. "Communities are created not given." Hence people must depend on their culture to find the knowledge needed for the creation of a community. Sindima is convinced that African cultures are capable of providing this

---

[46] H. J. Sindima, Religious and Political Ethics in Africa. A Moral Inquiry (London: Greenwood Press, 1998).

knowledge by way of symbols.[47] These symbols should be made the basis of a political ethic in Africa since an ethic is able to empower a people only when it draws directly on "what informs a people's way of life together.... True African political ethics, therefore, will have to be based on African concepts of the world and not on some borrowed concepts from outside Africa."[48]

From this African perspective, Sindima understands politics not as governance (which connotes the idea that politics is the business of a selected few) but as a conglomerate of ideas, meanings and behavioral patterns which enable people to live together. Besides the fact that religion (like other institutions of society) can influence community life and so has its role in politics, Sindima is of the opinion that politics as an "art" of living together is itself a spirituality.[49] He refers to the example of chieftancy among the Akan of Ghana, basing himself on the work of Pobee, to illustrate the ethical and religious implications of political authority. Sindima continues his discussion by drawing on two fundamental symbols *moyo* (life, in its universal cosmic meanings), and *munthu* (human life, or the prototype of all life) of the Malawi to postulate an essentially African political ethics. The discussion is completed by relating the symbols *moyo* and *munthu* to biblical and Christian interpretation in order to establish the relation between African values and Christianity and to define the moral obligation that befalls African Christians in politics.[50]

Sindima displays a good understanding of African concepts about the good and about ethics in general. His awareness of the value of indigenous African traditions with regard to community life and leadership are necessary for engaging meaningfully in an inculturation ethic. Especially the distinction he makes between politics and governance in the African perspective, and his attempt to relate the underlying symbols of community living to a Christian hermeneutic contribute greatly in furthering the discussion on ethics and inculturation. Despite these positive elements, Sindima's approach presumes the fundamental question, which, as has been argued in chapter three of this study, may not be overlooked in inculturation ethics. Given that there are such valuable symbols and systems of leadership in the African culture, why do they not function? It seems that we cannot continue to use indigenous traditions alone as a starting point for theorizing about African morality in general or political ethics in particular without begging the question. This view does not deny the value of African moral traditions but points to the fact that traditions, like laws or norms are often lifeless by themselves, unless they are enabled (made *dynamic* in the Greek sense of the word) by their bearers.

---

[47] Sindima, Religious and Political Ethics, pp. 167-168.
[48] Sindima, Religious and Political Ethics, p. 169.
[49] Sindima, Religious and Political Ethics, p. 169.
[50] Sindima, Religious and Political Ethics, pp. 171-176.

Another weakness of the authenticity approach is the fact that human beings are not only cultural. They are also institutional, in consequence of their sociality. Human beings are historical; they live on their past experiences and project into the future, but they are also bound to the limits of time. Human beings yearn to maximize their humanness not only by way of sharing life together, but also by working on their environment together and using the things of the world for their survival and improvement. They make use of new developments in science and technology to facilitate this cultivation of their natural milieu, and they share the fruits of their labor together. Thus besides the aspect of community living (together), co-existence, which Sindima quite rightly proposes as a grounding principle for political ethics, there are the other aspects of co-operation and co-participation.[51] To these should be added the aspect of ambiguity that characterizes human actions, making people in a community have different interests and priorities.

In Africa especially, political activity must consider the multiplicity of cultural groups, language and ethnic groups, religious affiliations and attitudes. Finally, human beings are not just spiritual, they are also conscious beings. African cultural history makes a consideration of the cultural psychology a *conditio sine qua non* in an ethic of inculturation.[52] Since some of these points are taken up later, we shall now turn briefly to the second approach used in analyzing the problem of political leadership in Africa.

4.4.2 The Responsibility Approach

This approach is related to the authenticity approach in respect of the appeal it makes to culture or to African communities in trying to analyze the socio-political problems of Africa. In contrast to the authenticity approach, however, the responsibility approach would seem to doubt that African cultures have anything good to offer for the advancement of African peoples. In some cases specific evils are attributed to African cultures particularly. But the basic argument of this approach is that the problems Africans face is a result of their irresponsibility and lack of sound moral systems to support their attempts at social organization. Africans are therefore told almost scornfully to stop blaming the outsider, do their home work and put their house in order. This for example is the approach of O'Donohue, referred to mostly in chapter two of this study. A recent essay that marks similar sentiments is the article of Richard Dowden, entitled, "What's wrong with Africa?"[53] There are striking

---

[51] See chapter one of this study, where the ideas of Janssens concerning the adequate consideration of the human person are discussed.
[52] See chapter one, especially the section on the existentialist model of inculturation.
[53] Dowden, 'What's Wrong with Africa', pp. 72-73.

similarities of thought between this essay and the views of O'Donohue. Dowden gives the impression that there is a special tendency in African communities for people to operate in matters concerning the state on the principle of "the winner takes all." He argues that leadership problems stem from or at least relate closely to the nature and culture of African societies: "I used to think that Africa was simply unlucky; wonderful people, terrible leaders. But then it began to occur to me that it could not be coincidence that so many of Africa's leaders were so bad all at the same time... The people may not quite get the rulers they deserve, but there must be a connection between the rulers and the ruled."[54]

It has been explained (see chapter two) that if this type of argument is to be understand as a plea for the consideration of the current political situation first and foremost from an intra-cultural perspective, then the plea is legitimate. But the manner in which this plea is made is rather ineffectual for engaging meaningfully in dialogue with Africans. Communication is obstructed because the responsibility approach tends to use the old categories that perniciously apply a synchronic and an ahistorical consideration of African peoples. Dowden portrays this inattentiveness to history when he says: "Each African country is very different, but common to all is an attitude to politics which begins and ends with power and wealth. Doesn't it in every nation? But in Africa there is nothing else."[55] To say that there is nothing else in African politics but the search for wealth and power explains little about the complex levels of relations and historical facts about African peoples as well as other peoples in the world. Instead such a statement betrays the tendency to use the long term effects of the traumatic experiences of Africans in history to judge, *a fortiori,* the moral constitution of African peoples. This procedure is worrisome and damaging to the self-image of Africans. One way of avoiding these unsuitable aspects of the responsibility approach would be to consider the problem integrally. Dowden would seem to accept implicitly such an integral analysis of the situation since he attempts to relate the African situation to given international conditions in which he sees a certain connection between "African societies and Africa's artificial nation-states and between those nation-states and the rest of the world."[56]

Paying attention to the connections between African societies, their history and the processes leading to the creation of modern nation-states in Africa, the role of the international community in shaping these nation-states politically, economically and technologically is a more resourceful approach to the problem of political leadership in Africa. Attending to these various

---

[54] Dowden, 'What is Wrong with Africa', p. 72; compare O'Donohue, New Wine and Old Bottles, pp. 151-156; see also earlier references to the same author in chapter two of this study.
[55] Dowden, 'What's Wrong with Africa', p. 73.
[56] Dowden, 'What's Wrong with Africa', p. 73.

aspects will prevent us from satisfying ourselves with some form of pre-judgmental kit of recipes for converting African cultures from their failings.[57] From a personalist perspective, inculturation ethics must show awareness of the complex issues involved in African politics. For instance, what are the effects of attempting to form democracies in Africa, and what is the period allowed for the maturation of such a political system, if it should function adequately in communities that lacked previous traditions to support a democratic system of politics? What is the caliber of people who qualify to hold political office and what are their inner dispositions to public office regarding the colonial foundations of current systems of politics in Africa? We can continue to add many more questions. Briefly put, many of the reservations expressed concerning the authenticity approach apply in the case of the responsibility approach also. The basic claim of a personalist criterion for doing ethics is that an African political ethic will be useful if it succeeds in helping Africans to study themselves in as much as they are conscious, attending to the operations of the various levels of their consciousness and seeking to understand how these levels relate, not in opposition to a world community to which they do not belong, but as a result of belonging to such a community. Africans must seek to understand themselves and their problems not apart from the world, but as part of the world.[58] We shall now try to analyze the problem of political leadership in Africa, applying a more integral consideration of the situation.

4.5 Reviewing the Problem of Leadership in Africa Today in the Light of the Personalist Criterion

The structures of public office in their current form in Africa are directly traceable to the colonial machinery. From the onset public office was strictly the reserve of the colonial master. The purpose of the colonial master however was not to serve the Africans but to rule and lord it over them.[59] The poorer

---

[57] See chapter one of this study, pp. 46 & 47; W. Bühlmann, The Coming of the third Church (London: 1976), pp. 300ff.

[58] Compare B. Lonergan, The Aquinas Lecture for 1968, delivered March 3, 1968 (Marquette University: Wisconsin-Alpha Chapter of Phi Sigma Tau: 1968), in: B. Lonergan, A Second Collection, pp. 69-86, here p. 73.

[59] Compare O'Donohue, New Wine and Old Bottles, pp. 150ff. O'Donohue believes that "Modern Africa has preserved the appearance of government as service, inherited from the colonial era, but it has really returned to the traditional formula of government as negative and repressive power" (p. 152). A few paragraphs before the one just quoted O'Donohue discourses: "How, we may now ask, did Africa conceive of the positive functions of government? There can be only one answer: it hardly conceived of them at all" (p. 151). It beats any stretch of imagination to understand how Africans could have inherited

and deprived the African looked, the more he or she resembled the picture of the "Niger" in the colonial master's fantasy.[60] If the African ever dared to step in the office of the colonial authorities, it was to ask for "favors" and not to demand service. And the colonial master was in no way accountable to the African over whom he ruled. This conception of public office as the position of the "boss" whose role was to have pity on the poor African masses, even while living off the sweat and labor of the same masses would seem to have become an indelible stamp on the minds of many an African. Many Africans in public office including the clergy would seem to operate sub-consciously from this image of the "boss". Hence whereas Africans have reason to complain about *neo-colonialism*, they must in many instances take responsibility for being their own *neo-colonial masters*.[61]

The average Ghanaian would identify this 'colonial' attitude on all levels of civil service in the country in contemporary times. The attitude would be recognized by the school boy who asks to buy a few stamps at the post office, the pedestrian who seeks help from a police officer, the illiterate mother who seeks audience with the school teacher, the village teacher who visits the bank and seeks to withdraw his or her own money, the patient before the nurse, let alone the doctor, the customer who seeks help from his or her insurance company and even the customer who purchases from a sales girl in a shop. In each of these cases, the one seeking service cannot help leaving with the feeling of having had to wait on the mercy of those who have to serve him or her. And yet there is a biting irony about the situation since these workers, in their various capacities, are described as *civil servants*![62]

This orientation to public office becomes more overt when the economic situation gets tougher. The one at the receiving end must really endeavor (probably by *greasing the palms* in Ghanaian jargon) to court the "favors" of the civil servant, or perhaps better to say the civil-boss, in order to obtain the requisite attention. Could it be that this disposition already bears the seed of corruption?

'government as service' from the colonial era!

[60] Compare A. Césaire, Discourse on Colonialism, translated from the French by J. Pinkham, (New York: Monthly Review Press, 1972).

[61] See B. Bujo, African Theology in its Social Context (Düsseldorf: Patmos Verlag GmbH, 1986), pp. 54-55, here find reference to A. Césaire, Une Saison au Congo (Paris: 1966). See also A. Césaire, Discourse on Colonialism.

[62] Many are the Ghanaians who tell stories of how they approached civil and government officials with trembling and fear, especially in the period soon after independence. My own mother tells me several stories of how she was mishandled, disgraced and left unaided on the many occasions she had to bring me to the hospital. The hospital staff was usually Ghanaian - "black Ghanaian men and women, wearing snow white dresses and shoes", my mother would say. She would usually end her story by saying, "I feared them, because they always embarrassed me."

A second attitude, directly related to the one above, is the difficulty people have in identifying with the government in Africa. The government is often conceived of in the very dichotomous categories on which colonialism flourished. Gyekye has aptly illustrated the point using the situation in Ghana as an example. Gyekye refers to the Akan maxim which says: "We do not carry the government on our heads; we drag it on the floor" (*aban womfa unsoa, wotwe no daadzie*) and explains that many Ghanaians see the Government as "them" different from "us". Gyekye explains: "The maxim has negative implications and consequences: it could whittle down the commitment of public officials to matters of state -including state property; it is a mandate for regarding public or governmental matters as inconsequential, as maters not worthy of great care or attention or respect; it is a sure recipe not only for political and administrative indolence but also corruption and irresponsibility."[63]

The attitudes described above, would seem to slither through the operations of many Africans in their daily commerce with each other, and with the world. But the experience is so subtle that even while many consciously demur such attitudes, the *master-servant* orientation to public office has remained a lingering colonial disposition '*acculturated*' and '*enculturated*' by many Africans. If we take the human constitution seriously, it is difficult to hold that such an orientation would lend itself easily to cure by sporadic and unrelated eruptions of protest from individuals or groups. It also looks too simplistic to believe that these attitudes would die out as a matter of course since Africans hate colonialism. For acculturation and enculturation (even when that in this case means the borrowing and learning of certain traits as a result of culture domination), confirm the fact that human beings are animals of habit,[64] and habits die hard.[65]

As Tönnies explains, what we do in the form of habit is always first learnt through repeated practice. Habit paves the way for desire and overcomes any oppositions and frictions. Habit belongs to the nature of evil or burden (as in the case of the colonial mentality) as well as to the nature of virtue (as in the case of justice and respect for human dignity).[66] In the Greek tradition, Aristotle showed his conviction about the power of practice when he

---

[63] Gyekye, Political Corruption, p. 6.

[64] See Berger and Luckmann, The Social Construction of Reality (London: Anchor Books, 1966); F. Tönnies, Die Sitte (Frankfurt am Main: Rütten & Loening, 1909).

[65] For much of what is discussed in this chapter on the attitudes of Africans to public office (and to certain values in general) resulting partly from the experiences of domination and humiliation in history, a critical reading of the work of Gustav Jehoda might provide a good starting point. His research, however, was limited to Ghana, and one would have to be cautious not to extend his findings arbitrarily to other African countries. See G. Jehoda, White Man. A Study of the Attitudes of Africans to Europeans in Ghana before Independence (London: Oxford University Press, 1961).

[66] Tönnies, Die Sitte, pp. 1-13.

proposed the actual repetition of moral operations as the best method for moral training.[67]

It looks reasonable, from the above analysis, to surmise that in many instances the actual completion of a given operation by many Africans who hold public office flows from a certain disposition that is often sub-conscious as a result of long years of practice. What is worse, habit especially in its form as 'burden' (bad habit) is also experienced as an inner tyrannical force, a 'passion'.[68] In that state habit could even take the place of the will, and become a relentless force and master that must be obeyed. Long years of humiliation must have robbed Africans not only of what they have, but what they are.[69] Could it be that this inner burden of humiliation accounts to a great extent for the spiral of tyranny, a passionate continuation of self-humiliation (call it habitual self-humiliation, if you will) experienced on the African political scene? Could it be that the tragic procedures of African leaders are themselves a desperate cry for a liberation from an inner experience of the tyranny of humiliation? In order to see how these questions concretely apply to African leaders, it will be helpful to turn our attention now to some examples. We shall apply the personalist criterion in three perspectives: the subjective, objective and contextual principles, drawing on the methods of Janssens and Komonchack as worked out in chapter three.

4.5.1 Subjective Principle: Who Becomes a Leader in Africa?

Two main forces inadvertently contributed to the creation of political leaders in Africa in the period leading to independence and thereafter. These were the colonial governments and the missions. Both depended on Western education for the attainment of their respective aims in the colonies. For the colonialist, education in Africa was to create a reservoir of qualified indigenous Africans for the use of the colonial government. For the Christian missionaries on the other hand, education was to serve as a means of evangelization and to hasten the growth of the church. However these Western trained Africans became potential nationalists who finally challenged colonial presence in Africa. Due to the fact that both colonial governments and Christian missions were using

---

[67] Aristotle, Nichomachean Ethics, translated with an Introduction by D. Ross (London: Oxford University Press, 1954, first published 1925). There are in Ghana several proverbs that underscore the same lesson about the effects of practice. The Ewes for instance say, "Zâ si mebua nu gbo mo o." This means the hand does not miss its way to the mouth even in the dark (as a result of regular practice). See N. K. Dzobo, African Proverbs: Guide to Conduct. The Moral Value of Ewe Proverbs (Cape Coast: Cape Coast University Press, 1973), p. 60.
[68] Tönnies, Die Sitte, pp. 9-10.
[69] See F. Fanon, The Wretched of the Earth (New York: 1968), pp. 212ff.

the same means of education for their purposes, "sometimes it was touch-and-go whether a particular educated African became a priest or a politician."[70] There is the example of Nkrumah who seriously considered the possibility of becoming a priest and even studied theology in the United States. Nkrumah later embraced the gospel of Pan-Africanism and African Liberation and so became the first president of Ghana.[71] Some African leaders did actually combine both religious and political leadership. Busia was the president of the second republic of Ghana and maintained an active Christian life as a Methodist preacher. Like Busia, C. Banana was both president of his country and an ordained minister.[72]

Another group of professionals that seems to have taken on political responsibility at the wake of independence and thereafter were teachers. Mazrui confirms that by the 1960s, the number of politicians with experience in teaching was striking. In Ghana and Nigeria about 30% of legislature were teachers. Mazrui refers to an observer who attributed the situation to the fact that primary school teachers had a high position in the bush village and therefore were placed on a high social standing and had great influence. "The high prestige inherent in the new western style secular education, as well as the prerequisite of the English language for national political career, converted teachers into highly eligible parliamentarians."[73] The influence and prestige of politics established in the 1940s and 50s made politics become a career dream for many young Africans.

By and large, Western education was the only way Africans could become a part of the political machinery and the tool for political influence was oratory. The Western trained elite now constituted the social group from which African leaders grew. This group did not succeed, however, in initiating a smooth transition from the older indigenous forms of leadership to the new forms of the modern state. Rather the elite became an institution that run parallel to the existing institutions of leadership in Africa. Mazrui observes that this situation affected "a much wider range of social variables."[74] In short there ensued a certain disharmony in the functioning of many African communities.

---

[70] A. Mazrui, Political Values and the Educated Class, p. 1.
[71] Mazrui, Political Values and the Educated Class, p. 2.
[72] Caanan Banana was a Methodist Minister and theology professor until 1980 when he became the first ceremonial president of Zimbabwe after the country obtained independence in 1980. He combined his ministry with his post as President from 1980 until 1987. Following his conviction and subsequent sentencing for homosexual assault in the later part of 1998 and early part of 1999, his Church relieved him of his ministerial status. See 'The Chronicle' (Bulaw, Zimbabwe: 18th December, 1998).
[73] J. H. Price, West Africa, 26 May, 1956, p. 325; Coleman, Politics of Developing Areas, p. 341-2, in: Mazrui, Political Values, p. 4.
[74] Mazrui, Political Values, p. 16.

Beside the Western educated elite is the military whose appearance on the political scene has led to disastrous consequences in African politics. Mazrui observes that unlike the Western trained elite model which was an innovation in African political organization, the involvement of the military in politics is based on the "warrior-leader" model, which is an older phenomenon in Africa. There were many African societies without any writing at all. But there was hardly any without some form of military experience. Defense of the tribe was an important concern. "The warrior complete with initiation which went towards producing such a fighter, featured prominently in the organization of African political life."[75] This type of leadership, however, operated in its context and time in correspondence to needs of the people.

In contrast to this old warrior-leader model, when the new warriors (the military) sought to replace the educated elite on the political scene, many African countries were faced with a problem because the new warriors were themselves a colonial creation which did not directly serve the situation of Africa. Colonial policy tended more to inscribe the illiterate or less educated rural folk into the army in order to ascertain total loyalty and control. Thus when they took up power they lacked both the wisdom that was part of the training of the pre-colonial African warrior and the pen and oratory of the post-colonial African nationalist.[76]

As Abdulai observes, in the wake of independence many of the men in the armies of African nations were non-commissioned offices.[77] It was the new African leaders that elevated the soldiers to the officer class. Nkrumah, for instance, boasts of having reorganized the army and the navy from the scratch. He writes: "I know, that there are many in my armed forces who are loyal to me ... I should know this, because the Ghana Armed Forces is my own creation. I reorganised [sic] the Army myself, founded the Ghana Air Force, and established the Navy from the scratch." [78] Lumumba also promoted a number of Congolese non-commissioned officers to the officer class when he became Prime Minister of the Congo in June 1960. Similar moves were made by other African leaders, as was the case in Rwanda, Burundi, Uganda and Central African Republic.[79]

In many of these cases, these presidents found themselves overthrown by the new military officers they had created. Kotoka removed Nkrumah from power in Ghana; Idi Amin ended the Obote regime in Uganda and Mobutu brought the Lumumba era to an end in the Congo. A recent example of the caliber of leadership of these new warriors in Africa was the Abacha regime

---

[75] Mazrui, Political Values, p. 15.
[76] Mazrui, Political Values, p. 16.
[77] N. Abdulai, "Background to the Crisis [in the Congo] (I)", in: West Africa, 31 March - 6 April 1997, p. 506.
[78] K. Nkrumah, Voice from Conakry (London: Panaf Books Ltd., 1967), p. 6.
[79] Abdulai, 'Background to the Crisis (I)', p. 506.

in Nigeria. Abdulai quotes Yoweri Museveni of Uganda as saying that these new military officers were "just a colonial levy of riflemen with a low level of education and literacy."[80] Thus these new warrior-leaders were disposed to nothing else but share force and brutality in their bid to secure and legitimize their authority.

4.5.2 Objective Principles: What Justifies Leadership Authoritatively?

The caliber and disposition of the people who become leaders in Africa is just one (the subjective) aspect of the general principle[81] for normatively evaluating leadership as a moral value. There is also the objective aspect, i.e. those elements commonly accepted by the community, which justify the position of the leader authoritatively. These points of common consensus constitute the mediated sources of the leader's authority in the community. As we saw earlier, sources of authority may be codified into a legal system, or operate on a system of intra-communal relations sealed by bonds of kinship expressed in religious symbolism and practice. In both ways the intention is basically the provision of objective instances from which political action is authoritatively evaluated and justified. Here, we may remind ourselves of Komonchak's ideas on the objective principles which together with the subjective form the generative principles for moral discernment and action.[82] In the case of fundamental Christian morality, such objective principles are Scripture, moral traditions, examples of person and action. These constitute culturally, historically and contextually mediated points of reference. Together with the individual Christian as an originating value, they constitute the principles that generate moral discernment. In the case of a political ethic, objective principles would include an accepted legal code, say a constitution in the case of democracies, or kinship ties, ancestors, stools and tradition in the case of chiefdoms. The individual leader is able to act appropriately in so far as he or she correlates with these common points of consensus. These objective principles do not only influence his political discernment, they also legitimize his actions and make them authoritatively binding.

On this level of objective principles also there are problems in contemporary Africa. It would seem that many African leaders find themselves before multiple possibilities, some of which contradict each other,

---

[80] Abdulai, 'Background to the Crisis (I)', p. 506.
[81] Recall the methods of Janssens and Komonchak respectively. See chapter three of this study, sections 3.2.1 to 3.2.4.
[82] The ideas of Komonchak have been represented in chapter three, section 3.2.1 of this study.

as a result of the multiple African heritage.[83] It is difficult to determine when African leaders seek legitimization as indigenous chiefs or as Western democrats or as Islamic religio-political leaders. It is highly probable that part of the problem of leadership in Africa lies in the difficulty of integrating these multiple systems for engaging in political activity in Africa. Often all three sources (the indigenous, Arabic and Western) are manipulated or abused for the personal purposes of the leader concerned. Let us take the example of the use of royalty and liberationist propaganda in the regimes of some African leaders to illustrate the point.

4.5.2.1 Royalty as a Source of Political Authority

The use of royalty by African leaders as a source of authority in modern politics in Africa is illustrative of this problem. Pobee demonstrates this craving on the part of African leaders in the case of Nkrumah. Pobee informs us that Nkrumah actually got himself made Tufunhene of Nkroful and 'enstooled' Chief of Nsuem on the 7th of April 1962 in succession to Nana Adu Kwadaa.[84] It is said that Nkrumah literally followed the indigenous ceremony of the 'enstoolment' of chiefs when he became the first president of the Republic of Ghana in 1960.[85] Nkrumah's titles and honorific appellations were: 'His High Dedication, the Osagyefo Dr. Kwame Nkrumah, Kokoduruni, Kantamanto, Oyeadieyie, Osuodumgya, Kasapreko, Abrofusuro, Asomdwehene'.[86] Drawing on royalty for political authority also provides part of the background for understanding the whole complex phenomenon of the 'one-party system' and 'life presidency' in African politics. One sees a close connection to the local axiom that the institution of chieftaincy never dies. The same nostalgia for royalty lies behind the Nkrumahist motto: "Nkrumah never dies" and the so-called cult of Nkrumah.[87]

Similarly, the 1961 amendment of the criminal code was aimed at actually consolidating the president as a glorified chief. By that amendment it became an offence to undertake any activity that created hatred, disrepute or ridicule for the president. Mr. A. Ofori Atta, then minister of Justice said: "the Head of State of Ghana is a sacred person, irrespective of the party to which

---

[83] See chapter two of this study on Mazrui and 'the triple heritage' of Africa. With direct reference to the theology of Incarnation, Mudimbe speaks of African, Muslim and Euripean heritage, closely related to Mazrui's idea modell the indigenous, the Arabic and Western heritage. See V. Y. Mudimbe, The Invention of Africa (Bloomington and Indianapolis: Indiana University Press, 1988), pp. 59ff.
[84] Pobee, Religion and Politics, p. 31.
[85] Pobee, Religion and Politics, p. 32.
[86] Pobee, Religion and Politics, p. 31.
[87] Pobee, Religion and Politics, p. 32.

he belongs".[88] Anyone conversant with the traditional chieftancy system would recognize this maneuver for its inherent reference to the local rubrics of chieftancy.

Like Nkrumah, Mobutu began a nationalist rhetoric in 1972 under the ideology of "authenticity". This later became "Mobutuism" and "the president renamed himself Mobutu Sese Seko Kuku Ngbendu wa Zabanga."[89] His honorary titles were: "president-founder of the Party, president of the Republic, commander in chief of the armed forces." Mobutu also had a personality cult like Nkrumah. The media presented Mobutu as the "Father of the Nation, the Helmsman and the Messiah."[90] In several instances it was clear that Mobutu saw himself as a great King and father of the nation, upon whom all must depended for their life. He did not only pose as a chief to whom the whole wealth of the community belonged symbolically, but actually took possession of the wealth of the nation, making no difference between public and private property.[91] Is it possible that African politicians become autocratic because they wish to gain by sheer force of power the respect and high degree of legitimacy which local chiefs enjoyed as a matter of course?

The use of royalty as a source of authority in the contemporary political machinery in Africa, however, can be nothing but a mask. The pose of royalty by African leaders lacks the internal sanctity that it had in the local setting. For several reasons (which cannot be treated here) chieftancy has been supplanted and in its place the legal system of political authority planted.[92] In order to fill in the vacuum the rule of force instead of the force of law is applied. This was the case of the 1961 amendment of the criminal code that more or less sacralized the president and promulgation of the preventive detention act under Nkrumah. Parallel practices could be found in the history of Mobutu's regime. Pobee rightly concludes: "What African leaders do not have by birth or through a sacral role they contrive through a whole extensive machinery to achieve."[93]

By consolidating their cravings for spontaneous and absolute acceptance from their communities, while using the rule of force, the relational effect of the leadership activities of African leaders ends up in the total subjugation of

---

[88] Cited in Pobee, Religion and Politics, p. 32.
[89] Abdulai, 'Background to the crisis', p. 507.
[90] A. Zarembo and M. Mabry, "Mobutu's Legacy", in Newsweek, Vol. CXXIX, No. 21 (New York: Newsweek Inc., May 26 1997), p. 4. This article explains Mobutu's name, "Sese Seko Kuku Mgbendu wa za Banga", to mean "the all-powerful warrior who, because of his endurance and inflexible will to win, will go from conquest to conquest leaving fire in his wake" (same article, p. 4). Abdulai on his part explains the same name to mean "the cockerel who jumps on all the chickens in the farmyard" (Abdulai, 'Background to the Crisis', p. 507).
[91] See Dowden, 'What's Wrong with Africa'.
[92] See Pobee, Religion and Politics, pp. 24ff.
[93] Pobee, Religion and Politics, p. 32.

their communities. For even where the people feel displeased about their leader, they have no way of removing him from office because they are intimidated through the means available to the leader. Even in cases where the leaders operate by the force of law the results are usually not different. In the case of the rule of force the community is powerless before the army. In the case of the force of law, the community is still powerless because of the high percentage of illiteracy.

In the local system "the chief was bound by custom to act only with the concurrence and on the advice of his council. If he acted arbitrarily, without consultation and approval of his counsel he could be deposed. That was one way in which the chief's powers were curbed. ... Those who elected the chief also had the power to depose him if he did not perform the duties of his office satisfactorily."[94] In contemporary politics however the leader tends to have a council which exists only in name. In a sense it is difficult not to see in many an African leader the portrait of the colonial administrator to whom all "natives" were responsible, who however was responsible to no one within the colonial territory, at least not to the "natives"!

4.5.2.2 Liberationist Propaganda as a Source of Political Authority

Besides royalty, many African leaders assume power feeling that they have a liberator's vocation, an ideology also branded as a reason for the legitimacy of authority. Many style their governments with strong tendencies of political Messiahnism, and some even adopt overt (Christian?) religious overtones. In Ghana, Nkrumah posed as the Messiah of the people. In the wake of the military *"take-overs"*, governments were formed under captions such as National *Liberation* Council, and National *Redemption* Council. At the peak of his revolution, Rawlings was sometimes referred to as "Junior Jesus".[95] Many of these leaders feel called to lead the African to authenticity, self-reliance, political rectitude and accountability. Yet some of these leaders seem to reveal an inner confusion about their own subjective states in relation to this avowed political vocation.

The example of Mobutu is once again fitting. In the wake of his ideology of authenticity, he abrogated the use of European names and enforced a particular style of dress. He lashed out against Westernization and preached Africanization. At the same time Mobutu would seem to have been far from accepting himself as an African. He robbed his country to purchase Villas in Europe, a sign of his own nostalgia for, and a subtle but real attraction to, the Western heritage. In Mobutu, we probably had a bundle of a

---

[94] Busia, The Position of the Chief, p. 47, in: Pobee, Religion and Politics, p. 47.
[95] See Assimeng, Religion and Social Change.

warrior, a fictive chief, a Westerner, a politician after the style of the rule of force, all combined in the same and one African personality.

4.5.3 The Contextual Principle: Where do African Leaders Operate?

Generative principles operate in a given context. They are manifested concretely in a given world and relate to the moral actions that they produce in and through their given context. Simply put, generative principles are mediated realities bound to a history and a context. The context in which African leaders have to operate is therefore an important element that must be considered when we try to understand the problem of leadership in Africa. Much of the context has been described at various sections of this study, but it is useful to sketch once more some of the important aspects so as to collate the individual points scattered at different places into a unified whole.

African communities are in transition, religiously, socially, culturally, economically, scientifically and technologically. Besides the factor of transition is that of plurality. Pluralism in Africa is not an idea, it is a daily reality. Interests are as many and varied as there are interest groups. There are numerous languages, language groups and ethnic groups. Different religious attitudes abound, and the extent to which religion influences socio-political life varies.

The African context is also characterized by the fact that African communities are still battling for the basic equality of all human persons. They have to work to convince the international community about the common vocation of all human beings, and the fact that all share the same origins and destiny. But the ever increasing dependency of African nations on the rich nations makes the attainment of this goal rather laborious. Dependency in turn disposes African communities to international manipulation. The role of some Western nations in the "creation" of leaders in Africa may not be underestimated.

There is also the aspect of poverty, disease and illiteracy. These conditions make it difficult for many Africans to be directly involved in politics. Although it is proper to say that all are leaders in a society that functions well, for many African peoples, this axiom is only partly true. Few are properly informed about their own rights and duties, let alone the institutions of governance. This lack of shared knowledge about political life is itself a potential source of abuse of power and social dysfunction.

Paradoxically, however, there are also many positive aspects to the context in which African leaders have to operate.[96] The African continent is

---

[96] See A. Mazrui, The African Condition: A Political Diagnosis (London: Cambridge University Press, 1980).

geographically central and has all the chances to influence international politics. The continent has human and natural resources, it has rich cultural and religious traditions, a point that has been reiterated by many scholars. The community spirit found among many African peoples is a valuable potential for political initiative in the search for social cohesion, the distribution of goods and responsibilities and for sustaining political systems based more on consensus than on force.

By applying these three principles of "subjectivity", "objectivity" and context, the horizons for evaluating the problem of leadership have been extended beyond the popular manner in which this evaluation is undertaken. It cannot be said, however, that the personalist criterion, based on the adequate consideration of the human person has been exhaustively applied to study the problem of political leadership in Africa. What the attempt has achieved is the presentation of an alternative approach. The application of the personalist criterion shows that good African traditions alone do not suffice as a solution at all levels of the problem. But the personalist criterion also shows that rashly dismissing African cultures will not achieve much. An exaggerated concentration on culture, one way or the other might end up in the already existing spiral of resignation and frustration. It takes more than culture and responsibility to be human and to act morally. Human beings are more complex and so are human moral problems. We shall conclude the chapter by considering the concrete contribution that an inculturation ethic can make with regard to the problems we have studied in these paragraphs.

4.6 The concrete contribution of Inculturation ethics

Christianity concerns our response to God's gift of himself to us in Jesus. It is also about the way he empowers us through the gift of his Spirit in our attempts to respond to his love. Jesus made this love concrete in his person and through his words and actions. Central to Jesus' actions and proclamation is the establishment of the Kingdom of God and its ultimate realization as the fulfillment of God's love in and for us.

The Kingdom of God, however is no utopia. It concerns human history in all its aspects. In the light of the Person of Jesus and in his proclamation we are able to see the evil in human history. Through our faith in the incarnation and in the passion, death and resurrection of Jesus, we realize that we have to be open to God's own solution in the face of our own impotence in many respects. But our faith in Jesus also challenges us to take human agency in the unfolding of human history seriously. We must take ourselves and our history just as seriously as God takes us seriously and draws us to himself in Jesus. Agency in this sense is not to be understood just to mean responsible actors, but also knowing subjects, conscious-selves. The contribution of inculturation ethics will depend very much on its ability to support these two aspects of human openness to God and human agency in the life of African Christians. By emphasizing openness to God and human agency, inculturation ethics, as part of Christian ethics in general points to the fact that the solution to the evil in the world implies our attainment of fullness of humanness by being drawn into the person of Jesus. Morality has to do with humanization and humanization has all to gain from the incarnation of Jesus.

In view of the aspects of openness to God and human agency, inculturation ethics can help the African Church to become the 'community of narrative' in which Africans find room and attention to tell and celebrate their own story whenever they enact the story of Jesus. In order to heal the spiral of humiliation, resulting from alienation (the state of amnesia) in the conventional narrative, the African Church must endeavor to relate the eucharistic "re-membering" of the Jesus story to a concrete theology of anamnesis that heals the African of his or her amnesia.[97]

Inculturation ethics would achieve much by enabling Africans to remember, and to integrate their memory consciously in their daily choices and actions. As mentioned earlier, no one can narrate who cannot remember. In this connection inculturation ethics can make a major contribution by challenging African Christians to take the "do this in memory of me" as seriously as they can.[98] Africans cannot claim to be the memorial community of Jesus, if remembering the Jesus event does not yield in the remembrance of themselves and their concrete history.

Rather than describe African moral systems, or seek to formulate new moral norms, inculturation ethics demands from the African Church to take Africans seriously and make their experiences the imperative that determines the moral operations of African Christians. The African Church must become conscious of the history that has brought Africans to this point and insist that this history is not like a dress that Africans once tried to see if it fits, which they have since put down.[99]

What the Church needs in order to reflect on moral issues relating directly to Christian communities in Africa is a method that allows for an analysis of the dispositions of African Christians as a result of their experiences in history. Inculturation ethics could assist the church in this regard by developing possibilities which help the church to communicate with the modes of self-knowing and self-evaluation of African peoples. Such possibilities would help to interpret behavior not on the bases of abstract

---

[97] See Bujo, Die ethische Dimension der Gemeinschaft, p. 131; J. B. Metz, Glaube in Geschichte und Gesellschaft. Studien zu einer praktischen Fundamentaltheologie, (Mainz:1992).

[98] Compare Bujo, Die ethische Dimension der Gemeinschaft, pp. 131, 191ff.

[99] Compare M. Frisch, Mein Name sei Gantenbein (Frankfurt am Main: Suhrkamp, 1964).

norms, but on the basis of the dignity of humanness revealed in the incarnation of Jesus. In working out such possibilities inculturation ethics would draw on already existing values and relate them to the specific state of African communities.[100] What might be new in the development of such possibilities would probably not be the content of morality as such, but the methods of interpretation.[101] Briefly put, within the African Church, the basic contribution of inculturation ethics would be an uncompromising call to self-awareness.[102]

Leadership does not arise in a vacuum; it arises to meet a 'situation'…a subjective and cultural interpretation of objective experiences of people.[103] As such communities usually develop systems of leadership arising from their specific cultural resources. These resources are themselves influenced by the situations of the communities in question. With regard to leadership, inculturation ethics demands from African Christians to initiate the process of liberation from the spiral of humiliation. This initiative will not depend on some blueprint external to the experience of African Christians. The African Church is in the best position to know that the evangelizing Church could quickly become the colonizing Church. African Christians and especially leaders of the African church can draw on their own experiences to adopt appropriate forms of leadership which help to free the African will, the African heart, and the African soul from the spiral of habitual humiliation.[104]

A painful tragedy that can befall the African Church is for her leaders themselves to perpetuate a 'colonial disposition'. The Christian leadership of African clergy may not supplant the importance of indigenous leaders. They may not adopt approaches to leadership which run parallel to or sidestep the existing leaders in the local communities of which they are pastors.

Inculturation ethics can also contribute by pointing out those aspects of leadership which hinder the ultimate good of African communities. It belongs to the Christian vocation to denounce evil and to demand a spirit of perseverance in the effort to do good. It is in place for the church to raise her voice against the social and political evils that afflict the continent. This is regularly done through the letters of the conferences of bishops and other church institutions. These letters, however, tend often to address crisis or conflict situations. But this prophetic task may not be reduced to a kind of crisis management. Instead inculturation ethics must seek out those elements, situations and challenges that induce a feeling of insecurity and lack of self confidence in African leaders. This failure to trust in their own competence, their search for acceptance and legitimacy are partly responsible for the use of

---

[100] See Bujo, African Christian Morality, p. 71.
[101] See Tracy, Plurality and Ambiguity, p. 8; see also this study, chapter two, pp. 35ff.
[102] See earlier reference to Ela, My Faith as an African, p. xvi.
[103] Compare M.-F. Jassy, Leadership, p. 4; cited in Hevi, Indigenous Leadership, p. 255.
[104] Compare earlier reference to Sarah, 'Den aufrechten Gang finden', p. 248. See also Hevi, Indigenous Leadership, pp. 332ff.

force, inappropriate acquisition of wealth and intolerance for any form of opposition or political difference. In view of the challenges facing many African leaders, it is important for the church to discover ways of ministering to, assisting and reassuring African leaders in the discharge of their daily responsibilities. This service to people in public office is more effective if it is provided before crises develop. The exhortative (*paranesis*) aspects of the church's prophetic duty remain very closely linked to the advocative, encouraging and strengthening (*paraclesis*) role of the church as the sacrament of God's presence in human history.

We should also not overlook the reciprocal communication of life and effort that exists between the leader and the community. The moral responsibility of the leader redounds on the community and vice versa. Leadership functions within a complex net of relations, and a conglomerate structure of communication. Inculturation ethics can contribute by studying und understanding this structure of communication and offering useful suggestions as to how the Christian church can serve as an axis for socio-political dialogue in Africa. To be at the service of socio-political dialogue it is important to be in touch with the masses at the grassroots of African communities. The church will be promoting socio-political dialogue by cherishing and supporting the network of groups, individuals and initiatives committed to the emancipation and integral liberation of African peoples. In Ghana, the Catholic Youth Organization (CYO), for instance, served this function at its beginnings. Today, this aspect of conscientization towards civil awareness and emancipation would hardly be found on the agenda of the organization where it still exists. Where the organization has died out, nothing more appropriate has been found to take its place. Other movements such as Pax Christi, though useful and meaningful when properly adopted to the African situation, are reserved to a privileged group of literate African Christians and are hardly found at the grassroots.

The communal and collective aspects of moral responsibility acquire a place of importance among African communities. It is essential for the local community to be able to determine how the political innovation in vogue serves the good of the community and of individuals. The challenge to the African church to develop a political ethic, therefore, presupposes this practical aspect of making local communities politically functional by giving birth to individuals, groups, organizations and initiatives committed to emancipation. These groups need to be supported with appropriate information and literature so that they become the Christian core of resistance against oppression.[105]

---

[105] The Essay of G. Baum, "An Ethical Critique of Capitalism: Contributions of Modern Catholic Social Teaching", in: M. Zweig (ed.), Religion and Economic Justice (1991), has been of great use to me in formulating my ideas in this paragraph. The same Essay appears in C. E. Curran and R. A. McCormick (ed.), John Paull II and Moral Theology: Readings in

The role of the community as subjects of political activity is founded on Christian thinking and the church's social teaching.[106] But the idea receives special emphasis in the context of inculturation in African perspectives. Inculturation presupposes a normative concept of humanness by postulating the incarnation of Christ as paradigm and goal in our attempts to redress the anthropological poverty of Africans and to promote their process of humanization. This normative concept provides inculturation ethics its point of departure for engaging in social criticism. Alienation in Africa is not just an alienation from what we produce (labor),[107] but an alienation from what we are.[108] Political leadership will continue to be normatively detrimental to Africans as long as it continues to deny the people at the grassroots the opportunity of being the subjects of their society. By encouraging people to bridge the gab between the leader and the led, the church will be providing the axis for socio-political dialogue proposed earlier.

The consequences for the church in trying to denounce and at the same time minister to autocratic and sometimes brutal dictatorships, and the need to support the people at the grassroots to be subjects of their societies is not only paradoxical, it is also precarious. But this unimaginable nature of the task is the revolutionary aspect of doing ethics. The words of Richard McCormick are appropriate for ending this discussion on the contribution of inculturation ethics: "Moral awareness and judgements are fuller and deeper than "rational arguments" and rational categories. They are the result of evidence in the broadest sense – which includes a good deal more than mere rational analysis. While moral judgements must continually be submitted to rational scrutiny in an effort to correct and nuance them, in the last analysis, rooting as they do in the intransigence and complexity of reality, they remain deeper and more obscure than the systems and arguments we devise to make them up."[109]

Moral Theology No. 10 (New York: Paulist Press, 1998), pp. 237-254.

[106] See John Paul II, Laborem Exercens, in G. Baum, The Priority of Labor: A Commentary on Laborem Exercens (New York: Paulis Press, 1982); John Paul II, Solicitudo Rei Socialis, in The Logic of Solidarity: Commentaries on Solicitudo Rei Socialis, ed. G. Baum and R. Ellsberg (Maryknoll: Orbis Books, 1989). These sources were acquired from Baum's Essay referred to above.

[107] See K Marx. "Alienated Labor", in K. Marx: Early Writings, ed. T. B. Bottomore (New York: McGraw-Hill, 1964), pp. 120-134.

[108] See chapter one of this study, with reference to Martey and the Ecumenical Association of Third World Theologians.

[109] R. C. McCormick, Ambiguity in Moral Choice (Milwaukee: Marquette University Press, 1973), p. 106.

5. Conclusion

When we do theology, we do not only reflect on religious reality, we also mediate between culture and the significance of religion within that culture.[110] Our manner of theologizing also determines what we apprehend as religious reality and how we evaluate the significance of that reality in a given culture. In various ways, our reflection is subject to the laws that shape our humanness. For example, the language we use to formulate and give expression to our reflections limits our perception to certain given forms of description, interpretation and evaluation. But we are also able to break through the limitations that characterize our reflection because we make new experiences that challenge us and make us critical of the perceptions of reality that we hold on to at one time or the other. Hence we do not have to experience the conditions that structure our perception and relation to meaning as a kind of prison.

Our openness to the tension between past and present experiences makes us attentive to the glimpse that every new experience gives us into the inexhaustible intelligibility that underlies our humanness. We must, therefore, sustain a continuous correlation between experience and reflection if we wish to survive and to transform ourselves. The way in which we are able to sustain this correlation is to engage in a life long task of interpretation.[111] Interpretation presupposes communication, dialogue, conversation, the sharing of narratives between individuals as well as between groups of persons. There are rules to guide us in communication and to aid our interpretation and understanding. Tracy reminds us of the "transcendental imperatives" formulated by Lonergan: "Be attentive, Be intelligent, Be reasonable, Be responsible."[112] These transcendental precepts are fundamental because they concern the manner of our "knowing" and our morals. They challenge our bias, demand flexibility, openness to others, accuracy of conception and expression, capability to accept conflict and a willingness to change our mind when there is enough reason and evidence for change.[113] To be human, we must dialogue, sharpen our skill of interpretation and be constantly busy with interpretation and re-interpretation.[114]

The connection between the four chapters of this study, which pulls them together into a coherent development of thought, is the element of interpretation. From this perspective, the study claims that it is important for African scholars to delve more into the subjective aspects of African Christian

---

[110] Lonergan, Method, p. xi.
[111] See Tracy, Plurality and Ambiguity, referred to in chapter two of this study.
[112] Lonergan, Method, p. 231; See Tracy, Plurality and Ambiguity, p. 19.
[113] See Lonergan, p. 231; Tracy, Plurality and Ambiguity, p. 19ff.
[114] See Tracy, Plurality and Ambiguity, p. 9, referred to in chapter two of this study.

ethics. They must pay attention to the processes necessary for promoting the struggle of African Christians to become true subjects in Christ. In this connection, what Lonergan says about the precepts we need to follow in becoming moral subjects applies in the African context. It is crucial for an inculturation ethic to study Africans and how they evaluate the data relating to any set of specific moral questions they are confronted with.[115] A fruitful inculturation ethic must also seek to understand how the African is known and how the African knows what he or she knows about himself or herself.[116] In both cases we shall be engaged at profound intellectual and psychological levels in making sense of the complex cultural, historical, religious, and anthropological experiences of Africans.

This search for meaning is an unavoidable condition for a moral and religious conversion. In order to fulfill this condition, it is mandatory for us to deconstruct all previously given conceptions about the African, and seek to reconstruct a new consciousness, using the incarnation of Jesus not only as a paradigm, but also as a norm and as God's gift and empowerment for the attainment of our "subjectivity". One would therefore look in vain for a description of moral systems in Africa or of morality in general in this study. No direct attempt has been made to sort out good or bad African moral traditions, and no suggestions have been offered as to how good African moral traditions could be used to develop an African Christian ethic. There are instead four movements of "re-interpretation"—of inculturation, of Africanness as the underlying premise and aim of inculturation, of the Christian religious foundations of an African Christian ethic, and of the problem of political leadership.

Inculturation, Africanness (authenticity) and the religious foundations of Christian morality for the African church are three major domains which ramify into the multiple aspects and individual topics involved in the study of African Christian morality. By attempting to engage these broad areas in the process of reinterpretation, the study has touched on a large number of topics which, however, could not be discussed at length. Certain parts of the discussion have therefore remained rather general and incomplete in their exposition. The idea of considering ethics as a hermeneutic of behavior, however, introduces an innovative slant that offers perspectives for developing a beneficial methodology for doing African Christian ethics. Such a

---

[115] See Lonergan, Method, Chapter 1; D. H. Johnson, "Lonergan and the Redoing of Ethics", in: Continuum 5, (1967-1968), pp. 211-20; J. A. Raymaker, The Theory-Praxis of Social Ethics: The Complementarity Between Hermeneutical and Dialectical Foundations Milwaukee, Wis., Marquette University, Diss., 1977), pp. 340-352. Raymaker also cites D. Johnson and criticizes him for overstressing the importance the subjective pole in ethical inquiry. See Raymaker, p. 341, footnote 6.

[116] This is a reference to Lonergan's idea of 'intellectual conversion'. See Lonergan, Method, chapter one.

methodology will be useful for the African church of today and of the future since it will complement the normative, ethnological, historical, and descriptive-comparative approaches that are currently used in the study of African Christian morality.

It is true that morality consists of what people actually do, i.e. the actual application of specific moral laws or conventions. Morality also involves the canons for measuring the essentially good, which implies the composition of moral principles into a coherent system of evaluation and right behavior. But there is also the important aspect of ethics which is the investigation of "the presuppositions that inform the various ethical theories behind particular patterns of behavior."[117] On this level we need a sound hermeneutic. A methodology that studies ethics as a hermeneutic of behavior would make inculturation ethics a valid aspect of an integral African theology which emphasizes a hermeneutic of suspicion.[118] Unless inculturation is accompanied by a radical renewal of memory, it is bound to become itself a masque that covers the concrete suffering of Africans, the crisis in which they find themselves. In this way inculturation will be blind to the challenges of the present as a result of the past and to the solution of such challenges in view of the future. In the midst of the tensions, humiliation and conflicts that characterize African history, inculturation will contribute to the liberation of Africans, if it leads us to the depths of our historical consciousness.

The incarnation makes us as Africans wake up to the many conditions which have mediated the reality in which we are compelled to achieve our humanness. We realize that many of these mediations have actually distanced us from the love and purpose of God for us. These mediations engendered religious, cultural, political, and economic circumstances. These circumstances in turn provided the basis for structures, operations and modes of communication which obliterated a sense of being and belonging to the family of people created in the image of God in the heart and mind of many Africans. Thus inculturation cannot concern itself just with the religious aspects of life, but seek an integral liberation and transformation of the African in all aspects of life. One way in which inculturation can initiate this total liberation is by helping Africans to begin consciously to tell their own story, become convinced of their life-story and be able to identify with it. Inculturation should nurse an intensive dialogue in which Africans actually engage in communication with themselves, with others and with God.

Among some Ghanaian peoples it was the practice for the chief or an indigenous priest to narrate the village saga at important festivals. It often happened that the narrator ended up in ecstasy. Some elders explain that

---

[117] J. A. Raymaker, The Theory-Praxis of social Ethics: The Complementarity Between Hermeneutical and Dialectical Foundations Milwaukee, Wis., Marquette University, Diss., 1977), p. 340.

[118] See chapter one of this study and earlier references to Martey, and Ela.

ecstasy is necessary for the narrator to identify with his story. The elders maintain that ecstasy is a moment of a new self-awareness, a state which the individual had hitherto not enjoyed. At that point the narrator and his or her story become identical. The more the narrator attempts to convince the audience, the more convinced the narrator becomes of his or her own story. Ecstasy is, in this sense, as much important for the one who experiences it, as it is for those who observe the experience. Christian dialogue must produce this moment where the interlocutors get to know themselves not only through the people with whom they communicate, but also by understanding themselves for what they are as a result of the dialogue. Someone working with an indigenous Ghanaian concept might call this renewed knowledge of self that results from Christian dialogue ecstasy, whereas conventional theology might call the same experience conversion. When this happens, we would have achieved much, if not all of what Christian ethics and Christianity are about – conversion.

BIBLIOGRAPHY

ABDULAI, N. "Background to the Crisis [in the Congo] (I)", in West Africa, 31 March-6 April 1997.

ABRAHAM, K. C. (ed.), Third World Theologies: Commonalities and Divergences, Maryknoll, N.Y.: Orbis Books, 1990.

ACHEBE, C. No Longer at Ease, New York: Anchor Books, reprinted 1994.

ACKAH, C. A. Akan Ethics, Accra: Ghana Universities Press, 1988.

ADOTEVI, S. Négritude et Négrologues, Paris: Plon, 1972.

ADZAKPE, T. Penance and Expiatory Sacrifice among the Ghanaian-Ewe and their Relevance to the Christian Religion, Rome: Tipografia Olimpica, 1982.

AGBETI, J. K. West African Church History (2 vols.), Leiden: E. J. Brill, 1986.

AKOI, P. Religion in African Social Heritage, Rome: 1970.

ALLEN, R. C. When Narrative Fails, in: Journal of Religious Ethics, vol. 21, no. 1, 1993.

ALUKO, T. M. Chief the Honorable Minister, London: Heinemann, 1985.

AMEWOWO, W. A Study of the Biblical Foundations of Liberation Theology (unpublished Dissertation), Rome: Faculty of Theology, Pontificia Universitas Gregoriana, 1976.

ANDERSON, J. N. D. (ed.), The World's Religions, London: Inter-Varsity Press, 1975.

ANDERSON, W. The Living World of the Old Testament, England: Longman, 1984.

APPIAH, K. A. In My Father's House: Africa in the Philosophy of Culture, New York: Oxford University Press, 1992.

APPIAH-KUBI, K. and TORRES, S. (eds.), African Theology En Route, Maryknoll: Orbis Books, 1979.

ARISTOTLE, Nichomachean Ethics, translated with an Introduction by Ross, D. London: Oxford University Press, 1954.

ARRUPE, P. Letter to the Whole Society on Inculturation, in: Studies in the International Apostolate of Jesuits, 7 June 1978.

ASSIMENG, M. Religion and Social Change in West Africa, Accra: Ghana Universities Press, 1989.

AUBENAS, R. and RICHARD, R. La Chiesa e il Rinascimento, Torino, 1972.

AUER, A. Autonome Moral und christlicher Glaube, Düsseldorf: Patmos Verlag, 1971.

AUSTIN, D. and Luckham, R. Politicians and Soldiers in Ghana, London: Frank Cass, 1975.

BARBIERI Jr., W. A. Ethics and the Narrated Life, in: The Journal of Religion, vol. 78, no. 3 July 1998.

BARTON, J. (ed.), The Cambridge Companion to Biblical Interpretation, Cambridge: Cambridge University Press, 1998.

BASCOM, W. R. Ifa Divination: Communication between Gods and Men in West Africa, Bloomington: Indiana University Press, 1969.

BEATTIE, J. Other Cultures: Aims, Methods and Achievements in Social Anthropology, London: Cohen & West, 1964.

BEAUCHAMP, P. The Role of the Old Testament in the Process of Building up of Local Churches, in: Inculturation (III), Bible and Inculturation, Rome: 1983.

BEDIAKO, G. M. Primal Religion and Biblical Religion: Addressing a Problem of Relationship, Sheffield: Academic Press, 1997.

BENTLEY, P. (general ed.), The Hutchinson Dictionary of World Myth Oxford: Helicon Publishing Limited and Duncan Baird Publishers, 1995.

BERGER, P. L. and LUCKMANN, T. The Social Construction of Reality, New York: Anchor Books, 1966.

BETTENSON, H. (ed.), The Early Christian Fathers, Oxford: Oxford

University Press, 1956.

BONINO, J. M. Doing Theology in a Revolutionary Situation, Philadelphia: Frotress Press, 1975.

BOTSOE, E. Y. [Personal Letter to the Bremer Mission], Bremen: Bremer Staatsarchiv, Stab 7, 1025-43/4.

BOXER, C. R. The Portuguese Seaborn Empire 1415-1825, London: Hutchinson, 1969.

BRAUER, J. C. (ed.), The Impact of the Church upon its Culture, Chicago: Chicago University Press, 1968.

BREMER MISSION, Gemeinde Ordnung, Bremen: Bremen Staatsarchiv, Stab 7, 1025-77/6.

BROWN, P. The World of Late Antiquity from Marcus Aurelius to Muhammad, London: Thames & Hudson, 1971.

BÜHLMANN, W. Afrika. Die Kirche unter den Völkern, Mainz: Matthias-Grünewald-Verlag, 1963.

BÜHLMANN, W. The Coming of the Third Church, Slough: St. Paul Publication, 1976.

BUJO, B. African Christian Morality at the Age of Inculturation, Nairobi: St. Paul Publicaations, 1990

BUJO, B. African Theology in ist Social Context, Nairobi: St. Paul Publications, 1986.

BUJO, B. Die ethische Dimension der Gemeinschaft. Studien zur Theologischen Ethik, Freiburg Schweiz, 1993.

BUSIA, K. A. The Position of the chief in the Modern Political Systems of Ashanti, London: Frank Cass, 1968.

BUTE, E. L. and Harmer, H. J. P. The Black Handbook: The People, History and Politics of Africa and the African Diaspora, London and Washington: Cassell, 1997.

CABRAL, A. Unite et Lutte, Paris: Maspero, 1967.

CAROTHERS, J. C. The African Mind in Health and Sickness: A Study in Ethnopsychiatry, Geneva: World Health Organization,

1953.

COCHRANE, C. N. Christianity and Classical Culture, London: Oxford University Press, 1957.

COLLET, G. Inkulturation, in: Eicher, P. Neues Lexikon der theologischen Begriffe, Bd. 3, München: Kössel-Verlag, 1991.

CRONIN, K. Rights and Christian Ethics, Cambridge: Cambridge University Press, 1992.

DANQUAH, J. B. The Akan Doctrine of God, London and Redhill: Lutterworth Press, 1942.

DAVIDSON, B. et al., The Growth of African Civilisation. A History of West Africa 1000-1800, London: Longman, 1965.

DIEMER, A. (ed.), Africa and the Problem of its Identity. International Philosophical Symposium on Culture and Identity of Africa, Frankfurt: Verlag Peter Lang, 1985.

DIXON, R. The Building of Cultures, New York: 1928.

DOWDEN, R. What's Wrong with Africa, in: The Tablet, London: The Tablet Publishing Company Limited, January 16, 1999.

DULLES, A. Models of Revelation, Maryknoll: Orbis Books, 1983.

DULLES, A. Models of the Church, Dublin: Gill and McMillan, 1974.

DZOBO, N. K. African Proverbs: Guide to Conduct. The Moral Value of Ewe Proverbs, Cape Coast: Cape Coast University Press, 1973.

EISENSTADT, S. N. Some Observations on the Dynamics of Traditions in: Comparative Studies in Society and History IX (4), 1969.

ELA, J. M. African Cry, Maryknoll: Orbis Books, 1986.

ELA, J. M. My Faith as an African, Maryknoll: Orbis Books, 1988.

ELIADE, M. and J. KITAGAWA (eds.), The History of Religions, Chicago, University of Chicago Press, 1959.

EVANS-PRITCHARD, E. E. The Theories of Primitive Religion, Oxford: Clarendon Press, 1965.

FANON, F. Studies in a Dying Colonialism, New York: Monthly Review Press, 1965.

FANON, F. The Wretched of the Earth, New York: Grove Press, 1965.

FLANNERY, A. (ed.), Vatican Council II: The Conciliar and Post Conciliar Documents, Leominster: Fowler Wright Books Ltd., 1975.

FORD, D. (ed.), African Worlds. Studies in the Cosmological Ideas of African Peoples, London: Oxford University Press, 1954.

FRISCH, M. Mein Name sei Gantenbein, Frankfurt am Main: Suhrkamp, 1964.

GENERAL CATECHETICAL DIRECTORY, London: Catholic Truth Society, 1971.

GIDDENS, A. Tradition, 1999 Reith Lectures, BBC Radio 4, Homepage.

GILL, R. Christian Ethics in Secular Worlds, Edinburgh: T & T Clark, 1991.

GOODY, J. Literacy in Traditional Societies, Cambridge, 1968.

GOODY, J. The Domestication of the Savage Mind, Cambridge, 1977.

GOODY, J. The Interface Between the Written and the Oral, Cambridge, 1987.

GOUTHS, K. World Revolution and the Science of Man, in: Roszak, T. (ed.), The Dissenting Academy, New York, NY: Random House, 1968.

GREMILLION, J. Proceedings of the Catholic Theological Society of America 38, 1981.

GROVES, C. T. The Planting of Christianity in Africa (4 vols.), London: Lutterworth, 1948-58.

GUTIERREZ, G. A Theology of Liberation, Maryknoll: Orbis Books, 1973.

GYEKYE, K. Political Corruption. A Philosophical Analysis of a Moral Problem, Accra: Sankofa Publishing Co. Ltd., 1997.

GYEKYE, K. Tradition and Modernity: Philosophical Reflections on the African Experience, Oxford: Oxford University Press1997.

HABERMAS, J. Theorie des Kommunikativen Handelns, Bd. 1, Frankfurt am Main: Shurkamp, 1981.

HALEBLIAN, The Problem of Contextualization, in: Missiology, 11 (1983).

HÄRING, B. Free and Faithful in Christ, Middlegreen: St. Paul Publications, 1981.

HARRIS, M. The Rise of Anthropological Theory, Columbia University: Harper Collins Publishers, 1968.

HARRIS, M. The Rise of Anthropological Theory, New York: Harper Corlins Publishers, 1968.

HASELBARTH, H. Christian Ethics in the African Context, Ibadan: Daystar Press, 1976.

HATCH, E. Culture and Morality: The Relativity of Values in Anthropology, New York: Columbia University Press, 1983.

HAY, D. Europe: The Emergence of an Idea, Edinburgh: Edinburgh University Press, 1957.

HEGEL, G. W. The Philosophy of History, New York: Prometheus Books, 1991.

HEIDEL, A. The Babylonian Genesis, Chicago & London: University of Chicago Press, 1974.

HERTZ, A., KORFF, W., et. al. (eds.), Handbuch der christlichen Ethik, Freiburg: Herder, 1993.

HEVI, J. Indigenous Leadership among the Ewes of South-Eastern Ghana as a Moral Responsibility (unpublished Dissertation), Rome: 1980.

HODGEN, M. T. Early Anthropology in the Sixteenth and Seventeenth Centuries, Philadelphia: University of Pennsylvania Press, 1964.

HONDERICH, T. (ed.) The Oxford Companion to Philosophy, Oxford: University Press, 1994.

HOWELL, L., and LINDERMAYER, V. (eds.), Ethics in the Present Tense: Readings from Christianity and Crisis 1966-1991, New York: Friendship Press, 1991.

IDOWU, E. B. Olodumare, God in Yoruba, London: Longmans, 1962.

JANSSENS, L. Artificial Insemination: Ethical Considerations, in: Louvain Studies, vol. viii, no 1, (1980), pp. 3-29.

JASSY, M. -F. P. Leadership, Kampala: Gaba Publications, 1974.

JEANNIÈRE, A. S.J. Corps Malièable, in: Cahiers Laennec, 29 [1968].

JEHODA, G. White Man. A Study of the Attitudes of Africans to Europeans in Ghana before Independence, London: Oxford University Press, 1961.

JOHN PAUL II, Address to the Italian National Congress of the Ecclesial Movement for Cultural Commitment (16 January 1982), 2: Insegnamenti V/ (1982).

JOHN PAUL II, Apostolic Exhortation, Catechesi Tradendae, 1979.

JOHN PAUL II, Post Synodal Apostolic Exhortation, *Ecclesia in Africa*, (Nairobi: Paulines Publications. 1995), pp. 41-56.

JOHNSON, D. H. Lonergan and the Redoing of Ethics, in: Continuum 5, 1967-1968.

KAMPHAUS, F. Eine Zukunft für Alle, Freiburg: Herder, 1995.

KEEN, M. The Pelican History of Medieval Europe, Harmondsworth: Pelican, 1969.

KELLY, K. T. New Directions in Moral Theology: The Challenge of Being Human, London: Geoffrey Chapman, 1992.

KENNEDY, T. Doers of the Word: Moral Theology for Humanity in the Third Millennium, vol. 1, Middlegreen: St. Pauls, 1996.

KERN, W., POTMEYER, H. J., SECKLER, M. Handbuch der Fundamentaltheologie, 4Bd., Tübingen: Franke Verlag, ²1999.

KING, N. Q. The Emperor Theodosius and the Establishment of Christianity, London: SCM Press, 1961.

KI-ZERBO, J. and NIANE, D. T. (eds.), General History of Africa - Vol. 4: Africa from the Twelfth to the Sixteenth Century, Paris: UNESCO Publishing, 1997.

KLUXEN, W. Ethik des Ethos, Freiburg/München: Verlag Karl Alber GmbH, 1974.

KOCH, T. Kriterien einer Ethik des Politischen, in: A. Herz, W. Korff, et. al. (eds.), Handbuch der christlichen Ethik, Bd. 2, Freiburg: Herder, 1993.

KOHLBERG, L. and COLLBY, A. Das Moralische Urteil: Der kognitionszentrierte entwicklungspsychologische Ansatz, in: Sterner, G. (ed.), Kindlers Psychologie des 20. Jahrhunderts, Bd. 1, Weinheim und Basel: Beltz Verlag, 1984.

KOMONCHAK, J. Moral Pluralism and the Unity of the Church, in: Concilium 150 (10/1981), pp. 89-94.

KUDADJIE, J. N. Aspects of African Ethics, in: Pobee, J. S. (ed.), Religion, Morality and Population Dynamics, Legon: University of Ghana, 1977.

KUDADJIE, J. N. Does Religion Determine Morality in African Societies? —A Viewpoint, in: Ghana Bulletin of Theology, vol. 4, No. 5, Dec. 1973.

LACAPRA D. (ed.), The Bounds of Race: Perspectives on Hegemony and Resistance, London: Cornell University Press, 1991.

LEWIS, M. M. Language, Thought and Personality, London: George G. Harrap & Co. Ltd., 1963.

LOGLO, J. West African Traditional Religion for A Level Religious Studies, Accra, 1984.

LONERGAN, B. Method in Theology, London: Darton Longman & Todd Ltd., 1972.

LONERGAN, B. The Aquinas Lecture for 1968, delivered 1968 (Marquette University: Wisconsin-Alpha Chapter of Phi Sigma Tau, March 3, 1968.

LORNEGAN, B. A Third Collection, Paulist Press, 1985.

LUIJPEN, W. A. Eixstential Phenomenology, Pittsburg: Duquesne University Press, 1960.

LYOTARD, J. -F. Das postmoderne Wissen: ein Bericht, Bremen: Impulse & Association, 1982.

LYOTARD, J. -F. Die Moderne redigieren, Bern: Benteli Verlag, 1988.

MACINTYRRE, A. After Virtue: A Study in Moral Theology, Notre Dame Indiana: University of Notre Dame Press, 1981.

MAGESA, L. African Religion: The Moral Traditions of Abundant Life, Maryknoll: Obis Books, 1997.

MAMATTAH, C. M. K. History of the Ewes of West Africa, Keta: Volta Research Publications, 1978.

MANNONI, O. Prospero and Caliban: The Psychology of Colonization, translated by Powesland, P. Ann Arbor: University of Michigan Press, reprinted, 1990.

MARKUS, A. R. Christianity in the Roman World, London: Thomas & Hudson, 1974.

MARTEY, E. African Theology: Inculturation and Liberation, Maryknoll: Orbis Books, 1994.

MASOLO, D. African Philosophy, Edinburgh: Edinburgh University Press, 1994.

MAZRUI, A. Political Values and the Educated Class, London: Heinemann, 1978.

MAZRUI, A. The African Condition. A Political Diagnosis, London: Cambridge University Press, 1980.

MAZRUI, A. The Africans: A Triple Heritage, London: BBC Publications, 1986.

MAZRUI, A. The Moving Cultural Frontier of World Order: From Monotheism to North-South Relations, World Order Models Project, Working Paper No. 18, New York: Institute for World Order, Inc., 1982.

MBITI, J. African Religions and Philosophy, 2nd ed., Ibadan: Heinemann Educational Books, 1990.

MBITI, J. Concepts of God in Africa, Heinemann, 1970.

MCKENZIE, J. Authority in the Church, London: Chapman, 1966.

METZ, J. B. Glaube in Geschichte und Gesellschaft. Studien zu einer praktischen Fundamentaltheologie, Mainz: Matthias-Grünewald Verlag, 1992.

MIETH, D. Narrative Ethik, in: Freiburger Zeitschrift für Philosophie und Theologie, 22, (1975).

MIETH, D. Dichtung, Glaube und Moral: Studien zur Begründung einer narrativen Ethik; mit einer Interpretation zum Tristanroman Gottfrieds von Strassburg, Mainz: Grünewald, ²1983.

MILL, J. S. Dissertations and Discussions, Vol. 3, London: Longmans, Green, Reader & Dyer, 1875, reprinted 1967.

MOMIGLIANO, A. (ed.), The Conflict between Paganism and Christianity in the Fourth Century, Oxford: Clarendon Press, 1963.

MONTAGU, A. (ed.), The Concept of the Primitive, New York: Free Press, 1968.

Mordstein, F. Menschenbild und Gesellschaftsidee. Zur Krisis der politischen Ethik im 19. Jahrhundert, Stuttgart: Kohlhammer, 1966.

MUDIMBE V. Y. (ed.), The Surreptitious Speech, Chicago: University of Chicago Press, 1992.

MUDIMBE, V. Y. The Invention of Africa, Bloomington and Indianapolis: Indiana University Press, 1988.

MUGAMBI, J. N. K. and NASIMIYU-WASIKE, A. (eds.), Moral and Ethical Issues in African Christianity: Exploratory Essays in Moral Theology, Nairobi: Initiatives Publishers, 1992.

MUGAMBI, J. N. K. Jesus in African Christianity: Experimentation and Diversity in African Christology, Nairobi: Initiatives Publishers, 1989.

MÜHLMANN, W. Homo Creator: Abhandlungen zur Soziologie, Anthropologie und Ethnologie, Wiesbaden: Otto Harrassowitz, 1962.

MUZOREWA, B. The Origins and Development of African Theology, New York: Orbis Books, 1985.

MVENG, E. Récents Développements de la Théologie Africaine, in: Bulleting of African Theology vol. 5, no.9, 1983.

NGONGO, L. P. Pourvoir Politique Occidental dans les Structures de l'Eglise en Afrique, in: Civilisation Noir et Eglise Catholique: Colloque d'Abidjan, 12-17 Septembre 1977, Paris: Présence Africaine, 1978.

NILSSON, M. P. Geschichte der Griechischen Religion, Bd. 2, München: C. H. Beck, 1967.

NOCK, A. D. Conversion: The Old and the New in Religion from Alexander to Augustine of Hippo, Oxford: Oxford University Press, 1933.

NOULDIN, H. Questiones Morales: De Principiis Theologiae, 1899.

O'DONOHUE, J. New Wine and Old Bottles: A Study of the Concepts of Traditional Africa and of Their Continuing Influence Today, Upsala: Reprocentralen HSC, Upsala University, 1994.

ODUYOYE, M. A. and KANYORO, M. R. A. (eds.), The Will To Arise: Women, tradition, and the Church in Africa, Maryknoll: Orbis Books, 1992.

OGOT, B. A. (ed.), General History of Africa, vol. 5, Paris: UNESCO Publishing, 1997.

ONOGE, O. Revolutionäre Forderungen an die afrikanische Soziologie, in: Jestel, R. (ed.), Das Afrika der Afrikaner:

Gesellschaft und Kultur Afrikas, Frankfurt am Main: Suhrkamp Verlag, 1988.

OPOKU, A. K. West African Traditional Religion, Hong Kong: FEP International Ltd. 1978.

OPPENHEIM, F. E. Moral Principles in Political Philosophy, New York: Random House, 1968.

OPPONG, C. Growing up in Dagbon, Tema: Ghana Publishing Corporation, 1973.

ORUKA, H. O. African Philosophy: A Brief Personal History and Current Debate, in: Contemporary Philosophy. A new Survey, vol. 5, Dordrecht/Boston/Lancaster: Martinus Nijhoff Publishers, 1987.

OWEN, G. E. L. Logic, Science, and Dialectic: Collected Papers in Greek Philosophy, edited by, Nussbaum, M., London, 1986.

PANNENBERG, W. Anthropology in Theological Perspective, Edinburgh: T. & T. Clark Ltd., 1985.

PARRINDER, G. African Mythology, London, Hamlyn, 1967.

PARRINDER, G. West African Religion. A Study of Beliefs and Practices of Akan, Ewe, Yoruba, Ibo and Kindred Peoples, London: 1961.

PARSONS, T. The Churches and Ghana Society 1918-1955, Leiden: E. J. Brill, 1963.

PÉNOUKOU, E. -J. Églises d'Afrique Propositions pour l'Avenir, Paris: 1984.

PETZOLDT, L. Kleines Lexikon der Dämonen und Elementargeister, München: Verlag C.H. Beck, 1990.

PIEPER, A. (ed.), Geschichte der neueren Ethik, 2Bd., Tübingen und Basel: Franke Verlag, 1992.

POBEE, J. S. Religion and Politics in Ghana, Accra: Asempa Publishers, 1991.

POBEE, J. S. Towards African Theology, Nashville, TN: Abingdon, 1979.

PURCHAS, S. Purchas His Pilgrimes, Hakluyt Society Extra Series, 1905.

RADER, D. A. Christian Ethics in an African Context, Frankfurt am Main: Peter Lang, 1991.

RAHNER K. and VORGRIMLER, H. Kleines Konzilskompendium, Herder: 1966.

RAHNER, K. (ed.) The Concise Sacramentum Mundi, Kent: Burns & Oates, paperback ed. 1993.

RATTRAY, R. S. Ashanti Proverbs, Oxford: Clarendon Press, 1916.

RATTRAY, R. S. Ashanti, Oxford: Clarendon Press, 1923.

RATTRAY, R. S. Religion and Art in Ashanti, London: Oxford University Press, 1927.

RAYMAKER, J. A. The Theory-Praxis of Social Ethics: The Complementarity Between Hermeneutical and Dialectical Foundations, Milwaukee: Wis., Marquette University, Diss., 1977.

REHBERG, K. –S. (ed.), A. Gehlen, Gesamtausgabe, Bd. 3, Teilband 1, Der Mensch: Seine Natur und seine Stellung in der Welt, Frankfurt a. M.: Vittorio Klostermann, 1993.

RICOEUR, P. Freud and Philosophy: An Essay on Interpretation. Tr. Denis Savage, New Haven, Conn.: Yale University Press, 1977.

RUSSELL, D. Kenneth Kaunda. Zambia Shall be Free, London: Longman, 1978.

SACK, O. The Man Who Mistook His Wife for a Hat, and Other Clinical Tales, New York: Harper & Row, Perennial Library, 1987.

SARAH, R. Den aufrechten Gang finden, in: Herderkorrespondenz (HK). Monatshefte für Gesellschaft und Religion, Heft 5, Freiburg: Mai, 1994.

SARPONG, P. A. Ghana in Retrospect, Tema: Ghana Publishing Corporation, 1974.

SARTRE, J. P. L'Existentialisme est un Umanisme, Paris: Gallimard, 1954, reprinted 1996.

SCHAUMBERGER, C. and MAAßEN, M. (eds.), Handbuch Feministische Theologie, Münster: Morgana-Frauenbuchverlag, 1986.

SCHELSKY, H. Zur Theorie der Institution, Bertelsmann Universitätsverlag, 1975.

SCHILLEBEECKX, E. Christ the Sacrament of our Encounter with God, London: Sheed and Ward, 1963.

SCHILLEBEECKX, E. Christ, the Christian Experience in the Modern World, London: Sheed and Ward, 1980.

SCHILLEBEECKX, E. Gasammelte Schriften Bd. 1, Offenbarung und Theologie, Mainz: Matthias-Grünewald Verlag, 1965.

SCHINELLER, P. A Handbook on Inculturation, New York: Paulist Press, 1990.

SCHMIDT, L. Die Ethik der alten Griechen Bd. 1, Stuttgart: Frommann, 1882, reprinted 1964.

SCHMÖLZ, F. M. Chance und Dilemma der politischen Ethik, Köln: Bachem, 1966.

SCHREITER, R. J. Constructing Local Theologies, Maryknoll: Orbis Books, 1996.

SCHÜSSLER FIORENZA, E. Brot statt Steine. Die Herausforderung einer feministischen Interpretation der Bibel, Freiburg/Schwiez: Ed. Exodus, 1988.

SEMPEBWA, J. W. African Traditional Norms and Their Implication for Christianity: A Case Study of Ganda Ethics, St. Augustin: Steyler Verlag, 1983.

SHARKEY, N. Incarnational Theology, in: New Catholic Encyclopedia, Vol. 7, New York: McGraw-Hill Book Company, 1981.

SHARPE, E. J. Comparative Religion: A History, London: Duckworth, 1975.

SHARPE, E. J. Understanding Religion, London: Duckworth, 1983.

SHORTER, A. Toward a Theology of Inculturation, Maryknoll:

Orbis Books, 1986

SIKER, J. S. Scripture and Ethics: Twentieth–Century Portraits, New York and Oxford: Oxford University Press, 1997

SINDIMA, H. J. Religious and Political Ethics in Africa. A Moral Inquiry, London: Greenwood Press, 1998.

SMITH, E. African Ideas of God: A Symposium, London: Edinburgh House, 1955.

STAMER, P. F. Islam in Sub-Saharan Africa, Estella: Editorial Verbo Divino, 1995.

STRENG, F. J. (ed.), Understanding the Religious Life, California: Dickenson Publishing Company, 1976.

SUNDERMEIER, T. Den Fremden verstehen: Eine praktische Hermeneutik, Goettingen: Vandenhoeck & Ruprecht, 1996.

SUNDERMEIER, T. Nur Gemeinsam Können Wir Leben, Gütersloh: Gütersloher Verlaghaus, 1988.

TAYLOR, J. V. The Primal Vision, London: SCM Press, 1963.

TEMPELS, P. Bantu-Philosophie: Ontologie und Ethik, Heidelberg: Wolfgang Rothe Verlag, 1956.

THIELICKE, H. Theologische Ethik II/1, Tübingen: Mohr, 1959.

TÖNNIES, F. Die Sitte, Frankfurt am Main: Rütten & Loening, 1909.

TOWA, M. Léopold Sédar Senghor: Négritude ou Servitude, Yaoundé: Cle, 1971.

TRACY, D. Plurality and Ambiguity: Hermeneutics, Religion, Hope, San Francisco: Harper & Row, 1987.

TRACY, D. translated by Klinger, S. Theologie als Gespräch: Eine Postmoderne Hermeneutik, Mainz: Matthias-Grünewald Verlag, 1993.

TRIMINGHAM, J. S. Islam in West Africa. Oxford: Claredon Press, 1959.

TURKSON, P. and F. WIJSEN (eds.), Inculturation: Abide by the

Otherness of Africa and the Africans, Kampen: 1994.

TYLOR, E. B. Researches into the Early History of Mankind and the Development of Civilization, 1878.

VANSINA, J. Kings in Tropical Africa, in: Beumars, E. and Koloss, H. - J. (eds.), Kings in Africa. Art and Authority in Central Africa: Collection Museum für Völkerkunde Berlin, Utrecht: Foundation Kings of Africa, 1993.

VILLA-VICENCIO, C. and De Gruchy, J. (eds.), Doing Ethics in Context: South African Perspectives, Maryknoll: Orbis Books, 1994.

WA THIONGO, N. Moving the Centre: The Struggle for Cultural Freedoms, London: J. Curry, 1993.

WALLIGO, J. M. et al., Inculturation: Its meaning and Urgency, Nairobi: St. Paul Publications, 1986.

WATT, W. M. The Influence of Islam on Medieval Europe, Edinburgh: Edinburgh University Press, 1972.

WEBER, M. Wirtschaft und Gesellschaft, Tübingen: Mohr, 1922.

WEBSTER, J. B. and BOAHEN, A. A. The Growth of African Civilisation. The Revolutionary Years: West Africa since 1800, London: Longmans, 1967.

Webster's New Encyclopedic Dictionary (revised Edition), New York: Black Dog & Leventhal Publishers, 1993.

WELCH, W. Unsere postmoderne Moderne, Weinheim: VCH Verlagsgesellschaft, 1991.

WELTKIRCHE: Dokumente aus Afrika, Asien und Lateinamerika, München: Missio, 1996-1999.

WESTERMANN, D. Afrika als europäische Aufgabe, Berlin: Dt. Verlag, 1941.

WESTERMANN, D. Afrikanische Tabusitten in ihrer Einwirkung auf die Sprachgestaltung, Berlin, 1940.

WILLIAMS, N. P. Tradition, in: Hastings, J. Encyclopaedia of Religion and Ethics, Vol. 12, Edinburgh: T & T Clark, 1908-1926.

WILLIAMS, S. The Faith of a Politician, in: The Tablet, London: The Tablet Publishing Co. Ltd., 14. August 1999.

WILSON, R. (ed.), Rationality, Oxford: Blackwell, 1974.

WINTHROP, R. H. Dictionary of Concepts in Cultural Anthropology, New York: Greenwood Press, 1991.

WIREDU, K. Morality and Religion in Akan Thought, in: Oruka, O. and Masolo, D. (eds.), Philosophy and Cultures, Nairobi: Bookwise Publishers, 1983.

WIREDU, K. Philosophy and an African Culture, Cambridge: Cambridge University Press, 1980.

ZAREMBO, A. and MABRY, M. Mobutu's Legacy, in: Newsweek, Vol. CXXIX, No. 21, New York: Newsweek Inc., May 26, 1997.

FORUM INTERDISZIPLINÄRE ETHIK

Herausgegeben von Gerfried W. Hunold

Band 1 Jean-Pierre Wils: Verletzte Natur. Ethische Prolegomena. 1991.

Band 2 Dorothee Beckmann/Karin Istel/Michael Leipoldt/Hansjörg Reichert (Hrsg.): Humangenetik - Segen für die Menschheit oder unkalkulierbares Risiko? 1991.

Band 3 Peter Kaufmann: Gemüt und Gefühl als Komplement der Vernunft. Eine Auseinandersetzung mit der Tradition und der phänomenologischen Ethik, besonders Max Schelers. 1992.

Band 4 Gerhard Droesser: Freiheitspraxis im Prozeß. Zur geschichtsanthropologischen Grundlegung einer Theologie des Ethischen. 1992.

Band 5 Andrea Redeker: Abweichendes Verhalten und moralischer Fortschritt. Zur Steuerungsfunktion der Normkritik in der theologisch-ethischen Reflexion. 1993.

Band 6 Elke Hümmeler: Erfahrung in der genetischen Beratung. Eine theologisch-ethische Diskussion. 1993.

Band 7 Walter Schaupp: Der ethische Gehalt der Helsinki Deklaration. Eine historisch-systematische Untersuchung der Richtlinien des Weltärztebunds über biomedizinische Forschung am Menschen. 1994.

Band 8 Alfons V. Maurer: Homo Agens. Handlungstheoretische Untersuchungen zum theologisch-ethischen Verständnis des Sittlichen. 1994.

Band 9 Berthold Saup: Zur Freiheit berufen. Zur Dimension des Ethischen im Marchtaler Plan. 1994.

Band 10 Dorothee Beckmann: Hippokratisches Ethos und ärztliche Verantwortung. Zur Genese eines anthropologischen Selbstverständnisses griechischer Heilkunst im Spannungsfeld zwischen ärztlichem Können und moralischer Wahrnehmung. 1995.

Band 11 Gerfried W. Hunold / Dorothee Beckmann (Hrsg.): Grenzbegehungen. Interdisziplinarität als Wissenschaftsethos. 1995.

Band 12 Helga Willinger: Ethische und rechtliche Aspekte der ärztlichen Aufklärungspflicht. 1996.

Band 13 Wilfried Lochbühler: Christliche Umweltethik. Schöpfungstheologische Grundlagen · Philosophisch-ethische Ansätze · Ökologische Marktwirtschaft. 1996.

Band 14 Anton Georg Schuster: Finaler Rettungsschuß. Theologisch-ethische Untersuchung zum finalen Rettungsschuß als lex specialis. 1996.

Band 15 Gerhard Bachleitner: Die mediale Revolution. Anthropologische Überlegungen zu einer Ethik der Kommunikationstechnik. 1997.

Band 16 Gerhard Gansterer: Die *Ehrfurcht vor dem Leben.* Die Rolle des ethischen Schlüsselbegriffs Albert Schweitzers in der theologisch-ökologischen Diskussion. 1997.

Band 17 Elmar Kos: Verständigung oder Vermittlung? Die kommunikative Ambivalenz als Zugangsweg einer theologischen Medienethik. 1997.

Band 18 Manfred Waltl: Eigennutz und Eigenwohl. Ein Beitrag zur Diskussion zwischen Soziobiologie und theologischer Ethik. 1997.

Band 19 Jürgen in der Schmitten: Die Entscheidung zur Herz-Lungen-Wiederbelebung. Studie im deutsch-amerikanischen Vergleich. 1998.

Band 20 Gunter M. Prüller-Jagenteufel: Solidarität – eine Option für die Opfer. Geschichtliche Entwicklung und aktuelle Bedeutung einer christlichen Tugend anhand der katholischen Sozialdokumente. 1998.

Band 21 Michael Pindl: Versöhnung mit dem Leiden. Leidfreiheitsideologie und Gewalt gegen behinderte Menschen aus der Sicht eines im christlich-buddhistischen Dialog gründenden Ethos. 1998.

Band 22 Wolfram Winger: Personalität durch Humanität. Das ethikgeschichtliche Profil christlicher Handlungslehre bei Lactanz. Denkhorizont – Textübersetzung – Interpretation – Wirkungsgeschichte. 1999.

Band 23 Christa Schnabl: Das Moralische im Politischen. Hannah Arendts Theorie des Handelns im Horizont der theologischen Ethik. 1999.

Band 24 Thomas Laubach: Lebensführung. Annäherungen an einen ethischen Grundbegriff. 1999.

Band 25 Manfred Maßhof-Fischer: Ethik und Vorurteil. Moralpsychologische Studien zu den Legitimationsstrategien soziokulturellen Handelns im Konfliktfeld von Mythos und Rationalität. 2000.

Band 26 Simon Kofi Appiah: Africanness – Inculturation – Ethics. In Search of the Subject of an Inculturated Christian Ethic. 2000.

Laurent W. Ramambason

Missiology: Its Subject-Matter and Method

A Study of *Mission-Doers* in Madagascar

Frankfurt/M., Berlin, Bern, New York, Paris, Wien, 1999. 208 pp.
Studies in Intercultural History of Christianity. Edited by Richard Friedli, Jan A. B. Jongeneel, Klaus Koschorke, Theo Sundermeier, Werner Ustorf.
Vol. 116
ISBN 3-631-34602-6 · pb. DM 65.–*
US-ISBN 0-8204-4320-4

Missiology is the study of *mission-doers*, the persons who are active in Christianisation, with methodological attention to the dialectic of personhood. Mission, in this approach, is what a mission-doer thinks it is. Mission-doers are potential facilitators as well as potential hinderers of the cause of Jesus Christ. They emerge in particular contexts; as the contexts change they converge and diverge. New contexts for Christianisation may require new ways of doing it, which in turn may require new people to carry them out. That is why individual and corporate mission-doers emerge, are renewed and eventually fade away. The understanding of missiology is illustrated with reference to the Church of Jesus Christ in Madagascar under the impact of the Gorbachev transition (1985-93).

Contents: The study of *mission-doers* · Persons who are active in Christianisation · Methodological attention to the dialectic of personhood · Study of '*mission-doers*' in Madagascar under the impact of the Gorbachev transition (1985-93)

Frankfurt/M · Berlin · Bern · Bruxelles · New York · Oxford · Wien
Distribution: Verlag Peter Lang AG
Jupiterstr. 15, CH-3000 Bern 15
Fax (004131) 9402131
*incl. value added tax
Prices are subject to change without notice.